Mindful Machines, Masterful Humans

The Role of Innovations, AI and Tech Mastery in Organizational Transformation

Robert Munjoma

Dedication

To my grandmother, Erica, and her cherished husband, Mathias—now at peace.

You believed in me when I couldn't see my own potential and had unshakable faith that I would navigate uncharted waters and rise beyond every boundary.

Your love and unwavering confidence remain my compass and my strength.

This is for you, with all my love.

Acknowledgment

This book would not have been possible without the support and encouragement of incredible individuals who have guided and inspired me along this journey.

To **Arnold**, thank you for motivating me to take the leap and create this work. Your wisdom and support have been instrumental in shaping the direction of this book.

A special thanks to my former professor and advisor, **Dr. Professor R. Glenn Cummins.**

To my children, I am deeply grateful for your unwavering belief in me. You are my constant motivation and source of strength.

To my parents, thank you for your boundless love and care.

Finally, to all those who have played a role in shaping my personal and professional journey—whether large or small—my heartfelt thanks. To my third-grade teacher, the late Ms. Ngulube, whose encouragement laid the foundation for my future, and Dr Jeskinus Mukonoweshuro, aka JK, who set my professional journey for success through roles that provided opportunities and challenges that prepared me to excel, your belief in me has been invaluable. Thank you for your unwavering support and encouragement along the way!

About the Author

Rob is an experienced Organizational Change consultant, team-building expert, and trainer of trainers with expertise in strategic communication and business leadership, innovations, responsible AI, and technological transformation. With a Masters in Mass Communication from Texas Tech University, an MSc. in Strategic Management, and a PhD in progress, Rob has spent over two decades researching and guiding organizations through complex changes, helping them align teams and technological innovations responsibly with business goals.

Rob's career began in banking and finance, where he specialized in product development, systems integration, and business development. He transitioned to corporate consultancy following a bank acquisition, where he was invited to lead the change management process. This marked the start of his extensive consulting career, during which he led transformative projects across Africa, Asia, and the Americas. His expertise spans multiple industries, with a focus on strategic change and breakthrough innovation strategies, responsible AI leadership, and training fostering sustainable growth.

In addition to his professional achievements, Rob is passionate about the intersection of technology and human impact, which inspired his book, *"Mindful Machines, Masterful Humans: The Role of Innovations, AI and Tech Mastery in Organizational Transformation."* He draws from his own experiences in consulting and corporate leadership to explore the pivotal role of AI in shaping the future of organizations.

Rob currently resides in Virginia, USA, where he balances his professional life with being a proud father to his three children.

Preface

This book was born from a desire to empower leaders at all levels to embrace the opportunities and challenges brought by AI. It's for executives steering large enterprises, team managers overseeing daily operations, and emerging leaders looking to make their mark in the world.

In a world where technology is evolving at breakneck speed, the role of leadership is undergoing a profound transformation. Artificial intelligence, automation, and data-driven decision-making are no longer the future—they are the present. As these tools change industries, redefine jobs, and challenge traditional business models, leaders must adapt and grow in ways that go beyond what previous generations have ever imagined. It is a guide for this new era, where agility, foresight, and ethical responsibility are the cornerstones of effective leadership.

This book goes beyond technical know-how, emphasizing the importance of ethical leadership and responsible AI adoption. As AI tools become more integrated into our lives and work, questions of privacy, fairness, and accountability are no longer optional; they are essential. Leaders today have a responsibility to ensure that AI-driven decisions respect individual rights and contribute to society's well-being.

It is my hope that this book serves as a compass and a resource, inspiring you to lead confidently and responsibly in a world transformed by AI.

Contents

Introduction

A mid-sized company CEO faced a critical decision as her team spent months evaluating a new AI system that promised to automate several key business processes. This could increase efficiency and reduce costs. The data showed that implementing AI could boost productivity by 30% and give the company a competitive edge. By doing so, they can generate significant revenue growth.

However, there was a catch. This new system would likely reduce the need for some jobs, which would potentially displace a portion of the workforce. Thus, the CEO raised a difficult question. Should she move forward with the technology when she knows it would bring about financial gains but also cause disruption to employees' livelihoods? Or should she maintain the current operations, avoiding layoffs but possibly falling behind competitors embracing automation?

Many leaders are now confronting this kind of decision in the age of AI. As AI continues to transform industries, leaders must navigate these complex dynamics. It could be said that AI is itself redefining leadership.

Therefore, business and organizational development leaders and practitioners must master how innovations impact organizational development. This includes knowing what AI really is and how it is evolving quickly. Through this, you can find compatibility with this tool and effectively integrate it into existing business systems. You can use these tools for growth, profitability, and survival.

AI's rapid development has created a skills gap noticeably as there is a shortage of professionals with expertise in AI-related fields. This could be both a challenge and an opportunity for individuals to acquire in-demand skills. Therefore, choosing to ignore this fast-dominating phenomenon is plainly proving to be counterproductive very soon.

What Is AI & What Can It Do?

AI is essentially a branch of computer science. It focuses on creating systems or software that can perform tasks that typically require human intelligence. Problem-solving, learning, understanding natural language, recognizing patterns, and making decisions are some such tasks. AI technologies aim to simulate human cognitive functions in machines. This allows them to think, reason, and act in ways that mimic human intelligence. However, it is a broad and multidisciplinary field with various subfields. We will discuss the subfields in detail in the prevailing chapters.

Setting the Stage

It's imperative to grasp the impact of AI in the context of organizational transformation in our modern business landscape. The digital age has ushered in a profound paradigm shift. It has reshaped how organizations and the economy at large function. This transformation entails both challenges and opportunities of immense magnitude.

As of 2024, the Global Innovation Index (GII) ranks the most innovative economies, emphasizing their ability to adopt and leverage new technologies for growth and development.

As at 2024, the Top 10 Most Innovative Economies ranked based on their Global Innovation Index (GII) scores had Switzerland leading the ranking with the highest score of 67.5, followed by Sweden at 64.5 and the United States at 62.4. Singapore fourth with 61.2, while the United Kingdom and South Korea closely followed with scores of 61.0 and 60.9, respectively.

Other highly innovative economies included Finland (59.4), Netherlands (58.8), Germany (58.1), and Denmark (57.1), rounding out the top ten. These countries have demonstrated strong capabilities in research, technology, and innovation-driven growth, solidifying their positions as global leaders in innovation.

One cannot overlook the fierce competition in acknowledging this terrain. The ever-evolving customer expectations and the breakneck speed of technological innovation. It's an environment characterized by uncertainties that makes it essential for organizations to adapt and pivot.

But there's more to this narrative than challenges and uncertainties, such as the success stories that serve as an optimistic outcome. They reveal how organizations that have embraced AI have triumphed in this new era. These stories serve as a wellspring of inspiration, reinforcing the urgency of the message.

So, the stage is set! And it's set with purpose where the call to action is clear. Mastering AI and tech isn't an option anymore. It's the priority.

"While technology is evolving at an unprecedented pace, organizations that do not keep up with these advancements can quickly fall behind, while those that master the latest tech can gain a significant competitive edge."

—Gartner. A leading research and advisory company in the technology and business sector.

This alludes to the reality that the disconnect between the intent to innovate and actioning those plans does have a direct and significant impact on a company's revenue growth, profitability, and ultimate survival. AI is indeed expanding business.

In fact, it's a rapidly growing industry that is transforming the way businesses operate. According to a report by **Harvard Business Review**, digital innovation spurred by COVID-19 has put AI and analytics at the center of business operations. AI and analytics are boosting productivity and delivering new products and services. This accentuates corporate values, addresses supply chain issues, and fuels new startups (McKendrick, AI Adoption Skyrocketed Over the Last 18 Months, 2021). [1]

Forbes Advisor surveyed 600 business owners who are using or planning to incorporate AI into their businesses. The results revealed that businesses are employing AI in a variety of ways to improve efficiencies, save time, and decrease costs. With its continued advancements, AI is quickly becoming a precious resource for companies across industries.

The most popular applications include customer service, with 56% of respondents using AI for this purpose, and cybersecurity and fraud management, adopted by 51% of businesses. Other notable uses of AI are customer relationship management (46%), digital personal assistants (47%), inventory management (40%), and content production (35%) (IBM, 2024). [2]

Moreover, recent generative AI advances have generated optimism in the tech sector. For instance, the ChatGPT chatbot has been leading the way in generative AI breakthroughs (Muhammad Usman Tariq, 2021)[3].

---

[1] AI adoption skyrocketed over the last 18 months. (2021, September 27). *AI Adoption Skyrocketed Over the Last 18 Months*. Retrieved October 8, 2024, from https://hbr.org/2021/09/ai-adoption-skyrocketed-over-the-last-18-months

[2] Ibm. (2024, September 12). AIOps. *What is AIOps?* https://www.ibm.com/topics/aiops

[3] Tariq, M. U., Poulin, M., & Abonamah, A. A. (2021). Achieving operational excellence through artificial intelligence: driving forces and barriers. *Frontiers in Psychology, 12*. https://doi.org/10.3389/fpsyg.2021.686624

It has demonstrated the effectiveness of transformer-based models for language tasks. This has encouraged other AI researchers to adopt and refine this architecture (Marr, 2023).[4]

The Homo Magister Concept

Leadership is undergoing a fundamental transformation right now. A leader is no longer simply a decision-maker or strategist. The complexities of AI-driven change demand that leaders adopt a new paradigm. One that positions them as teachers, mentors, and guides. This is where the concept of Homo Magister comes into play.

Homo Magister—meaning "the teaching human"—represents a leadership model where leaders are not just authority figures. They are facilitators of learning and growth. Leaders must guide their teams through transitions in this environment of rapid technological advances. It is their job to help employees acquire new skills and adopt new mindsets. Also, guide them on how to go through the emotional and ethical challenges AI brings.

AI can undoubtedly automate many routine tasks. However, it cannot replicate human judgment or empathy. Neither can it bring the creativity of humans. Leaders must, therefore, foster these qualities within their organizations

---

[4] Marr, B. (2023, May 19). *A short history of ChatGPT: How we got to where we are today.*
Forbes. https://www.forbes.com/sites/bernardmarr/2023/05/19/a-short-history-of-chatgpt-how-we-got-to-where-we-are-today/

and teach their teams how to work alongside AI rather than fear or resist it.

This new model of leadership requires a shift in focus. A change from top-down directives to empowering others to think critically and make informed decisions. The Homo Magister leader sees themselves as a lifelong learner. Someone who models adaptability and encourages a growth mindset among their teams. In doing so, they ensure their organizations are equipped to prosper in a constantly evolving AI world.

The Convergence of Human Wisdom and AI

Effective leadership in the AI era entails the ability to merge human wisdom with AI's unparalleled capacity for data processing and pattern recognition. AI excels at analyzing vast amounts of data and offering insights that humans may overlook. However, it is the leader's human intuition, creativity, and ethical judgment that give context and meaning to those insights.

For example, AI might suggest an optimal course of action based on performance metrics. The leader must assess whether that course aligns with the organization's values and ethical standards or not. If not, then the leader has to guide the AI with certain prompts that are sensitive and provide a personal touch. Similarly, while AI can identify patterns in customer behavior, only a human leader can creatively envision how to turn those patterns into innovative, meaningful customer experiences.

In this way, the future of leadership lies not in choosing between human wisdom or AI but in learning the art of integrating both. This convergence will define how we lead and create sustainable and human-centered progress.

AI Fears 'Bold' Claims

AI has a wide range of applications across various industries. It has the potential to revolutionize many aspects of our lives, from improving productivity to addressing complex societal challenges. However, it also raises important ethical and social considerations that need to be carefully managed.

Thus, AI has generated both fears and bold claims. Here are some key points related to this impact:

1. Automation and Job Displacement: AI and automation technologies can automate routine and repetitive tasks. This can lead to the displacement of certain jobs, which could be a major concern for workers in industries where such tasks are prevalent. So, several workers can lose their jobs and the opportunity to earn their wages. It may necessitate a shift in job roles or reskilling to remain employable. However, AI can also create new job opportunities in fields related to AI development and maintenance. In fact, even ethical oversight can only be dealt with by a human.

According to a report by McKinsey Global Institute, between 400 and 800 million jobs around the world will possibly be gone by 2030. Robotics would usurp people's jobs. Self-driven cars and customer service software will also replace the current vehicles and services. The study found that up to one-third of the 2030 employees may need to learn new skills and find new work in more advanced economies like the U.S. and Germany (James Manyika, 2017).[5]

The midpoint estimate suggests 15% (400 million workers) could be affected. A portion of the workforce may need to switch occupations, with estimates ranging from 3% (75 million workers) at midpoint to 14% (375 million workers) in the fastest adoption scenario.

Still, it is bold to claim that AI will have the ability to think like humans by 2050. It is difficult and, quite frankly, too early to predict it for now, but we can simply not dismiss it as being a possibility—regardless of how much one might want to. Though AI has made noteworthy strides in recent years, it is still far from achieving human-like intelligence.

2. Ethical Concerns: The use of AI in decision-making, particularly in areas like hiring, lending, and criminal justice, has raised ethical concerns about bias, fairness, and transparency. It is essential to address these issues to ensure AI is used responsibly and equitably.

---

[5] Manyika, J., Lund, S., Chui, M., Bughin, J., Woetzel, L., Batra, P., Ko, R., & Sanghvi, S. (2017). Jobs lost, jobs gained: What the future of work will mean for jobs, skills, and wages. In *McKinsey & Company*. https://www.mckinsey.com/featured-insights/future-of-work/jobs-lost-jobs-gained-what-the-future-of-work-will-mean-for-jobs-skills-and-wages

3.   Bold Claims: AI has generated bold claims, such as the potential for super-intelligent AI or AI surpassing human capabilities. While these claims fuel excitement and innovation, they also raise concerns about safety and control, prompting discussions on ethical AI development and regulation.

4.   Economic Impact: AI has the potential to boost economic growth and competitiveness, but it may also exacerbate income inequality if not implemented equitably. Governments and organizations need to consider the broader economic implications of AI adoption.

By 2030, research indicates artificial intelligence is expected to have a significant global economic impact, with China experiencing the greatest benefit, contributing $7 trillion to its economy. North America projected to see a significant boost of up to $3.7 trillion from AI-driven advancements. Northern Europe expected to gain $1.8 trillion, while Southern Europe is projected to benefit by $0.7 trillion. In developed Asia, countries like Japan and South Korea are expected to see an AI-driven economic growth of $0.9 trillion. Latin America, $0.5 trillion. Outside these major regions, the rest of the world, is estimated to see an impact of $1.2 trillion. These projections underscore AI's transformative role with China and North America anticipated to benefit the most from its integration into various industries.

5. Privacy and Security: The increased use of AI in data analysis and decision-making processes raises concerns about data privacy and security. Protecting sensitive information and ensuring secure AI systems are paramount. As AI becomes more integral to data analysis and decision-making, concerns surrounding data privacy and security intensify. Safeguarding sensitive information and ensuring the security of AI systems are, therefore, critical priorities.

Hence, AI has the power to transform the workforce in terms of the jobs it affects and the new opportunities it creates. Responsible AI development and addressing the associated challenges are crucial so that we can increase the benefits and mitigate the risks.

Part I: Grasping the AI Opportunity

Chapter 1: Recognizing Digital Shifts

A retail company had been a primary gift shop in its community for decades. It was the kind of place where customers had grown used to being greeted by name, where you could find that perfect gift just in time for the holidays, and where Saturday mornings felt like a small-town reunion as neighbors caught up in the aisles.

But things changed for that company. Over the last few years, the company faced a steady decline in foot traffic and sales. Meanwhile, e-commerce giants like Amazon were thriving. More and more people preferred the convenience of ordering products online and having them delivered right to their doorsteps. The once-busy aisles of that store now seemed empty, save for a few loyal customers who hadn't fully embraced the digital shift.

The company was struggling to keep up. They felt the pressure to adapt but were caught in the rapid change, including changing customer behaviors, the speed of technological advancements, and the aggressive pricing strategies of online competitors. They had tried a few things, including launching a website, offering discounts, and even hosting special in-store events, but the results were modest at best. Eventually, the store had to close permanently.

This situation is a perfect example of how disruptive forces could turn a familiar business environment on its head. The challenge was clear for traditional companies like this: adapt or risk being left behind.

The pace of technological change is accelerating rapidly, and it continues to gain speed. One key concept that explains this trend is Moore's Law. Gordon Moore, a co-founder of Intel, introduced this idea in the 1960s. He predicted that the number of transistors on a microchip would double approximately every two years. This means that computers consistently become more powerful while simultaneously decreasing in cost at a predictable rate.

For a while, that idea held steady, and even today, we still see this trend in how tech improves so quickly. Think about your smartphone, for example. Ten years ago, the phones we carried couldn't do half of what today's models can. But it's not just about more powerful chips; it's about the effect this tech has across industries from retail to healthcare.

The speed at which businesses adopt new technology has increased significantly. In the past, major advancements took years or even decades to gain widespread acceptance. Today, however, the adoption process moves much faster. Consider the evolution from dial-up internet to streaming HD videos; what once required patience now happens easily.

The acceleration is even more evident when looking at how quickly new platforms reach massive audiences. Television took about 13 years to reach 50 million users. In contrast, Facebook achieved that milestone in just over a year, while Pokémon Go reached 50 million users in only 19 days. This rapid adoption highlights the faster pace of technological integration in our current era, demanding that businesses stay agile and responsive to remain competitive.

Businesses have to keep up with this accelerating pace, or they risk falling behind. They have to understand how technology can transform entire industries.

AI and automation have quickly transitioned from futuristic concepts to essential business tools. Only a few years ago, using AI to analyze data or interact with customers felt revolutionary. Today, it has become an industry standard. The pace at which companies adopt these technologies continues to accelerate, creating challenges for those who are not ready to adapt.

The challenge for businesses now extends beyond simply staying informed about new technologies; they must learn how to adapt and integrate them efficiently.

Technology is more than just a helpful tool in today's digital age. It is the basis for future growth. Knowing how to use AI and other technologies opens new opportunities and helps solve problems that once seemed too difficult. These skills allow companies to turn challenges into strengths, keeping them a step ahead.

Key Technologies Restructuring Businesses

Several key technologies are reshaping the way businesses operate, opening up new opportunities and driving change across industries. Among these, AI, IoT, blockchain, and cloud computing stand out as some of the most influential. Each of these technologies offers unique benefits that can transform how organizations work, compete, and grow.

Artificial Intelligence (AI)

Artificial Intelligence (AI) allows businesses to analyze data, automate processes, and make smarter decisions. By learning from vast amounts of information, AI can improve customer service through chatbots, streamline supply chains, and even predict market trends. Its ability to identify patterns and optimize operations makes it a powerful tool for efficiency and innovation.

The Internet of Things (IoT)

The Internet of Things (IoT) connects everyday devices to the Internet, enabling them to collect and exchange data. This technology helps organizations monitor equipment, track inventory, and improve logistics. For example, IoT sensors in manufacturing can predict when a machine needs maintenance, reducing downtime and saving costs. It creates a more connected and responsive business environment.

Blockchain

Blockchain provides a secure way to record transactions and track assets across a network. Its transparency and tamper-resistant nature make it ideal for industries like finance, supply chain, and healthcare. Businesses use blockchain to ensure secure transactions, verify the authenticity of products, and streamline complex processes, all while reducing the risk of fraud.

Cloud Computing

Cloud Computing offers businesses access to vast computing resources without the need for heavy investment in physical infrastructure. It allows companies to store data, run applications, and scale their operations flexibly. Cloud services make it easier to collaborate, enable remote work, and support business continuity, giving companies the agility to respond to market changes quickly.

These technologies help organizations become more efficient, responsive, and innovative, ensuring they stay competitive in a rapidly changing world. By embracing these tools, companies can unlock new levels of performance and open up opportunities for future growth.

Key Subfields in Artificial Intelligence (AI)

AI is a broad and multidisciplinary field with various subfields, some of which are mentioned below:

1. **Machine Learning**: A subset of AI that involves training machines to learn from data and improve their performance on specific tasks without being explicitly programmed. Machine learning algorithms are used in applications like recommendation systems, image recognition, and natural language processing.

2. **Deep Learning**: A subfield of machine learning that uses artificial neural networks to model and solve complex tasks. Deep learning has made significant advancements in areas like image and speech recognition.

3. Natural Language Processing (NLP): NLP focuses on enabling machines to understand, generate, and interact with human language. It is used in chatbots, language translation, and text analysis.

4. Computer Vision: This field is concerned with enabling computers to interpret and understand visual information from the world, such as images and videos. It's used in facial recognition, autonomous vehicles, and medical image analysis.

5. Robotics: AI is essential in the development of intelligent robots that can perform tasks in the physical world. This includes industrial robots, service robots, and autonomous drones.

6. Expert Systems: These are AI systems designed to mimic human expertise in specific domains. They use rule-based systems to make decisions and solve problems.

7. Speech Recognition: AI is used to convert spoken language into text, which is useful in applications like virtual assistants and transcription services.

8. Autonomous Systems: AI is a critical component of autonomous systems like self-driving cars and drones, enabling them to navigate and make decisions in real-world environments.

9. Reinforcement Learning: A type of machine learning where an agent learns to make decisions by interacting with an environment and receiving feedback in the form of rewards or penalties. It's used in gaming, robotics, and recommendation systems.

10. AI in Healthcare: AI is increasingly used in healthcare for tasks like diagnosing diseases, predicting patient outcomes, and drug discovery.

11. AI in Finance: In finance, AI is used for algorithmic trading, fraud detection, risk assessment, and customer service.

12. AI in Education: AI is used to develop personalized learning platforms, intelligent tutoring systems, and automated grading systems.

13. AI in Agriculture: AI is making significant strides in agriculture, with applications in precision farming, crop monitoring, and automated machinery. It helps farmers make data-driven decisions about planting, irrigation, and crop health.

14. AI in Mining: The mining industry utilizes AI to improve safety and efficiency. AI-powered drones and robots are used for exploration, and data analytics help discover and monitor mining operations.

15. AI in Pharmaceuticals: AI is revolutionizing drug discovery by analyzing vast datasets, predicting potential drug candidates, and streamlining clinical trials. It accelerates the development of new medications and treatments.

16. AI in Sports: AI plays a role in enhancing sports performance analysis. It's used for player tracking, injury prediction, and the development of coaching tools. In sports broadcasting, AI enhances the viewing experience through real-time data and analysis.

17. AI in Team Building: AI also addresses various concerns related to team compatibility and job skills training. Here's how AI contributes to these areas:

- *Team Compatibilities:* Assembling and optimizing teams by analyzing individual strengths, weaknesses, working styles, and personalities. It helps in creating more harmonious and effective teams. For example, AI algorithms can consider factors like communication styles and preferred working hours to ensure a well-matched team composition.

- *Job Skills Training:* Job skills training has evolved with the rise of personalized programs, often referred to as microlearning. AI plays a crucial role in this as it analyzes each individual's skills, competencies, and learning preferences to design tailored training modules. This approach ensures that the content and pace of training match the specific needs of each team member, making skill development more effective and knowledge acquisition more efficient. By focusing on what each person needs, AI-driven microlearning enhances overall learning.

- *Performance Assessment:* Monitors team performance and provides real-time feedback to both team members and leaders. It helps identify areas that require improvement and enables targeted training interventions by tracking key performance indicators, such as productivity, collaboration, and goal achievement.

- *Skill Gaps Identification:* AI can analyze the skill sets within a team and identify gaps or areas where certain skills are lacking. This information is invaluable for decision-makers and allows them to effectively prioritize training and development efforts to overcome these gaps.

- *Resource Allocation:* Leaders can allocate resources more efficiently by assessing team members' skills and availability. This approach ensures that the right people with the right skills are assigned to the right tasks, boosting overall team performance and productivity.

- *Predictive Analysis:* Leaders can also use predictive analysis to identify potential issues within a team, such as conflicts or skill gaps, before they escalate. This foresight allows them to proactively address problems, leading to smoother team dynamics and improved productivity.

AI's data-driven insights and adaptability make it valuable for optimizing team building and job skills training. Focusing on the individual needs and compatibilities of team members contributes to more cohesive and high-performing teams.

Tech Mastery encompasses a range of competencies and skills, including:

1. Understanding AI and Technology: This involves having a deep comprehension of AI and other relevant technologies, their capabilities, limitations, and their potential impact on various aspects of an organization.

2. Strategic Integration: Tech mastery means strategically integrating technology into an organization's processes and operations. It involves identifying the areas where AI and other technologies can deliver the most value, creating a clear implementation plan, and ensuring that these efforts align with the organization's overall goals. This approach helps businesses leverage technology effectively, turning it into a driver of growth and efficiency.

3. Innovation: It relates to the ability to innovate using technology. This involves creating new applications, solutions, or business models that leverage AI and tech to drive transformation and competitive advantage.

4. Change Management: Successful tech mastery also includes the skills to manage the organizational change that comes with technology adoption. This entails guiding employees and stakeholders through the transition, addressing concerns, and ensuring a smooth adaptation to new tools and processes.

5. Data and Analytics Proficiency: Tech mastery often involves a strong understanding of data and analytics, as these are critical components of AI and tech-driven decision-making.

6. Continuous Learning: Technology is constantly evolving, so tech mastery requires a commitment to continuous learning and staying updated on the latest advancements in AI and tech.

7. Ethical and Responsible Use: Mindfully using technology, especially AI, is a critical part of mastering it. This means paying close attention to ethical and responsible practices. This includes considering issues like bias, privacy, and security.

8. Leadership: Those with tech mastery should be able to lead teams and organizations through the process of adopting and leveraging technology effectively.

Mastering technology and AI has a crucial role in building high-performing teams and driving organizational success. AI assesses performance, identifies skill gaps, and predicts potential challenges. This allows leaders to make informed, data-driven decisions that improve team dynamics and boost productivity. Organizations can adopt AI technology and turn these advancements into a competitive advantage.

AI's Impact on Business Processes

Artificial Intelligence (AI) is bringing a new level of efficiency, precision, and customer focus by reshaping business processes across industries. Its impact spans from customer service to supply chain management and product development, fundamentally changing how companies operate.

Mentioned below are the ways AI is transforming these key areas and some specific examples of its applications:

Customer Service

AI has revolutionized customer service by enabling businesses to provide faster and more personalized support. Chatbots and virtual assistants have become common, handling routine inquiries and resolving common issues 24/7 without human intervention. For example, companies like *Bank of America* use their virtual assistant, Erica, to assist customers with account information, transaction history, and financial advice. These tools reduce wait times and ensure customers receive quick responses, which has led to higher customer satisfaction levels.

Beyond chatbots, AI-powered sentiment analysis tools help businesses understand customer emotions during interactions, whether in emails, social media, or chat sessions. This allows customer service teams to identify dissatisfaction early and address issues before they escalate. For instance, *Zendesk* uses AI to analyze customer conversations, prioritize urgent issues, and offer agents suggestions to improve responses.

Supply Chain Management

AI also plays an essential role in optimizing supply chains by improving demand forecasting, inventory management, and logistics. Predictive analytics powered by AI help companies anticipate demand shifts, which helps them adjust production and inventory levels accordingly. *Amazon* is a prime example of using AI to analyze purchasing patterns and adjust stock levels in its warehouses. This reduces overstock and stockouts, ensuring customers get what they need when they need it.

AI-driven robotics and automation streamline the picking, packing, and shipping processes in warehouses. It increases speed and accuracy. *Walmart* has implemented AI robots to manage inventory levels by scanning shelves and alerting staff when products need restocking. This reduces human error and ensures that shelves remain stocked. Additionally, AI helps optimize routes for delivery trucks, saving fuel costs and reducing delivery times, as seen with companies like *UPS*.

Product Development

AI is transforming product development by enabling businesses to analyze market trends and consumer preferences faster and more accurately. Companies can identify gaps in the market and develop products that better align with customer needs through AI-driven data analysis. For example, *Coca-Cola* uses AI to analyze customer feedback and identify trends in flavors, leading to the creation of new products that cater to evolving tastes.

AI also enhances the design and testing phase of product development. In industries like automotive manufacturing, *Tesla* uses AI to simulate real-world driving conditions and refine its autonomous driving software. This reduces the time and cost associated with physical prototyping and testing.

AI's impact on business processes is undeniable, as it has transformed the way companies interact with customers, manage their supply chains, and develop new products. With its ability to analyze vast amounts of data and automate complex tasks, AI allows businesses to operate more efficiently and stay competitive in a fast-paced market.

Transforming Business Decisions with AI

AI also brings accuracy, speed, and insight to the way organizations make decisions. Companies now have the power of AI to dig through massive amounts of data, spot patterns, and even make recommendations instead of relying solely on intuition or traditional analysis.

Data-Driven Insights

One of the biggest advantages of AI in decision-making is how it turns large amounts of data into actionable insights. In the past, businesses would have teams of analysts sifting through reports to find trends and make sense of what was happening. Now, AI can analyze customer behavior, market trends, and internal operations in real-time. This means leaders can make decisions based on what's happening right now rather than looking back at last quarter's numbers.

Take retail, for example. AI can analyze sales data and customer preferences to help stores decide which products to stock and when. This means fewer unsold items sitting on shelves and more of what customers actually want. In finance, AI models can predict market movements or even help assess risk, making investment decisions smarter and faster. It's all about using data to stay ahead of the curve.

Predictive Analytics

AI can help predict what's likely to happen next. Predictive analytics uses algorithms to look at past data and identify future trends. This is extremely helpful for businesses trying to plan for the future. For instance, a logistics company might use AI to predict delays in their supply chain and reroute shipments before a problem even occurs.

In healthcare, AI-powered predictive analytics can analyze patient data to predict the likelihood of certain health conditions, allowing doctors to intervene earlier and improve patient outcomes. This kind of foresight can mean the difference between reactive and proactive decision-making, helping organizations avoid costly mistakes and seize new opportunities.

Autonomous Systems

AI has also brought us autonomous systems, machines, or programs that can make decisions and act without constant human input. Think of self-driving cars, automated trading systems, or even AI managing energy use in a smart building. These systems are designed to optimize outcomes on their own, making split-second decisions based on the data they receive. This will help businesses save time on routine decisions and focus on strategic priorities.

Benefits and Potential Pitfalls

AI-driven decision-making also speeds up processes, eliminates human biases, and allows businesses to act on insights faster than ever. With AI's ability to see patterns that humans might miss, organizations can gain a competitive edge, fine-tune their strategies, and better meet customer needs.

But there are also some risks. AI systems are only as good as the data they're trained on. If that data has biases or gaps, AI can end up making decisions that are unfair or even harmful. For example, AI in hiring has sometimes shown biases against certain demographics because it learned from biased historical data. This means that businesses need to be careful about how they build and use AI systems, ensuring transparency and fairness.

Additionally, relying too heavily on AI can mean losing the human touch in decision-making. AI might know what the data says, but it can't always understand the bigger picture, like the nuances of a company's culture or the unique needs of its customers. So, you must maintain a balance between trusting AI insights and human oversight.

Recent research by **McKinsey & Company** underscores the transformative power of AI and technology in modern businesses. According to their study published in 2021, companies that have effectively integrated AI into their operations have seen a significant boost in productivity and efficiency. The research shows that AI-driven automation not only reduces labor costs but also leads to a 20-25% increase in output. It highlights the critical role of technology in optimizing processes, allowing organizations to achieve more with fewer resources.[6]

Additionally, a report from the World Economic Forum in 2020 highlights the importance of AI and technology in enhancing customer engagement. According to the report, organizations that use advanced analytics and AI-driven personalization techniques have experienced a 30% increase in customer satisfaction and loyalty. This research underscores how technology is reshaping the customer

---

[6]https://www.mckinsey.com/~/media/McKinsey/Business%20Functions/McKinsey%20Analytics/Our%20Insights/Global%20survey%20The%20state%20of%20AI%20in%202021/Global-survey-The-state-of-AI-in-2021.pdf

experience and making it more tailored and responsive to individual needs.[7]

Furthermore, a study published by the International Data Corporation (IDC) in 2022 showcases the global impact of AI and technology. It reveals that businesses that invest in digital transformation initiatives, including AI, are projected to capture an additional $1.2 trillion in revenue by 2025. This research underlines the economic implications of technology adoption, emphasizing that it's not just a matter of staying competitive but also driving significant financial growth.[8]

AI-driven decision-making is offering new levels of insight and efficiency. It enables organizations to make smarter, faster decisions, anticipate future trends, and even automate complex processes. But with this power comes responsibility. Businesses need to ensure they use AI thoughtfully, considering its potential and limitations.

The Changing Competition in Business

In today's global business world, gaining a competitive edge is a top goal for any company.[9] A competitive advantage is what sets a company apart, helping it boost profits and lead its industry by offering new features in its products or services.

---

[7]https://www.weforum.org/agenda/2020/12/ai-productivity-automation-artificial-intelligence-countries/

[8]https://www.mckinsey.com/capabilities/quantumblack/our-insights/the-state-of-ai-in-2022-and-a-half-decade-in-review?src_trk=em670554f2a39f94.13004265912974668

[9]https://www.researchgate.net/publication/305397486_Types_of_Competitive_Advantage_and_Analysis

Startups, for example, often gain an edge by focusing on innovation and applying new technologies in creative ways, even in traditional industries.[10]

Technology can enhance what a company offers, improve how it makes products, and streamline logistics. Such advancements can redefine entire industries and push the boundaries of what's possible. Innovations in engineering, the Internet, and new materials have even led to tools that tackle global challenges like climate change.[11]

Focusing on technology has helped create a new digital economy. This economy is created by globalization, local markets, partnerships between companies, insights into consumer needs, and the integration of the Internet into everyday devices. Therefore, in this fierce competition and rapid tech growth, companies need to adopt new technologies to stay ahead of rivals and capture a bigger share of the market.

Blurring Industry Boundaries

Technology has made it easier for companies to step outside their traditional roles and offer new services. Think about how *Amazon* went from selling books online to becoming a giant in cloud computing with AWS or how *Apple* moved from making computers to dominating the

---

[10]https://www.researchgate.net/publication/363480750_Estimating_the_dur ation_of_competitive_advantage_from_emerging_technology_adoption

[11]https://www.researchgate.net/publication/337333407_Critical_factors_for _the_successful_implementation_of_Industry_40_a_review_and_future_resear ch_direction

music industry with iTunes and then streaming with Apple Music. These moves might have seemed unlikely years ago, but technology made them possible. Now, every business needs to keep an eye on potential disruptors from unexpected places.

The boundaries between industries are no longer clear-cut. A car company isn't just competing with other automakers anymore; it's also competing with tech companies like *Tesla* that have redefined what a car can be. Technology has allowed companies to create entirely new experiences and value for customers, and that's where the competition gets fierce.

Platform Economies and Ecosystems

One of the key drivers of this shift is the rise of platform economies. Instead of just selling products or services, companies like *Airbnb* and *Alibaba* have built platforms that connect users directly with what they need. These platforms create a whole new way of doing business by acting as intermediaries, making money by facilitating connections rather than owning the actual service or product.

These platforms thrive on scale. The more users they attract, the more valuable they become, creating a network effect that's hard for traditional businesses to compete with. It's not just about having a better product anymore; it's about creating an ecosystem that users want to be a part of. This is why we see companies across all industries, from retail to banking, trying to build their own platforms and ecosystems to stay relevant.

New Entrants Disrupting Established Markets

It has now become easier for new entrepreneurs to enter industries that were once dominated by a few well-known companies. These newcomers bring fresh ideas, innovative approaches, and, often, new business models that challenge the status quo.

Unlike established companies, new entrants aren't held back by outdated systems or rigid processes. They can move quickly, adapt to changes, and implement the latest technology without having to overhaul old structures. This allows them to offer unique products or services that meet evolving customer needs, often at lower costs or with added convenience.[12]

These disruptions can reshape entire industries. The traditional players must adapt quickly to this new competition, as their market share and relevance can be at risk. The presence of new entrants pushes all companies to innovate and rethink their strategies to maintain their competitive edge. This shift in the market dynamics forces established companies to respond, either by adopting new technologies themselves, adjusting their business models, or finding new ways to add value for customers. Ultimately, the entry of new competitors keeps the market dynamic and

---

[12]https://link.springer.com/article/10.1007/s40171-024-00409-9

competitive, encouraging continuous improvement and better options for consumers.

For established businesses, keeping up with this changing competition means rethinking how they approach the market. It's no longer enough to stick with what's worked in the past. They need to be open to partnerships, think about building or joining platforms, and focus on delivering value beyond their traditional offerings. This might require you to enter new industries or even welcome competitors into their ecosystem to keep customers engaged.

Competition is extremely unpredictable, but it's also full of opportunities for those who can adapt quickly. The companies that can embrace this shift recognize the power of platforms and find ways to build their own ecosystems. Therefore, they will have a better shot of being successful in a time when technology keeps changing the rules.

General Electric (GE), a long-established industrial powerhouse, has effectively disrupted its traditional sectors through innovative use of the Industrial Internet of Things (IIoT). GE recognized the potential of IIoT early on, seeing an opportunity to transform how industries like manufacturing and energy operate by integrating digital capabilities into physical infrastructure.

As a traditional player in the aviation, energy, and healthcare sectors, GE faced growing competition and pressure to improve efficiency. They saw how digital transformation could change the game, especially through the application of IIoT. This approach involves connecting industrial machinery with advanced sensors, data analytics, and software to gain real-time insights and optimize operations. For GE, this was a way to move beyond just being a hardware provider to becoming a leader in digital industrial solutions.

GE began implanting sensors in a wide range of industrial equipment, from turbines to aircraft engines and medical devices. By collecting large amounts of data from these machines and analyzing it using advanced software, GE could monitor performance continuously. This allowed them to detect issues before becoming major problems and optimize equipment performance in real-time.

For example, in the energy sector, GE used IIoT to monitor turbines in power plants. By analyzing data on temperature, vibration, and other key metrics, they could predict maintenance needs before a failure occurred. This helped their clients reduce unplanned downtime and improve the overall efficiency of power generation. The same approach was applied in aviation, where GE monitored engines to ensure aircraft operated smoothly and safely, which helped them minimize delays and maintenance disruptions.

GE's investment in IIoT didn't just make their products more efficient but also allowed them to create new revenue streams. They introduced digital services such as predictive maintenance, where they offered their customers the ability to foresee equipment failures before they happened. This service added value for clients, as it reduced costly downtimes and kept operations running smoothly. These new digital offerings helped GE transition from a purely product-based company to one that also provides valuable digital services.

This transformation had a significant impact on the market. GE strengthened its competitive position in traditional industries like energy and aviation while also positioning itself as a leader in industrial digitalization. Their ability to merge hardware expertise with software capabilities allowed them to adapt to changes in the industry landscape and stay relevant amid technological shifts.

GE's use of IIoT shows how adopting technology can help even established companies redefine themselves. It also highlights how leveraging emerging technologies can lead to both operational improvements and new market offerings. It helps in ensuring long-term competitiveness in evolving industries.

Traditional Business Model Obsolescence

Technological change has rendered many traditional business models obsolete. Companies that once dominated their industries have struggled to keep up with new technologies and consumer expectations, which have reshaped the market. These shifts have often led to the downfall of businesses that failed to adapt quickly enough to the changing technology.

For instance, the rise of digital media led to the collapse of companies that relied heavily on physical sales, such as

Blockbuster, which dominated the video rental market. Blockbuster's inability to pivot to streaming services like *Netflix* embraced digital delivery early on, which ultimately caused its decline. The company stuck to its physical rental model for too long, failing to recognize the shift in how people consumed media.

Similarly, *Kodak*, once a giant in the photography industry, struggled to transition from traditional film to digital photography. Even though Kodak was one of the pioneers of digital camera technology, it hesitated to fully embrace digital products, fearing it would undermine its profitable film business. Meanwhile, companies that adapted to digital photography thrived, and Kodak eventually filed for bankruptcy, a victim of its own reluctance to change.

These examples highlight how traditional business models, focused on physical products and face-to-face customer interactions, are vulnerable in an age where digital alternatives provide convenience, speed, and global reach. Businesses that fail to adapt to these shifts are often overtaken by more agile competitors.

Organizational Structure Evolution

As technology advances, organizational structures must evolve with the business models. Traditional hierarchical structures, where decision-making is centralized and communication flows from the top down, often struggle to keep up with the pace of change in today's fast-moving markets.

The rise of digital communication tools, remote work capabilities, and data analytics has enabled companies to adopt more flexible and network-based organizational structures. Unlike rigid hierarchies, these new structures allow for faster decision-making, greater collaboration across departments, and the ability to quickly pivot when market conditions change.

For example, many tech startups embrace a *flat organizational structure* where employees have more autonomy and decision-making power. This setup encourages creativity, innovation, and a faster response to changes in technology or customer needs. Established companies like *Spotify* have adopted *agile methodologies* and created cross-functional teams that can focus on specific projects and adapt quickly as new priorities arise. These network-based structures support a more iterative approach to product development, which is crucial in industries driven by rapid technological advancements.

Even large corporations are rethinking their structures. For instance, *Microsoft* shifted from a highly siloed structure to a more collaborative model under CEO Satya Nadella's leadership. This change enabled the company to embrace cloud computing more effectively, making it a key player in the cloud market alongside competitors like Amazon Web Services.

This shift from hierarchical to flexible structures is driven by the need for speed and innovation in response to technological disruption. Companies that adapt their organizational models to be more dynamic and interconnected often perform well with new technologies, align with evolving customer expectations, and maintain a competitive edge in a constantly changing business environment.

Human Capital Implications

Technological change is fundamentally altering the nature of work and the skills required in today's job market. As automation, AI, and digital tools become more integrated into everyday business processes, the demand for traditional skills is decreasing, while the need for new competencies is on the rise. Among these, digital literacy and adaptability have become essential.

Digital Literacy

Today's workforce needs to be comfortable with a range of digital tools and platforms, from data analytics software to cloud-based collaboration tools. Employees must know how to use basic computer programs and also understand more complex systems like AI-driven platforms or data visualization tools. The ability to quickly learn new digital skills is becoming a core component of job readiness.

Adaptability

Adaptability is also crucial alongside digital literacy. With technology and industry needs changing so quickly, workers need to be open to continuous learning and upskilling. Jobs today require more than just technical know-how. They demand an ability to pivot when new technologies emerge. This need for flexibility has led to a rise in "lifelong learning" cultures within companies, where continuous training and skill development are prioritized to keep pace with industry shifts.

This puts pressure on both employees and employers. Workers must take the initiative to stay relevant, while companies need to provide the training and resources to help them do so. Those who adapt quickly to these changes can thrive in the modern workforce, while those who don't may find themselves at a disadvantage.

Ethical and Societal Impacts

The integration of advanced technologies like AI and automation does not just transform industries; it also brings about significant ethical and societal challenges. As these technologies reshape the world of work, they raise critical questions about job displacement, privacy, and economic inequality.

Job Displacement

Automation and AI are taking over tasks that used to be performed by humans, particularly in industries like manufacturing, logistics, and even customer service. This can lead to job losses, particularly for roles that involve routine, repetitive tasks. While technology also creates new jobs, they often require more specialized skills, which can leave some workers behind.

For example, Tesla's **Optimus robot** is a great case of how AI and robotics are advancing in manufacturing. Optimus, designed to perform physical tasks typically done by humans, can lift heavy objects, assemble components, and perform basic manual labor. This level of automation has the potential to reshape factory work, where repetitive tasks are often handled by human workers.

While technologies like Optimus can improve efficiency and reduce costs, they also raise concerns about job displacement. Workers who previously handled these manual tasks may find their roles eliminated or significantly reduced. At the same time, the introduction of such technology creates demand for new roles, but these often require more specialized skills, such as robotics programming, AI maintenance, or data analysis.

This transition presents a major challenge for society: how do we help workers adapt? The solution lies in reskilling programs that equip people with the knowledge and abilities to thrive in new tech-driven roles. By learning new skills, displaced workers can transition to roles that technology has not yet fully taken over.

Privacy Concerns

With the rise of AI and data analytics, there's a growing concern about privacy. Many of these technologies rely on large amounts of personal data to function effectively, whether for targeted advertising, personalized services, or AI training models. This raises questions about how data is collected, stored, and used, as well as the transparency of these practices. Individuals and regulators are increasingly questioning how much data companies should be allowed to collect and how it should be protected to avoid misuse.

Economic Inequality

Technology's role in deepening economic divides is another critical issue. High-skilled workers who can adapt to technological changes often find new opportunities and higher wages, while those without digital skills may struggle to find employment. It may result in increased economic inequality, where access to opportunities is tied to access to education and technology. Addressing these disparities requires a focus on inclusive policies that ensure all workers have access to training and the opportunity to participate in the digital economy.

As technology continues to advance, society must find a balance between leveraging these innovations for growth and addressing the challenges they bring. It's about creating a future where technology enhances human potential rather than replaces it, ensuring that progress benefits everyone.

Future Trend Projections

In the coming years, the forces of digital transformation, AI, and emerging technologies will continue to reshape how businesses operate. As AI evolves, we can expect even deeper integration into everyday business processes, making operations more efficient and decision-making more data-driven. Technologies like AI, blockchain, and the Internet of Things (IoT) will likely become standard across industries, which will help companies analyze massive datasets, automate routine tasks, and create smarter, more connected products.

Emerging Technologies

Technologies like quantum computing and advanced robotics could further transform industries. Quantum computing promises to solve complex problems far faster than today's best supercomputers, potentially revolutionizing fields like pharmaceuticals and financial modeling. Meanwhile, advanced robotics and autonomous systems are set to change manufacturing and logistics by allowing for fully automated factories and supply chains. AI-driven tools like natural language processing and machine learning will continue to improve, enabling more sophisticated customer interactions and predictive capabilities.

Impact on Organizations

This wave of technological advancement will push companies to innovate continuously. It's expected that companies that quickly adopt and integrate new technologies will gain a competitive edge, while those that lag behind may struggle to keep up. Additionally, the shift toward more remote work and digital collaboration tools, spurred by recent global trends, will remain a significant aspect of how organizations function. Businesses will need to be agile, capable of quickly adapting to new tech trends, and ready to leverage them for both internal efficiencies and enhanced customer experiences.

Leadership Imperatives

As these forces reshape industries, they also change what is required of organizational leaders. Effective leaders will need to develop a deeper understanding of technology and its implications for their business. This is where the earlier mentioned Homo Magister imperative becomes essential.

Need for Technological Literacy

Leaders must become more tech-savvy. This doesn't mean they need to become tech experts, but they should understand enough to make informed decisions about adopting new technologies. This knowledge will help them identify opportunities, assess risks, and understand how technology can be a driver for growth.

Adaptive Strategies

Leaders need to create organizations that can pivot quickly when needed, keeping up with new developments and shifts in the market. This means fostering a work environment where learning and innovation are part of the daily routine. To make that happen, companies must invest in training and development programs, helping their teams build new skills and stay up to speed with emerging technologies. It's all about staying ready to adapt and making sure that the workforce is prepared for whatever comes next.

Ethical Guidance

As technology advances, it's more important than ever for leaders to use it responsibly. They play a key role in guiding their companies through the ethical challenges that come with AI and automation. This means tackling issues like protecting data privacy, ensuring that AI makes fair decisions, and thinking about how automation might impact jobs and the wider community. When leaders make ethics a priority, they not only build a culture of trust within their organization but also earn the trust of their customers. This trust is essential for maintaining a strong reputation, especially as the world becomes more digital and connected.

In essence, the future of business will be shaped by those who are willing to embrace technological change and navigate the challenges it brings. Leaders who can combine tech knowledge with a strong ethical compass will be best positioned to guide their organizations into this future. The ability to adapt, learn, and lead with responsibility will define the successful companies of tomorrow.

To keep up with the rapid pace of technological change, leaders need to take actionable steps within their organizations. Mentioned below are a few tips you can follow:

1. **Audit Current Capabilities**: Start by evaluating the organization's existing technological strengths and weaknesses. This could include assessing current digital tools, processes, and skills among employees. Understanding where the organization stands is key to identifying areas for improvement.

2. **Invest in Training and Development**: Equip the team with the skills they need to adapt to new technologies. This might involve workshops, online courses, or even partnerships with tech firms for specialized training. The goal is to build a workforce that's not just aware of new technologies but capable of using them effectively.

3. **Prioritize Data Ethics**: Establish clear guidelines for handling data, ensuring privacy and transparency in AI decision-making processes. This step helps in building a framework that respects customer data and maintains ethical AI practices, fostering trust.

4. **Create an Innovation Culture**: Encourage teams to experiment with new tools and ideas. This could be

through pilot programs or hackathons, where teams get hands-on experience with new technologies.

5. **Regularly Review and Adjust Strategy**: The technology changes quickly, so it's important to revisit strategies often. Leaders should remain flexible and willing to pivot and adjust their plans as new opportunities or challenges arise.

Reflections:

To apply these ideas effectively, consider these questions:

- What technologies currently pose the greatest opportunity or threat to our business model?

- How well-prepared is our workforce to adopt new digital tools, and where are the biggest gaps?

- Are we handling customer data in a way that builds trust and meets regulatory standards?

- What changes in our industry could potentially disrupt our operations in the next few years?

- How can we better foster a culture that embraces innovation and continuous learning?

These questions can help leaders think better about where their organization stands and how they can adapt to thrive in a tech-driven future.

Today's digital world is complex, and leaders need to be proactive and strategic. Embracing new technology, building new skills, and focusing on using data responsibly are now must-haves for staying competitive. Leaders who encourage innovation and flexibility within their teams can help their organizations not only keep up with change but also excel in it.

Chapter 2: Embracing New Leadership Models

A tech company CEO led her team through a major AI implementation as a mentor and teacher. She understood that introducing AI wasn't just about installing new software; it was about changing the way the entire team thought and worked and making sure everyone understood not only what AI could do but how it could improve their day-to-day tasks.

She held regular workshops where she walked them through the AI tools step by step. She made complex ideas easier to grasp by using real-life examples from their own workflows to show how AI could make everyday tasks faster and smoother. During these sessions, she didn't just explain AI in theory but also demonstrated how it could solve their problems on the spot.

When someone struggled with a concept, she was right there, helping them figure it out in real-time, breaking it down further until everyone understood. Her hands-on approach built trust and eased the learning process, but it also revealed the bigger challenges the team faced.

The team's biggest challenges revolved around adapting to the complexities of AI and the mindset shift it required. At first, many team members were unsure how AI would impact their roles, and some worried about the possibility of job displacement. The CEO had to address these concerns head-on by reassuring the team that AI wasn't here to replace them but to enhance their work and productivity.

Next, the technical learning curve posed a significant challenge. For many, AI was an entirely new field as there were unfamiliar terms, concepts, and tools. The team had to quickly get up to speed on how AI worked, how to integrate it into their existing systems, and how to use it effectively in their day-to-day operations.

Another challenge was overcoming resistance to change. Some employees were comfortable with their current workflows and hesitant to adopt new technologies that could disrupt established routines. It was about breaking old habits and embracing new and more efficient ways of working.

Finally, collaboration across departments proved difficult at first. AI implementation required close cooperation between technical and non-technical teams, and there were initial struggles in communication and aligning goals. The CEO had to foster a more collaborative environment where everyone felt their input mattered, regardless of their technical background.

Through guidance and learning, the team eventually overcame these challenges, but they were significant hurdles at the start of the journey.

The CEO handled resistance by taking a thoughtful, empathetic approach. She knew that resistance often comes from fear, so her first step was to open up clear lines of communication. Instead of pushing the team to adopt AI without explanation, she made time to meet with employees, listen to their concerns, and address them directly. She explained how AI would enhance their work rather than replace them, showing that their roles would become more focused on creative problem-solving rather than repetitive tasks.

Instead of introducing sweeping changes all at once, the CEO implemented AI in phases, starting with smaller, less disruptive tasks. As the team saw AI improving their efficiency in these areas, their initial skepticism started to fade. These small successes build confidence and trust in the new systems.

The AI implementation brought several positive impacts to the company, transforming both how the team worked and the overall business operations.

First, there was a noticeable boost in efficiency. Routine tasks that used to take up significant time were automated, allowing employees to focus on more strategic and creative work. This led to faster project completion times and an increase in overall productivity. For example, data analysis tasks that once took days were now completed in hours, freeing up the team to focus on decision-making and innovation.

The AI also improved accuracy. By reducing human error in processes like data entry and forecasting, the company could make more informed and data-driven decisions. This had a direct impact on the quality of their services, which resulted in better customer satisfaction and fewer costly mistakes.

In addition to operational improvements, the AI brought valuable insights. With advanced data analytics, the company could better understand market trends, customer preferences, and internal performance metrics. This allowed them to tailor their strategies more effectively, leading to improved products and services that better met customer needs.

Overall, AI not only streamlined operations but also empowered the team to work smarter and innovate more effectively, positioning the company for future growth and success.

In this scenario, we see the concept of *Homo Magister* in action, the leader as both a visionary and a teacher. This approach doesn't just push the company forward in terms of technology; it creates a culture of learning and growth. Her team wasn't just following her lead. They were evolving with her and were ready to face the future of tech with confidence.

The concept of *Homo Magister* comes from the Latin words "homo," meaning human, and "magister," meaning teacher or master. In the context of modern organizations, particularly those embracing AI-driven change, *Homo Magister* represents a new kind of leader, one who embodies both the visionary leadership needed to work through the complex technological advancements and the nurturing role of a teacher guiding their team through these changes.

In today's developing business world, the traditional leadership model is no longer enough. Leaders are not only expected to make strategic decisions but also to cultivate a culture of learning and adaptability within their teams. This is where *Homo Magister* becomes significant. These leaders don't just instruct from above; they actively participate in learning processes, ensuring their teams understand how to integrate AI and other advanced technologies into daily operations.

The *Homo Magister* approach is centered on the belief that leadership and teaching go hand-in-hand. As AI continues to transform how businesses operate, leaders need to be mentors and help employees overcome their fears of new technology, upskill, and adapt. This dual role enhances team performance as well as the entire organizational culture and promotes an environment of continuous growth.

Leadership has gone through many changes over the years. In the past, the common model was command-and-control, where leaders gave orders, and employees followed without question. This top-down approach was all about strict authority, where leaders held all the power and decision-making, while employees had little input. It worked well for certain industries, especially during times when efficiency and discipline were key, like in manufacturing and military contexts.

Over time, as industries evolved and companies started valuing collaboration and innovation, leadership styles had to change. This is where servant leadership came in. Instead of being a commander, the leader's role shifted to serving their employees and helping them succeed. This style emphasizes listening, empathy, and supporting the team's needs. Leaders who practiced servant leadership believed that by empowering their team, the organization would thrive. This shift was especially useful in creative industries and those focused on problem-solving, where collaboration was critical.

Technology is moving faster than ever, and organizations need leaders who understand these changes and also guide their teams through them. The old command-and-control model doesn't work in this environment because employees need to adapt and innovate, not just follow orders. Even servant leadership, while effective in many ways, isn't enough by itself.

This is where a new leadership paradigm is needed that blends visionary leadership with the role of a teacher, like the *Homo Magister* concept. Leaders must now inspire their teams with a clear vision of how AI and technology will shape the future and help their employees understand and apply these tools.

In short, as leadership has evolved over time, we now need a new approach that fits the demands of the AI-driven world. Leaders must be more than just decision-makers; they need to be teachers, mentors, and guides who help their teams thrive in the face of technological change.

Homo Magister and servant leadership share some similarities, but they differ in key ways, especially in how they address the challenges of modern, technology-driven organizations.

Servant leadership is focused on putting the needs of the team first. A servant leader acts as a support system and provides resources, guidance, and empowerment to help their employees thrive. The leader's main goal is to serve their team and remove obstacles that may hinder their success. It's a bottom-up approach, where the leader prioritizes empathy, listening, and encouraging a positive, supportive environment. While this style is effective in creating a collaborative and inclusive culture, it doesn't necessarily emphasize the leader's role in guiding technological learning and innovation.

On the contrary, Homo Magister goes beyond just supporting the team. It combines visionary leadership with active teaching. In this model, the leader not only serves the team but also plays an essential role in mentoring and educating. This approach is especially relevant in today's tech-driven world, where employees need to continuously learn and adapt to new technologies like AI.

In the AI era, leaders face new challenges that require traditional leadership skills and an understanding of technology. The fast pace of innovation, handling ethical issues, and finding the right balance between human judgment and AI-driven insights create important obstacles for today's leaders.

AI Era Leadership Challenges

The rise of artificial intelligence (AI) has brought about significant changes in how businesses operate, requiring leaders to adapt to new challenges that previous generations of leaders didn't face. The AI era presents unique obstacles that require a different approach to leadership and blends technology with human insight.

Mentioned below are some of the major challenges that leaders face.

1. Rapid Technological Change

One of the biggest challenges for leaders today is the speed at which technology is advancing. AI and related technologies, such as machine learning and automation, are developing so quickly that it's difficult for businesses to keep up. Leaders must stay on top of these developments to make informed decisions about how to implement new tools effectively within their organizations.

This constant state of change creates several issues:

- **Keeping Skills Current**: Leaders need to ensure their teams are continuously learning and updating their skills. This means promoting a culture of continuous education and being proactive in offering training and development programs.

- **Decision-Making Speed**: With technology evolving rapidly, leaders are often pressured to make quick decisions about adopting new tools or processes.

Delays can result in falling behind competitors who may be faster at integrating these new capabilities.

- **Resource Allocation**: Leaders must balance investment in AI tools with other business needs. Deciding how much to invest in new technologies without disrupting existing processes can be a complex and delicate balancing act.

2. Ethical Dilemmas

The introduction of AI brings about new ethical concerns that leaders must address. These issues are often unprecedented, leaving leaders without clear guidelines to follow. Some of the key ethical challenges include:

- **Bias in AI Systems**: AI systems are only as good as the data they are trained on, and if that data contains biases, the AI may reinforce or even amplify those biases. Leaders need to ensure that AI systems are fair, inclusive, and free from discrimination, particularly in areas like hiring, customer service, and decision-making processes.

- **Privacy Concerns**: AI systems often rely on large datasets, some of which may include sensitive personal information. Leaders are responsible for ensuring that these systems comply with privacy regulations and that customers' and employees' data is handled securely and ethically.

- **Transparency and Accountability**: AI algorithms can be complex and difficult to understand, even for those working closely with them. Leaders must decide how transparent they should be about how AI-driven decisions are made and who is accountable when things go wrong, humans or machines?

These ethical dilemmas require leaders to be thoughtful and deliberate in how they approach AI, often setting new policies or adapting existing ones to ensure their organizations use AI responsibly.

3. Balancing Human and AI Capabilities

One of the most significant challenges in the AI era is finding the right balance between human and AI capabilities. AI can automate many tasks, freeing employees to focus on more strategic or creative work, but this shift also creates uncertainty about the future of human roles in the workplace.

- **Redefining Roles**: Leaders need to reassess their employees' roles in light of AI's capabilities. They must determine which tasks should be handled by AI and which require a human touch. This might involve redesigning job roles, upskilling workers, or even creating new positions that focus on managing AI systems.

- **Employee Resistance**: The fear of job loss due to automation is a real concern for many employees. Leaders must manage these fears carefully and provide reassurance that AI is there to enhance, not replace the human work. Transparent communication and a clear strategy for how AI will benefit both the company and its employees can help mitigate resistance.

- **Maintaining Human Creativity and Empathy**: While AI excels at handling repetitive or data-driven tasks, it cannot replace human creativity, intuition, or empathy. Leaders must ensure that their teams continue to bring these uniquely human qualities to the workplace, even as AI takes on more responsibilities.

4. Managing AI Integration Across the Organization

Implementing AI across various departments can create operational challenges, especially if some teams are more resistant to change or less technically savvy. Leaders must ensure smooth integration by:

- **Promoting Collaboration**: AI implementation often requires collaboration between technical and non-technical teams. Leaders need to promote a culture where both groups work together, ensuring that non-technical employees understand the value of AI and how to work with it.

- **Monitoring and Adjusting**: AI systems require ongoing oversight and adjustment to ensure they are delivering value. Leaders must put processes in place to monitor AI performance and make changes when necessary, whether it's fine-tuning algorithms or adjusting how the technology is being used within the organization.

The AI era presents a unique set of challenges for leaders, requiring them to stay ahead of rapid technological change, go through complex ethical dilemmas, and strike a careful balance between human and AI capabilities.

Homo Magister Key Attributes

The concept of *Homo Magister* embodies a leader who excels not only in guiding organizations through complex technological changes but also in fostering a culture of learning and ethical responsibility. In an era driven by AI and rapid innovation, *Homo Magister* leaders must possess certain key attributes to go through the challenges and ensure that both their people and the technology they use are aligned with the organization's goals. Here are the critical attributes of a *Homo Magister* leader:

1. Technological Literacy

Unlike traditional leaders who may delegate technical aspects to specialists, a *Homo Magister* engages with new technologies like AI, machine learning, and data analytics. They aren't necessarily experts, but they have enough knowledge to make informed decisions and guide their team through the integration of these tools.

By being technologically literate, these leaders can:

- Identify opportunities where AI or other technologies can create value.

- Understand the challenges and limitations of implementing new tools.

- Communicate more effectively with technical teams and bridge the gap between tech experts and non-technical staff.

2. Ethical Reasoning

In an age where AI raises new ethical dilemmas, a *Homo Magister* must excel in ethical reasoning. They are responsible for ensuring that the use of AI and technology aligns with the values of the organization and society. This means thinking critically about the impact of AI on privacy, fairness, and transparency.

A *Homo Magister* demonstrates ethical reasoning by:

- Addressing biases in AI systems and ensuring decisions made by AI are fair and just.

- Making sure data privacy and security are top priorities, especially as AI relies heavily on large datasets.

- Guiding the organization in building AI solutions that are transparent and accountable so the public can trust their use.

3. Adaptability

The *Homo Magister* thrives in an environment of constant change. The rapid development of AI and other technologies means that leaders must be flexible and willing to adapt their strategies, methods, and even their mindset to keep up. Adaptability is more than just adjusting to new tools; it's about leading teams through transitions and encouraging a culture that embraces change rather than fears it.

Adaptability in a *Homo Magister* leader includes:

- Learning new technologies and understanding how they impact the business landscape.

- Pivoting when strategies aren't working and being open to trying new approaches.

- Fostering an organizational culture that values continuous learning and innovation, making employees comfortable with evolving technology.

4. Ability to Inspire and Teach Others

One of the core attributes of a Homo Magister is their ability to inspire and guide their team in embracing new technologies and changes. Rather than simply instructing or directing, they take the time to mentor their employees and help them understand the value of the tools at hand and how to use them effectively.

They demonstrate this by:

- Breaking down complex technological concepts into understandable terms, making them accessible to all employees, regardless of technical expertise.

- Leading by example, showing their own willingness to learn and adapt, which encourages their team to do the same.

- Creating an environment where curiosity is welcomed and employees feel empowered to ask questions, take risks, and grow alongside the evolving technology.

5. Strategic Vision

A *Homo Magister* leader possesses the ability to not only understand current technologies but also foresee how they will shape the future. They are always thinking ahead, considering how AI and other innovations can be leveraged to keep the organization competitive. This strategic vision allows them to plan for the long term, ensuring that technological adoption aligns with the company's overarching goals.

The strategic vision includes:

- Identifying future trends and preparing the organization to adapt.

- Aligning the use of AI and technology with the company's core mission and values.

- Balancing short-term gains with long-term sustainability ensures that technological investments pay off over time.

A *Homo Magister* leader embodies a unique combination of technological understanding, ethical responsibility, adaptability, and the ability to inspire and teach others. These leaders are essential in the AI era, where rapid technological advancements and ethical dilemmas require leaders who can guide their organizations and also educate and empower their teams.

A key aspect of the *Homo Magister* leadership model is the leader's role as a teacher. As a teacher, a *Homo Magister* leader helps break down complex technologies and concepts, making sure everyone understands how these new tools can improve their work.

By acting as a mentor, a *Homo Magister* leader fosters a culture of continuous learning. This helps teams stay adaptable and prepared for future challenges, ensuring that the organization can keep up with technological advancements. Through their teaching, these leaders empower their teams to embrace new technologies.

In short, in the AI era, successful leaders are those who can teach and inspire their teams to grow alongside technology, making learning a core part of the company culture.

Balancing Human Intuition and AI Insights

In the AI era, leaders face the challenge of balancing human intuition with AI-driven insights. *Homo Magister* leaders understand that while AI provides powerful data and predictions, human judgment still plays a critical role in decision-making. The key to effective leadership lies in leveraging the strengths of both.

AI excels at analyzing vast amounts of data quickly, identifying patterns, and making accurate predictions. This can lead to more informed decisions, especially in areas like forecasting, risk assessment, and process optimization. However, AI has its limits. It lacks the ability to understand context, consider emotional or cultural factors, or think creatively in uncertain situations. This is where human intuition comes in.

Homo Magister leaders recognize the importance of combining AI insights with human intuition. They use AI as a tool to enhance decision-making, not to replace human judgment. By interpreting AI-driven data through the lens of experience, emotional intelligence, and an understanding of the broader context, leaders can make more nuanced and balanced decisions.

This balance allows organizations to benefit from AI's precision while tapping into the human ability to think critically, empathize, and adapt to changing circumstances. In this way, *Homo Magister* leaders promote a collaborative relationship between technology and human expertise, ensuring that both are used to their full potential.

A great example of a *Homo Magister* leader in action can be seen through a case study of a global industrial firm undergoing AI transformation. The company developed an analytics academy that trained its leaders to become both technological guides and mentors within the organization. This leader-driven training approach ensured that senior executives who were initially resistant or skeptical about AI learned the basics of AI and how it could impact their operations. These leaders then became champions of the technology, applying AI to optimize manufacturing processes, improve efficiency, and reduce operational costs across multiple sites.

The firm saw significant results from this strategy. Leaders used AI to predict operational parameters, such as machine settings, to reduce defects and improve production quality. The collaborative approach, with leaders acting as both visionaries and teachers, allowed the organization to bridge the gap between human expertise and AI capabilities. This approach not only improved business outcomes but also shifted the organizational culture toward one of continuous learning and technological adaptability.

By implementing these strategies, the company demonstrated how leaders embodying the *Homo Magister* model, combining teaching, technological insight, and leadership, can drive successful AI integration and foster a culture that embraces innovation.[13]

---

[13]https://www.mckinsey.com/capabilities/quantumblack/our-insights/the-analytics-academy-bridging-the-gap-between-human-and-artificial-intelligence

One well-known example of a company that has successfully bridged human capabilities and AI technology under strong leadership is Microsoft. Under the leadership of CEO Satya Nadella, Microsoft embraced AI to transform its products, services, and internal operations. Nadella exemplified the *Homo Magister* model by guiding the organization through a massive digital transformation while promoting a culture of learning and adaptability.

Microsoft integrated AI across its platforms—most notably with tools like Azure AI and Microsoft 365, which use machine learning and AI to improve productivity and automate routine tasks. Nadella not only advocated for AI's implementation but also prioritized upskilling employees to ensure they could use these new technologies effectively. He championed a culture of "learn-it-all" rather than a "know-it-all," emphasizing continuous learning and development across all company levels.

The impact was significant, as Microsoft positioned itself at the forefront of AI innovation, leveraging AI-driven insights to improve decision-making and product development. Under Nadella's leadership, Microsoft saw a resurgence in market growth, achieving a market cap of over $2 trillion while encouraging a collaborative, tech-savvy organizational culture.

Nadella's approach as a leader who not only drives technological innovation but also actively mentors and prepares his team for AI-driven changes is a prime example of *Homo Magister* leadership in action.

Developing Homo Magister Capabilities

Becoming a *Homo Magister* leader requires intentional effort and development across several key areas. Here are some practical strategies for developing the capabilities needed to manifest the *Homo Magister* leadership model:

1. Embrace Continuous Learning

To keep pace with technological advancements, *Homo Magister* leaders must commit to ongoing education. This means staying up to date on emerging technologies like AI, machine learning, and data analytics while continuously expanding their knowledge in leadership, strategy, and industry trends.

- **Action Step**: Dedicate time to personal learning by attending workshops, enrolling in online courses, or regularly engaging with industry thought leaders. Foster a culture that values curiosity and skill development within your organization to encourage a similar mindset.

2. Prioritize Ethical Training

As leaders adopt and implement AI, they face new ethical dilemmas that require thoughtful consideration. Ethical decision-making is essential to ensure that technology is used responsibly and fairly. Developing this capability involves understanding the ethical implications of technology and being able to face it in real-world situations.

- **Action Step**: Engage in ethics training that focuses on AI, data privacy, and responsible technology use. Establish clear ethical guidelines within your organization, and lead by example to demonstrate the importance of these principles.

3. Immerse Yourself in Technology

While leaders don't need to be technical experts, they must develop enough technological literacy to understand how emerging tools like AI can be leveraged for business success. When you work with technology, it allows you to communicate effectively with your team and make informed decisions, which will eventually help you identify opportunities for innovation.

- **Action Step**: Spend time working directly with tech teams and understanding the basics of AI, automation, and data analytics. Participate in hands-on experiences, such as testing new tools or exploring pilot projects, to gain an understanding of how these technologies impact your business.

4. Foster Collaborative Learning Environments

Homo Magister leaders recognize the importance of collective learning. By encouraging cross-functional collaboration, they enable teams to share knowledge, experiment with new ideas, and drive innovation.

- **Action Step**: Create opportunities for teams to collaborate on tech-driven initiatives. Host brainstorming sessions or innovation labs where employees from different departments can work together to solve challenges and explore new solutions.

Developing *Homo Magister's* capabilities requires a combination of personal commitment, ethical awareness, and technological engagement. By continuously learning, staying attuned to ethical concerns, and engaging themselves in technology, leaders can guide their organizations through the complexities of the AI era while fostering an environment of growth and innovation. The *Homo Magister* leader is not just a visionary but a teacher and a role model, ensuring that both technology and human potential are fully realized.

Organizational Culture Impact

The *Homo Magister* paradigm has a profound impact on shaping organizational culture, particularly in fostering innovation, ethical behavior, and adaptability. Leaders who embody this model serve not only as strategic decision-makers but also as mentors and teachers, influencing the values and behaviors of their teams.

1. Fostering Innovation

At the heart of the *Homo Magister* approach is the idea of continuous learning and growth. Leaders who adopt this mindset create an environment where experimentation is encouraged and innovation flourishes. By guiding their teams through new technologies like AI and promoting a culture of curiosity, *Homo Magister* leaders help employees feel empowered to explore new ideas and approaches.

- **Impact on Culture**: This focus on learning and innovation encourages a forward-thinking culture where employees are not afraid to take risks, try new things, or challenge the status quo. This helps organizations stay competitive and nimble in a fast-changing marketplace.

2. Promoting Ethical Behavior

Ethical considerations are more important than ever nowadays. *Homo Magister* leaders emphasize the responsible use of AI and data, ensuring that ethical standards guide decision-making at all levels of the organization. They lead by example, setting clear expectations about transparency, fairness, and accountability in the use of new technologies.

- **Impact on Culture**: By prioritizing ethical behavior, leaders foster a culture of integrity and trust. Employees are more likely to follow ethical guidelines when they see their leaders making responsible decisions. This creates an environment where everyone understands the importance of doing the right thing, even in complex tech-driven situations.

3. Building Adaptability

The rapid pace of technological change requires organizations to be flexible and adaptable. The *Homo Magister* leader plays a key role in developing this adaptability by encouraging employees to embrace change rather than resist it. Through continuous teaching and guidance, these leaders help their teams develop the skills and mindset to face the challenges.

- **Impact on Culture**: This emphasis on adaptability creates a resilient organizational culture that is better prepared to handle disruption. Employees become more comfortable with uncertainty and are more willing to learn new skills. This adaptability is essential for long-term success, especially in industries where technology is constantly evolving.

For instance, JP Morgan Chase, one of the world's largest and most established banks, found itself in a rapidly changing financial landscape due to the rise of fintech startups and evolving customer expectations. To stay competitive and relevant, the bank recognized the urgent need to innovate and embrace digital transformation.

Under the leadership of CEO Jamie Dimon, JP Morgan Chase made significant investments in its digital banking infrastructure and established strategic partnerships with fintech startups. These investments were aimed at enhancing their mobile banking capabilities and introducing new features such as mobile check deposits, digital wallets, and a more robust online banking platform. Additionally, the bank capitalized on fintech partnerships to incorporate the latest technological advances and deliver cutting-edge services to their customers.

To further improve efficiency and remain at the forefront of innovation, JP Morgan Chase also integrated artificial intelligence (AI) into its operations. One notable development was the creation of **COiN** (Contract Intelligence), an AI system designed to review legal documents. This tool significantly cut down on manual review time, reducing a task that used to take 360,000 hours annually to just seconds. This not only saved time but also reduced human error and operational costs.

By leveraging these fintech innovations and AI, JP Morgan Chase successfully modernized its services and provided a more convenient and efficient banking experience. This transformation allowed the bank to not only maintain its leadership in the financial industry but also attract tech-savvy customers and retain its existing client base, demonstrating how a traditional financial institution can effectively adapt to the digital era by fostering innovation and enhancing the customer experience.[14]

The *Homo Magister* leadership paradigm has a lasting impact on organizational culture by encouraging innovation, promoting ethical practices, and building adaptability. Leaders who embody this model create environments where employees feel empowered to learn, experiment, and grow.

---

[14]https://reports.jpmorganchase.com/investor-relations/2016/pdf/ar2016-lettertoshareholders.pdf

Homo Magister leaders can ensure their organizations are not only ready to face the challenges of the AI era but also positioned to thrive in it by shaping a culture that values continuous improvement and ethical responsibility.

Challenges in Adopting the Homo Magister Model

While the *Homo Magister* leadership model offers many benefits for the AI-driven world, its adoption is not without challenges. Shifting to this paradigm requires a transformation in both leadership style and organizational culture. Leaders and organizations may face several key obstacles as they attempt to integrate this model.

1. Resistance to Change

One of the most significant challenges in adopting the *Homo Magister* model is resistance to change, both from leaders and employees. Many organizations are rooted in traditional leadership models, such as top-down decision-making or command-and-control structures. Transitioning to a model where leaders are expected to teach, mentor, and collaborate requires a cultural shift that can feel uncomfortable for those used to more hierarchical structures.

- **Obstacle**: Employees and even leaders may resist the shift toward a more collaborative, learning-based culture, especially if they have thrived under older leadership styles.

- **Overcoming Resistance**: Clear communication and a gradual introduction of *Homo Magister* principles can help ease this transition. Leaders need to model the behavior they wish to see and build trust by showing the value of this new approach.

2. Lack of Tech Literacy Among Current Leaders

Another major hurdle is the varying levels of technological literacy among current leaders. The *Homo Magister* model requires leaders to not only understand emerging technologies like AI but also be able to teach and mentor their teams on how to use them. However, many established leaders may lack the necessary tech expertise or feel overwhelmed by the rapid pace of technological change.

- **Obstacle**: Leaders who are uncomfortable with technology may struggle to take on the teaching role required in the *Homo Magister* model.

- **Overcoming the Gap**: Providing opportunities for leaders to improve their technological skills through training programs, mentorship, and hands-on experience can help. Leaders don't need to become experts, but they must be confident enough to guide their teams and make informed decisions.

3. Short-Term Performance Pressures

Organizations often face intense short-term performance pressures, such as meeting quarterly financial targets or driving immediate revenue growth. The *Homo Magister* model, which focuses on continuous learning, ethical behavior, and long-term adaptability, may seem to conflict with these short-term demands. Leaders may feel torn between the immediate results that shareholders expect and the longer-term investment required to build a culture of learning and innovation.

- **Obstacle**: The pressure to deliver immediate results can discourage leaders from investing in the deeper cultural shifts required by the *Homo Magister* model.

- **Overcoming the Pressure**: It's important to strike a balance between short-term performance and long-term growth. Leaders can communicate the long-term benefits of the *Homo Magister* approach, such as improved innovation and resilience, to stakeholders. Small wins along the way—such as the success of new learning programs or tech implementations—can also demonstrate the value of this model.

Adopting the *Homo Magister* model presents challenges such as resistance to change, lack of tech literacy among current leaders, and the pressure for short-term performance. However, organizations can successfully integrate this leadership paradigm by addressing these obstacles through clear communication, training, and a balanced focus on both short-term and long-term goals.

Future of Homo Magister Leadership

As AI and other advanced technologies continue to evolve, the *Homo Magister* leadership paradigm is poised to grow in relevance. This model, which blends visionary leadership with teaching and mentoring, is well-suited to the demands of an increasingly digital and rapidly changing business. Looking ahead, several predictions can be made about how the *Homo Magister* paradigm may evolve and impact organizational structures and governance.

1. Greater Integration of AI in Decision-Making

As AI becomes more powerful and widespread, leaders will increasingly rely on AI-driven insights to make complex decisions. In the future, *Homo Magister* leaders will need to become even more adept at balancing human judgment with AI-generated data. While AI can process vast amounts of information and provide predictive insights, human intuition, and ethical reasoning will remain critical in interpreting these results and making final decisions.

- **Evolution**: The *Homo Magister* leader's role will expand to include not just teaching and guiding teams on AI usage but also understanding and shaping how AI-driven decisions impact broader strategic goals and ensure that these technologies align with human values and organizational ethics.

2. Flatter and More Agile Organizational Structures

As the *Homo Magister* model encourages continuous learning and adaptability, it is likely to lead to more decentralized and agile organizational structures. Traditional hierarchical models, where decisions are made at the top and trickle down, may give way to flatter organizations where teams are empowered to make decisions more independently.

- **Impact on Structures**: Leaders will act more as facilitators and mentors, creating environments where knowledge flows freely across the organization. This decentralized approach will allow businesses to adapt quickly to changes in technology and market conditions, fostering a more dynamic and innovative culture.

3. Shift in Governance Models

As the *Homo Magister* model grows, governance within organizations may also shift. Boards of directors and executive teams will need to evolve to include leaders with a strong understanding of technology and its ethical implications. Governance will need to reflect a balance between leveraging technology for growth and ensuring the responsible use of AI, data, and other emerging technologies.

- **Impact on Governance**: Companies may see the rise of technology-focused leadership roles, such as Chief AI Officers or Digital Ethics Officers, becoming integral to governance. These roles will support *Homo Magister* leaders in ensuring that technology is implemented with care, transparency, and accountability, reflecting the ethical standards of the organization.

4. Continuous Learning as a Core Organizational Value

As technology continues to change rapidly, the concept of continuous learning will become a foundational element of the *Homo Magister* leadership model. Leaders will not only need to stay on top of technological advancements themselves but will also have to ensure that their teams are equipped with the skills and mindset to adapt.

- **Impact on Culture**: Organizations may invest heavily in education and training, making learning a central part of their strategy. Learning and development programs will likely become more personalized and tech-driven, incorporating AI tools to tailor educational content to individual employees' needs. This emphasis on learning will help create a workforce that is more resilient and capable of evolving alongside technological changes.

5. Ethical Leadership as a Defining Feature

With AI and technology continuing to reshape industries, ethical considerations will become even more significant. The *Homo Magister* leader will be responsible for ensuring that AI is used responsibly, balancing innovation with societal impact. As technology plays a larger role in areas like decision-making, surveillance, and automation, leaders will need to address issues like bias, fairness, and transparency.

- **Evolution**: The future *Homo Magister* leader will likely become a champion of ethical AI, driving policies that ensure technologies are developed and used in ways that benefit both businesses and society. This will involve ongoing dialogue with stakeholders, including customers, regulators, and the public, to ensure trust and accountability.

The *Homo Magister* leadership paradigm is well-positioned to evolve alongside the rapid advancements in AI and other technologies. As organizations become more decentralized, agile, and focused on continuous learning, the role of the *Homo Magister* leader—as both visionary and teacher—will become even more critical. By balancing human judgment with AI insights and maintaining a focus on ethical responsibility, these leaders will shape the future of organizational structures and governance, driving sustainable innovation and success in the digital age.

Action Items for Aspiring Homo Magisters

For leaders looking to embrace the *Homo Magister* paradigm and develop the skills needed to lead in the AI-driven future, there are several practical steps to take. These actions will help build the technological, ethical, and teaching capabilities that define this new leadership model.

1. Commit to Continuous Learning

A *Homo Magister* leader must stay informed about the latest technological trends, especially in AI, data analytics, and automation. Continuous learning ensures that you can understand and leverage new tools to benefit your organization.

- **Action Step**: Enroll in courses or attend workshops on AI and emerging technologies. Make it a habit to read industry reports, follow tech leaders, and participate in discussions on future trends. This will help you stay ahead of the curve and make informed decisions.

2. Foster a Learning Culture in Your Organization

A key aspect of the *Homo Magister* paradigm is acting as a teacher and mentor. Leaders should foster an environment where learning is encouraged, mistakes are seen as opportunities for growth, and innovation thrives.

- **Action Step**: Set up regular learning sessions, workshops, or "lunch and learn" events where team members can share new knowledge or skills. Encourage employees to take courses and provide resources for continuous development. Lead by example by participating in these learning activities yourself.

3. Develop Ethical Decision-Making Skills

As technology, especially AI, becomes more integrated into decision-making, leaders will face new ethical dilemmas. Developing strong ethical reasoning will be crucial to ensuring that technology is used responsibly.

- **Action Step**: Engage in ethics training or discussions focused on AI, data privacy, and responsible technology use. Incorporate ethical considerations into your decision-making process by asking questions like, "How will this impact privacy?" or "Could this decision reinforce bias?" Develop guidelines for responsible AI use within your team or organization.

4. Build Technological Literacy

Leaders don't need to be experts in coding or AI development, but they must have a solid understanding of how these technologies work and how they can be applied. Being able to bridge the gap between technical teams and business strategy is essential for a *Homo Magister* leader.

- **Action Step**: Spend time working with technical teams to understand their tools and processes. Learn the basics of AI, automation, and data analytics so you can communicate effectively with both technical and non-technical staff. Consider taking a foundational AI course to strengthen your understanding.

5. Practice Adaptability and Agility

The speed of technological change means that leaders must be adaptable. This includes being open to new ideas, pivoting strategies when necessary, and encouraging your team to embrace change as a constant.

- **Action Step**: Regularly evaluate your current strategies and be willing to adjust them based on new information or technologies. Cultivate a mindset that sees change as an opportunity, not a threat, and encourage your team to do the same by highlighting the benefits of innovation and flexibility.

6. Encourage Cross-Disciplinary Collaboration

As a *Homo Magister* leader, fostering collaboration between departments, particularly between technical and non-technical teams, will be crucial for leveraging AI and other technologies effectively.

- **Action Step**: Facilitate regular meetings or projects that require teams from different areas of the business to work together. This cross-disciplinary collaboration helps build a culture where technology and strategy align, ensuring smoother implementation of AI-driven initiatives.

Becoming a *Homo Magister* leader requires intentional growth and a focus on continuous learning, ethical decision-making, and adaptability. By taking these practical steps, aspiring leaders can begin developing the skills necessary to guide their organizations through the complexities of the AI era. Whether through fostering a culture of learning, improving technological literacy, or encouraging collaboration, these actions will help you embody the *Homo Magister* paradigm and lead your organization toward a successful, innovative future.

Reflections:

To help you assess your current leadership style and how it aligns with the *Homo Magister* paradigm, consider these thought-provoking questions:

1. Are you staying informed about the latest technological trends, and do you actively explore how they can benefit your organization?

2. How often do you support your team's professional development and foster an environment where learning is prioritized?

3. Are you integrating AI data into your decision processes while still relying on your judgment, empathy, and experience?

4. Do you have processes in place to address ethical issues like data privacy, transparency, and fairness?

5. Are you open to new ideas and willing to adjust your strategies as technology and the business landscape evolve?

These questions are designed to help you reflect on how you currently lead and identify areas where you can grow in alignment with the *Homo Magister* leadership model.

Chapter 3: Building Technological Foundations

A mid-sized company was facing growing pressure to stay competitive since their competitors were upgrading their systems, and the CEO knew they needed to do the same to stay relevant. So when they heard about AI-driven predictive maintenance, a system that could predict when machines were about to break down, it seemed like the perfect solution. The promise of fewer breakdowns and smoother production was too good to pass up.

They quickly invested in the technology, confident it would transform their operations. But as soon as the system was installed, reality hit hard. The software was complicated, and the factory workers who had been maintaining machines manually for years were now facing confusing data and strange alerts from the AI. Every day, the system would flag potential issues, but no one knew what to do with the information.

One of the senior engineers, John, scratched his head as graphs and numbers flooded the screen. "What does this even mean?" he muttered under his breath. The training they had received wasn't enough, and they didn't have the technical expertise to make sense of the AI's warnings. To make matters worse, when the machines broke down, the team had no idea whether the AI had flagged the problem beforehand or not.

Weeks went by, and frustration built up across the factory floor. "We're still dealing with the same breakdowns, but now we have a fancy system that no one understands," said one of the maintenance workers, shaking his head. Eventually, the team started ignoring the AI alerts and went back to their old ways. They inspected the machines manually to try to figure out when something might go wrong.

The CEO, watching from the sidelines, realized they had made a critical mistake. The technology itself wasn't the issue; it was the lack of in-house expertise. They had invested in AI but hadn't invested enough in training their people to use it. The expensive system sat unused, and the company wasn't any closer to solving its problems.

It was clear now that just having the best technology wouldn't help if the team couldn't use it. The company needed more than AI. They needed people with the skills to make sense of it and apply it to their everyday work. Without that, they were stuck in the same spot, just with a more expensive problem.

This realization brings into focus the importance of tech mastery in any AI-driven transformation. It refers to the understanding of both the technical and strategic aspects of technology. It goes beyond just knowing how to use specific tools or software as it encompasses the ability to strategically leverage technology to drive innovation, improve efficiency, and solve complex business challenges. Therefore, if organizations want to succeed in today's competitive environment, they need to master both the practical and visionary sides of technology.

On the technical side, tech mastery includes proficiency in areas like AI, data analytics, machine learning, and automation. Individuals with tech mastery understand how these technologies work at a practical level, including how to set up, manage, and optimize them for specific organizational needs. This requires a solid grasp of programming, data science, and system integration.

However, tech mastery is not just about technical know-how. It also involves a strategic understanding of how technology can be used to achieve business goals. Leaders with tech mastery can envision the broader impact of AI on their organization, identify opportunities for its application, and align technological investments with the company's overall strategy. They know how to balance the benefits of automation with the need for human input and how to manage change as the organization adapts to new tech.

Before reaching this level of mastery, organizations must first assess their current capabilities. Understanding where the company stands in terms of technology is essential to determine the next steps, and conducting a current state assessment is the initial step.

Current State Assessment

Assessing an organization's current technology capabilities is an essential first step before going to any digital transformation. It helps identify where the organization stands. This process identifies existing strengths, highlights areas for improvement, and uncovers any gaps in skills or infrastructure that might hinder progress. A comprehensive evaluation sets the foundation for a more focused and effective tech strategy moving forward. Mentioned below are some tips to evaluate your company's tech readiness:

1. Conduct a Skills Audit

A skills audit is a way to measure whether your workforce has the technical expertise needed to handle new technologies like AI, data analytics, or automation. You can do this by:

- **Surveys and Self-Assessments**: Ask employees to rate their confidence in using specific tools or technologies. This helps gauge how comfortable the team feels about the current tech landscape.

- **Performance Evaluations**: Review past performance on tech-related projects to see where skills may be lacking.

- **External Experts**: Bringing in an outside consultant can offer an unbiased view of the team's capabilities and areas for growth.

The audit should help highlight knowledge gaps, allowing you to prioritize areas for upskilling or hiring.

2. Evaluate Technological Infrastructure

Next, assess the tools and systems your organization already has in place. Are your current technologies outdated or misaligned with your business goals? Look at:

- **Software**: Is the software you're using compatible with the newer technologies you want to implement? Make sure it's scalable and adaptable for future upgrades.

- **Hardware**: Check the health and performance of the hardware supporting your tech systems. Aging hardware may limit your ability to implement advanced tools like AI.

- **Cybersecurity**: Evaluate your cybersecurity protocols. New tech can introduce vulnerabilities, so it's important to ensure your infrastructure is secure and ready for expansion.

This evaluation helps you see whether your infrastructure can support the tech you plan to implement or if it needs an upgrade.

3. Identify Knowledge Gaps

Once you've audited skills and infrastructure, it's time to pinpoint specific knowledge gaps that could slow down or block successful tech adoption. You can do this by:

- **Workshops and Feedback Sessions**: Host sessions where employees can openly share where they feel less confident using current tools or systems.

- **Job Role Analysis**: Compare current job roles to the skills needed for future roles involving new technologies. This can help determine whether employees need training or if you'll need to hire new talent.

- **Benchmarking Against Competitors**: Research how similar organizations are using technology and compare your team's capabilities. This helps give a sense of where you stand within the industry.

Identifying gaps early will help you focus on the most critical areas for development, ensuring smoother implementation of new technologies.

Skills Required for an AI-Driven Future

We are living in a world with an AI-driven future where certain skills will be essential as the workplace continues to evolve.

As AI takes over routine tasks, the focus shifts toward more specialized, human-centered abilities. To succeed in this new environment, workers will need a different set of skills that complement technology rather than compete with it. Mentioned below are the skills that you must excel to thrive in the future:

1. **Data Literacy**: One of the most important skills is understanding and interpreting data. With AI generating large amounts of data, individuals must be able to make sense of it and draw meaningful conclusions. This includes

knowing how to work with data analytics tools and understanding how data impacts decision-making processes. The ability to read, analyze, and leverage data will be a basic requirement in most roles.

2. AI Understanding: Beyond just using AI, it's essential to grasp how AI works. This doesn't mean everyone needs to be an AI expert, but a basic understanding of how AI algorithms function, their capabilities and their limitations is crucial. Knowing what AI can and cannot do will help you apply it effectively in different business contexts.

3. Ethical Reasoning: Ethical issues will emerge as AI becomes more integrated into everyday processes. There will be challenges around data privacy, algorithm biases, and the impact on jobs. Individuals must develop strong ethical reasoning skills to face and conquer these challenges and make decisions that reflect fairness, transparency, and responsibility. Balancing the benefits of AI with its ethical considerations will be critical in ensuring that AI serves society well.

4. Adaptive Learning Abilities: The pace of change in an AI-driven world is fast, which means the ability to learn and adapt quickly is key. Employees will need to embrace continuous learning and stay curious about emerging technologies. Adaptability means being open to new tools, techniques, and evolving ways of working, as well as understanding that the skills required today may not be the same as those needed in the future.

Together, these skills will help individuals remain relevant and thrive in an AI-powered future. They bridge the gap between human expertise and machine efficiency, ensuring that technology complements human work rather than replacing it entirely.

For instance, Amazon has widely adopted AI and automation across its operations, particularly in logistics and supply chain management. Amazon uses AI-powered robots to manage warehouse tasks like sorting and packaging, which significantly improves efficiency by handling routine tasks.

However, alongside this shift to automation, Amazon recognizes the importance of human-centered skills. Employees who work in Amazon's fulfillment centers are trained to oversee and collaborate with the AI systems, ensuring they can troubleshoot, solve unexpected problems, and make decisions that require human judgment. Additionally, Amazon emphasizes adaptability and digital literacy by offering programs like *Amazon Career Choice*, which helps employees learn new skills and transition into higher-tech roles, such as machine learning or robotics experts.

This combination of automation with a strong focus on human skills shows how Amazon is preparing its workforce to thrive in an AI-driven world by balancing technology with the need for critical thinking, problem-solving, and adaptability.

Strategies for Rapid Skill Acquisition in Organizations

Organizations can use several strategies to help employees in acquiring new skills quickly and share knowledge effectively. These approaches not only make learning faster but also more engaging and accessible for everyone involved.

1. Micro-Learning

Micro-learning breaks down complex topics into small and manageable lessons. Instead of long training sessions, employees can learn in short bursts, sometimes just five to ten minutes. It is focused on one specific skill or concept. This approach works well because it fits into busy schedules and helps retain information better by focusing on one thing at a time.

2. Peer-to-Peer Teaching

Learning from colleagues can be a powerful tool. Peer-to-peer teaching allows employees to share their knowledge, whether it's in informal settings or structured programs. This method encourages collaboration and builds a strong learning culture within the organization. It also helps employees become more comfortable with new information since it's coming from someone they know and work with.

For example, an experienced employee could lead a workshop on a particular skill they have mastered, or teams could hold regular knowledge-sharing sessions where they exchange tips and insights about their work.

3. Immersive Learning Experiences

Immersive learning involves hands-on training or experiences that allow employees to learn by doing. This method can include simulations, virtual reality (VR), or real-life practice projects. Immersive learning makes the experience feel real, which helps with retention and understanding, especially for technical or complex tasks.[15]

For instance, companies might use VR simulations to train employees on equipment use or emergency procedures without any risk. This type of learning creates an engaging and practical environment where employees can experiment and gain confidence before applying new skills in real-world scenarios.

Building a Learning Ecosystem

Creating a robust learning ecosystem is key to fostering continuous tech skill development within an organization. Research from UNESCO on building effective learning ecosystems emphasizes the importance of partnerships between educational institutions, industry experts, and tech providers.

These ecosystems help organizations continuously develop their workforce's skills by providing access to

---

[15]https://itif.org/publications/2021/08/30/promise-immersive-learning-augmented-and-virtual-reality-potential/

relevant training, tools, and resources. By collaborating with educational partners, businesses can ensure that their employees remain current on technological advancements, while tech providers can offer hands-on experiences and support for the latest tools and innovations. This model fosters continuous learning, innovation, and knowledge sharing across all levels.[16]

1. Partnering with Educational Institutions: Collaborating with universities or technical schools provides employees with access to formal courses and certifications. This ensures they stay up-to-date with the latest technology trends and skills.

2. Collaborating with Tech Providers: Building relationships with tech companies allows for hands-on training with cutting-edge tools. Providers often offer workshops, certifications, or custom training modules tailored to an organization's specific needs.

3. Internal Knowledge Sharing: Establish peer-to-peer teaching, mentoring, and collaboration across departments. This not only spreads knowledge internally but creates a culture of learning and innovation.

By building a comprehensive learning ecosystem, companies can support the continuous development of tech skills, ensuring employees are well-equipped for future challenges.

---

[16]https://unesdoc.unesco.org/ark:/48223/pf0000375474

Customized Training Programs that include personalized microlearning courses help align employee development with an organization's goals and culture. These programs are tailored to meet specific needs, ensuring that the skills employees learn are directly relevant to their roles and the company's objectives.[17]

CDiGlobal works closely with leadership teams and shareholders to gain their support for cultural transformation. When leadership champions innovation and promotes knowledge-sharing, it sets the tone for the entire organization, fostering a positive learning environment.

One of CDiGlobal's key strategies is offering incentives for learning. This includes recognition programs, awards, and certificates that motivate employees to learn continuously. These programs aren't limited to just senior staff; they aim to empower employees at all levels, encouraging them to take charge of their professional growth.

Additionally, mentoring and coaching programs connect experienced employees with those eager to learn, facilitating knowledge transfer and fostering a culture of learning across the organization. These initiatives boost employee skills and help build strong internal networks, making it easier for employees to collaborate and grow.

Given that effective internal communication is crucial, CDiGlobal further formulates and implements

---

[17] https://aclanthology.org/W19-4434/

communication structures and systems that assist organizations in communicating the importance of curiosity, continuous improvement, and knowledge sharing to all employees. This includes regular updates, newsletters, and workshops. The implementation of knowledge-sharing digital platforms, ipso facto, makes it easier for employees to collaborate, share insights, and learn from each other, so CDiGlobal provides guidance for organizations in selecting and implementing such platforms. They not only provide access to a wealth of learning resources, including courses, materials, and platforms that support continuous learning but can also assist organizations in curating and creating their own learning resources.

Consultative work is not exclusive to feedback mechanisms, where employees can provide input on training programs and suggest areas where they would like to develop their skills further, such as employee engagement surveys. By helping organizations and individuals master AI and tech, CDiGlobal contributes to enhancing competitiveness. Those with a strong foundation in these areas can adapt to market changes, make data-driven decisions, and build resilience to uncertainties and disruptions.

By combining these strategies and engaging with all levels of the organization, CDiGlobal can promote a culture that values curiosity, continuous improvement, and knowledge sharing. This culture, in turn, empowers teams to embrace and harness the potential of AI and technology effectively, ultimately driving innovation and staying at the forefront of the digital age.

In summary, CDiGlobal's consultancy work and educational programs are instrumental in helping organizations build a dynamic and robust foundation for AI and tech mastery. This foundation extends beyond just knowledge; it encompasses adaptability, innovation, competitiveness, and a commitment to continuous learning. Therefore, CDiGlobal plays a pivotal role in shaping a more technologically proficient and resilient business landscape by empowering individuals and organizations to embrace the digital age.

Homo Magister Role in Tech Mastery

Leaders who embody the *Homo Magister* ideal play an essential role in driving tech mastery within their organizations. They guide their teams to understand and adapt to new tools. These leaders link human skills and technological innovation and ensure that their organizations are tech-savvy and adaptable.

Shantanu Narayen at Adobe provides a prime example of this. Under his leadership, Adobe transitioned to cloud-based services, developing the Adobe Creative Cloud and ensuring that employees learned to innovate within the digital space. His focus on training and upskilling employees has made Adobe a leader in digital transformation.

Another example is Mary Barra at General Motors. She drove the company's shift toward electric vehicles and autonomous driving technology. Barra championed this transformation and ensured that her teams were equipped with the knowledge and expertise to work with new technologies, positioning GM as a forward-thinking automotive leader.

Overcoming Barriers to Tech Mastery

Many organizations face significant barriers when trying to implement and scale technological advancements. Common obstacles such as resistance to change, budget constraints, and the rapid pace of technological evolution can prevent companies from fully integrating new tools and processes. Understanding these barriers and developing strategies to overcome them is key to achieving long-term success.

Resistance to Change

One of the biggest challenges organizations face is resistance to change. Many employees, particularly those comfortable with established methods, may fear the unknown or worry that technology will replace their jobs. This fear can lead to pushback, slowing down the adoption of new tools and systems.

Overcome Resistance: The key to overcoming resistance is clear communication. Leaders must explain the benefits of new technologies, emphasizing how these tools will make work easier and more efficient and ultimately lead to growth. For example, showing employees how AI or automation can take over repetitive tasks can ease concerns as it would help them to focus on higher-value work. Additionally, offering hands-on training and supportive learning environments can help employees feel more confident and capable of adapting to new tools. Leaders who promote an environment where questions are encouraged, and mistakes are seen as part of the learning process will find that their teams adapt more easily to change.

Budget Constraints

Another common barrier to tech mastery is budget constraints. Investing in advanced technology can be expensive, and many organizations are reluctant to make the leap, especially if they fear the return on investment (ROI) might not justify the costs. However, delaying or avoiding these investments can result in missed opportunities and falling behind competitors who are more willing to innovate.

Overcome Budget Constraints: Companies can overcome budget limitations by taking a phased approach to technology adoption. Instead of trying to implement a complete overhaul at once, organizations can focus on impactful changes that deliver measurable results. For instance, a company might start by implementing AI-driven analytics in marketing or customer service, where the benefits are clear and immediate, rather than adopting AI across every department. This approach can help justify further investment and secure additional budget down the line.

Additionally, organizations should consider leveraging partnerships with technology providers or educational institutions. Tech companies often offer training or support as part of their services, which can help the companies offset the cost of hiring external consultants or trainers. Universities or online learning platforms may also offer affordable training solutions for employees, helping them build the skills they need to manage new technologies without breaking the bank.

Rapid Technological Evolution

The fast pace of technological change is another significant challenge. As soon as companies adapt to one tool or system, a newer, more advanced version often becomes available. This constant state of flux can make it difficult for organizations to keep up and may eventually lead to **technology fatigue** or underutilized systems.

Overcome Rapid Technological Evolution: To manage the speed of technological advancement, organizations should prioritize continuous learning and flexibility. Building a learning culture where employees are encouraged to regularly update their skills is essential. Offering ongoing training programs or access to online courses can help ensure that teams remain up-to-date with the latest tools and trends. Moreover, creating dedicated innovation teams that focus on researching and experimenting with emerging technologies can allow companies to stay ahead of the curve without overwhelming the entire workforce.

Leaders need to remain strategically focused. Not every new piece of technology is a good fit for every company. You should evaluate each new advancement through the lens of the organization's unique needs and goals, choosing the tools that will have the most meaningful impact. This approach allows companies to stay relevant without chasing every trend that hits the market.

While barriers to tech mastery are common, they are not unconquerable. By addressing resistance to change with clear communication and support, approaching budget constraints with strategic investments, and building a culture of continuous learning to manage rapid technological evolution, organizations can successfully develop the tech mastery needed to succeed. Leaders who prioritize these strategies will be able to position their companies for technological success and encourage an adaptable workforce.

Measuring Tech Skill Development and Progress

Without the ability to measure tech skill development, organizations may find it challenging to gauge the effectiveness of their training and upskilling efforts. Therefore, it is crucial to have a robust mechanism in place for monitoring progress.

1. **Skill Assessments**: Regular skill assessments help identify areas where employees may require further training and allow organizations to tailor their programs accordingly.

2. **Certification Tracking**: Keeping track of the certifications and credentials earned by employees serves as a tangible indicator of progress and achievement.

3. **Key Performance Indicators (KPIs)**: Aligning tech skill development with specific KPIs can provide a quantitative measure of how improved tech skills translate into enhanced organizational performance.

4. **Feedback Loops**: Continuously gather feedback from employees to understand where they feel confident and where they need more support. Adapt your training based on this feedback to ensure continuous growth.

Take Google, for instance. It is a global technology giant and is renowned for its commitment to upskilling its workforce. Their approach provides an excellent case study for building tech skills within the organization.

Background: Google recognizes the fast-paced nature of the tech industry, and the company understands that to remain competitive and innovative, its employees need to continually upgrade their tech skills.

Strategies and Practices:

1. **Google's IT Support Professional Certificate**: Google partnered with Coursera to create this program. It provides training in IT support, helping individuals gain the skills necessary for tech roles.

The program offers a flexible and accessible way for employees to learn at their own pace.

2. **Machine Learning and AI Residency Program**: Google offers a one-year program that focuses on machine learning and AI. Participants work on cutting-edge projects and research, immersing themselves in these technologies.

3. **"Grow with Google"**: This initiative offers free training and tools to help people grow their careers or businesses. It includes courses on digital marketing, data analysis, and coding. Google's employees can access these resources, aligning their skill development with the company's goals.

Results: Google's upskilling initiatives have not only empowered their employees with tech skills but have also led to tangible benefits for the organization. They have a workforce that is equipped to navigate the ever-evolving tech landscape, contributing to Google's status as an industry leader.

The case of Google exemplifies how investing in upskilling and tech skill development can foster a culture of continuous learning and innovation within an organization. By providing a range of learning options and resources, Google not only ensures its workforce remains adept at the latest technologies but also aligns employee development with the company's strategic goals.[18]

---

[18]https://www.zavvy.io/hr-examples/employee-development-at-google

This case underscores the significance of ongoing upskilling and its direct link to organizational success in the tech-driven era. It serves as an inspiration for other organizations looking to foster tech mastery within their own teams, contributing to organizational transformation and adaptability in the digital age.

Building tech skills involves continuous learning, teamwork across departments, and clear ways to track progress. Developing tech mastery isn't a choice anymore, and it's essential for transforming a business and staying successful in the digital world. When companies invest in these skills, they invest in their future. Success now depends on how quickly and skillfully employees can adapt and apply new technology to keep the organization competitive and agile.

Ethical Considerations in Tech Mastery

As organizations work to develop tech mastery, it's important to think about more than just the technical side. Ethical considerations play a crucial role, especially when it comes to using advanced technologies like AI and managing large amounts of data. While building technical skills is essential, organizations must also focus on fostering ethical reasoning to ensure the responsible use of these powerful tools.

Responsible Use of AI

One of the biggest ethical challenges in tech mastery is ensuring the responsible use of AI. AI has the power to transform industries, but it also comes with risks, particularly when it comes to bias and fairness. AI systems are often trained on large datasets, and if these datasets are biased, the AI can reinforce or even magnify those biases. For example, an AI used in hiring could favor one demographic over another if it was trained on biased hiring data.

You must ensure that AI systems are regularly audited for bias and implement checks and balances to prevent harmful outcomes. In addition, transparency is key here. Employees and customers alike should understand how AI systems are making decisions and what data they are using. Organizations should be clear about the limitations of AI and avoid relying solely on automated systems without human oversight.

Data Privacy and Security

Another major ethical concern in tech mastery is the handling of data. With the rise of big data, organizations now have access to huge amounts of personal and sensitive information. While this data can be used to improve services and make better business decisions, it also comes with significant responsibility. Protecting this data from breaches, misuse, or unauthorized access is a critical aspect of ethical tech management.

Tech mastery must include a focus on data privacy and security measures. Employees should be trained on best practices for data protection, and companies should invest in secure systems to prevent cyberattacks. In addition to technical skills, organizations must also promote a culture of ethical data use. This means using data while respecting individuals' privacy rights and being transparent about how data is collected, stored, and used.

Furthermore, organizations need to comply with regulations like the General Data Protection Regulation (GDPR) or similar laws that govern data privacy. Ethical tech mastery involves not only following these regulations but also going beyond them to build trust with customers and stakeholders by treating their data with respect and care.

While technical skills are critical in today's digital world, developing ethical reasoning is equally important. Employees must be trained to think critically about the potential consequences of their technological decisions. For example, when developing new algorithms or systems, employees should be encouraged to ask, "What impact could this have on society? Are there any unintended negative consequences?"

Organizations can integrate ethical training into their tech programs by offering workshops or seminars that focus on real-world case studies where technology has both positive and negative effects. This can help employees understand the broader context of their work and the importance of making ethical choices.

Organizations must focus on the responsible use of AI, protect data privacy, and encourage ethical reasoning alongside technical skills. By addressing these ethical challenges head-on, companies can build trust with their employees, customers, and society. Ethical tech mastery is essential for long-term success in the digital age, ensuring that technology benefits everyone without causing harm.

Future-Proofing Tech Skills

It is essential for organizations to future-proof their tech skills to stay competitive. Simply focusing on current tools isn't enough because what's cutting-edge today might be outdated tomorrow. The key is to build a foundation of skills and foster adaptive learning capabilities that can keep up with constant change. Here's how companies can ensure that their tech mastery efforts remain relevant:

1. Focus on Foundational Skills

One of the best ways to prepare for future tech developments is to strengthen foundational skills that form the backbone of technology work. Skills like coding, data analysis, and problem-solving will remain relevant regardless of which new tools emerge. By focusing on these core areas, employees will have the essential knowledge needed to pick up new technologies more easily.

For example, programming languages like Python or Java are widely used across many different applications. Teaching employees these basics gives them the flexibility to adapt as new software or platforms come into play. Additionally, understanding data and how to analyze it is a critical skill in almost every industry today. Even if the tools for data analysis change, the ability to interpret and draw insights from data will always be necessary.

2. Encourage a Culture of Continuous Learning

Employees must be encouraged to keep learning. Organizations should provide opportunities for continuous education, whether through formal training programs, online courses, or workshops. The goal is to promote and encourage a mindset where learning is an ongoing process, not something that stops after a certain level of expertise is achieved.

Offering learning opportunities that are flexible and accessible is key. For example, microlearning, where employees can take short, focused lessons at their own pace, can be very effective. This allows employees to stay up-to-date with the latest technology trends without feeling overwhelmed. As learning becomes a routine part of work, employees will find it easier to adapt to new advancements.

3. Develop Adaptive Learning Capabilities

Future-proofing tech skills also means building the ability to learn and adapt quickly. Technology is evolving faster than ever, and employees need to be able to pivot as new systems, tools, and processes emerge. Adaptive learning focuses on teaching employees how to learn rather than just what to learn.

This can be done by encouraging critical thinking and problem-solving in everyday tasks. Instead of simply following procedures, employees should be taught how to assess situations and come up with innovative solutions. When employees are empowered to approach new challenges with curiosity and flexibility, they are better equipped to handle future shifts in technology.

4. Create Learning Pathways

Organizations should create clear learning pathways for their employees. These pathways provide a roadmap for acquiring new skills and advancing in their careers. By defining what skills are needed for different roles, companies can help employees see where they need to grow and how to get there. Learning pathways can be tailored to individual interests, allowing employees to pursue areas that align with their goals and the company's future needs.

For example, an organization might create a pathway for software engineers that starts with foundational coding skills, progresses to advanced AI or machine learning, and ends with specialized training in a specific industry application. This gives employees a clear direction and encourages them to continually improve their skills.

5. Leverage External Partnerships

To keep up with evolving technology, companies should also look beyond their own walls. Building partnerships with educational institutions, industry experts, and tech providers can give employees access to cutting-edge knowledge and resources. These collaborations ensure that training programs remain relevant and aligned with the latest industry trends.

For instance, a company might partner with a local university to offer tech certifications or collaborate with a leading tech provider to offer specialized training on the newest software. External partnerships not only provide valuable learning opportunities but also allow organizations to stay connected with emerging technologies.

6. Invest in Employee Growth

Investing in tech skill development is an investment in the future. By dedicating resources to training and development, companies show their employees that they value growth and innovation. Offering incentives, such as recognition programs, certifications, or even financial support for continuing education, motivates employees to stay engaged in their learning journey.

The return on this investment is a workforce that is agile, knowledgeable, and ready to tackle whatever challenges come with the next wave of technology. Companies that prioritize tech mastery now will be better positioned to navigate future disruptions and stay ahead of the competition.

Developing Tech Mastery Culture

Building a culture that values and promotes tech mastery requires strategic focus and commitment across all levels of an organization. Mentioned below are key strategies to foster such a culture:

1. **Leadership Support**: Leadership must promote tech mastery by encouraging innovation, continuous learning, and leading by example. When leaders show commitment to technological growth, it sets a clear tone for the entire organization.

2. **Recognition Programs**: Acknowledge and reward employees who excel in tech-related skills or who go the extra mile in learning new technologies. This could be through awards, public recognition, or even bonuses. Recognizing achievement not only motivates the individual but also signals to others that tech mastery is valued.

3. **Career Advancement Opportunities**: Employees are more likely to engage in skill development when they see a clear path for career growth. Offer promotions, new roles, or leadership opportunities to those who demonstrate tech expertise and continuous learning. This creates a strong incentive for employees to improve their technical skills.

4. **Provide Learning Resources**: Offer access to the latest training tools, courses, and workshops. Make it easy for employees to upskill by providing time and resources to learn new technologies. A company can also create a mentorship program where experienced employees can guide others in their tech development.

5. **Encourage Collaboration**: Create an environment where employees from different departments can collaborate on tech initiatives. Cross-functional teams promote knowledge-sharing and innovation, helping to build a broader understanding of how technology impacts various areas of the business.

By implementing these strategies, organizations can create a culture that values and promotes tech mastery.

Tips to Enhance Tech Mastery

Developing tech mastery within an organization requires a clear and structured approach. Here's a step-by-step guide to begin or enhance tech mastery initiatives:

1. **Initial Assessment**: Start by evaluating your organization's current tech skills, tools, and infrastructure. Conduct a skills audit and assess existing technology to identify gaps and opportunities.

2. **Set Clear Goals**: Define what tech mastery looks like for your organization. This includes identifying

key skills, tools, or technologies that align with your business objectives.

3. **Develop a Learning Strategy**: Create a structured plan for upskilling your workforce. This could include internal training programs, partnerships with tech providers, or online courses. Focus on both foundational skills and adaptive learning capabilities.

4. **Leadership Involvement**: Ensure leadership is actively engaged in promoting tech mastery. Leaders should champion learning, provide resources, and set an example by embracing new technologies themselves.

5. **Implement Recognition Programs**: Encourage participation by recognizing employees who achieve new certifications, complete training, or demonstrate tech leadership. Rewards can range from public recognition to financial incentives or promotions.

6. **Foster Collaboration**: Create opportunities for employees to collaborate on tech initiatives. Cross-functional teams help build a culture of shared learning and innovation.

7. **Measure Progress**: Regularly track and measure the impact of tech mastery efforts. Use metrics like skill development, productivity, or project outcomes to assess the program's success and make adjustments.

8. **Continuous Improvement**: Tech mastery is an ongoing process. Ensure the organization continues to evolve by providing ongoing learning opportunities and staying up to date with emerging technologies.

By following these steps, companies can successfully build and enhance tech mastery, empowering their workforce and staying competitive in a fast-changing digital landscape.

Reflections:

To apply these ideas effectively, consider these questions:

1. What is your organization's current level of tech mastery? Are there clear gaps in skills or technology?

2. How can leadership actively support and drive tech mastery within your organization?

3. What specific training methods or recognition programs could best motivate your employees to engage in continuous learning?

4. How adaptable is your organization to emerging technologies, and how could you improve that adaptability?

5. What key metrics will you use to measure the success of tech mastery initiatives?

By building tech mastery, organizations equip their workforce to handle rapid technological changes, keeping them agile and competitive. This mastery ensures that employees can adapt quickly to new tools and innovations, making the company more resilient in a fast-evolving digital landscape. Developing tech skills not only prepares the team for current demands but also positions the organization for future success. As we move into the next chapter, we will explore how cultivating an agile mindset further enhances a company's ability to thrive in today's tech-driven world.

Part II: Realizing AI's Potential

Chapter 4: Fostering Organizational Flexibility

A century-old manufacturing company relied on traditional methods that had worked for decades in the company's favor, and it thrived in its industry. But things began to change when tech-savvy startups entered the market. These new companies used advanced technologies and digital tools that gave them the edge in efficiency, cost reduction, and customer satisfaction.

These startups quickly adopted new technologies like AI and machine learning, which helped them predict market trends and respond instantly to customer needs. The older company, on the other hand, started losing ground due to its rigid structure and slower decision-making. They found it hard to implement such technologies at the same speed.

As a result, they were losing customers and market share to the more nimble and innovative startups. This put immense pressure on the company to rethink its processes and adapt if it wanted to stay competitive in this fast-moving digital age.

Leadership soon realized their slow decision-making processes and outdated systems were holding them back. They could no longer rely on past success. They needed to change how they operated to survive in this new era. They had to become more agile, more willing to adapt to new technologies, and open to experimenting with different working ways.

The situation highlighted the growing need for traditional companies to embrace an agile mindset if they wanted to remain competitive. Being open to change, fast to react, and ready to innovate became essential for the company's survival in the digital age.

Once they accepted this reality, the leadership became more open to innovation. They started encouraging faster decision-making and empowered their team to test new technologies without fear of failure. It created an environment where experimentation was welcomed. By encouraging a more flexible approach, the company ensured that they could adapt to new technologies and keep up with the competition.

This approach reflects the core principles of an agile mindset, which emphasizes flexibility, continuous learning, and the ability to pivot as needed.

Agile Mindset

The agile mindset refers to a way of thinking that emphasizes flexibility, adaptability, and continuous improvement. The agile mindset focuses on being open to change, collaborating often, and learning from small, iterative work cycles. Instead of sticking rigidly to a long-term plan, teams with an agile mindset adapt quickly to feedback, new information, and evolving circumstances. This approach encourages innovation, improves responsiveness, and helps organizations stay competitive in rapidly changing environments.

Agile Principles

1. **Flexibility**: Agile prioritizes the ability to respond to changes rather than sticking rigidly to a predefined plan. This is crucial for digital transformation, where technologies and market conditions shift quickly.

2. **Iterative Development**: Agile encourages breaking down projects into smaller, manageable pieces and delivering them incrementally. This allows for continuous improvement and quick adaptation to new trends or requirements.

3. **Collaboration**: Cross-functional teamwork is at the heart of agile. Collaboration across departments ensures that multiple perspectives come together to solve problems, which is vital for digital transformation initiatives.

4. **Customer-Centricity**: Agile focuses on delivering value to the customer. In digital transformations, aligning tech initiatives with customer needs ensures that solutions are relevant and impactful.

5. **Frequent Feedback**: Agile thrives on constant feedback from stakeholders, allowing teams to adjust their efforts based on real-time data and feedback, leading to better results.

Being agile allows companies to stay competitive in the era of rapid technological change. As digital transformation often involves navigating unknown territory, the ability to pivot, adapt, and respond quickly becomes crucial. Agile fosters a culture of innovation and flexibility and makes it easier for organizations to adopt new technologies, such as AI, and adjust their strategies when needed.

However, companies that fail to embrace these agile principles risk falling behind, as was the case with Yahoo. Once a dominant force in the internet industry, Yahoo struggled to adapt to the evolving digital world. One major obstacle was the lack of consistent leadership buy-in. Over a short period, Yahoo cycled through multiple CEOs, each introducing different strategies. This constant change and lack of a unified vision made it difficult for the company to compete effectively with emerging platforms like Google and Facebook. Without a solid leadership commitment to driving digital transformation, Yahoo couldn't capitalize on market opportunities.

Ultimately, Yahoo's inability to embrace uncertainty and secure strong leadership for digital transformation led to a significant decline in its relevance, culminating in its acquisition by Verizon. This example highlights the critical role that leadership buy-in and an agile mindset play in navigating uncertainty successfully.

Embracing uncertainty becomes a natural extension of agility. In rapidly changing markets, uncertainty is inevitable, but organizations that view it as an opportunity can drive innovation and growth. Agile methodologies create the mindset and structure needed to handle the unknown with confidence, allowing teams to experiment, iterate, and adapt quickly. Companies that view uncertain market conditions as opportunities often find creative solutions and pivot successfully. When businesses step into the unknown with a willingness to adapt, they can gain a competitive edge.

Flexibility and adaptability are essential for organizations aiming to succeed with agile transformation. These qualities help companies respond to ever-changing challenges. Listed below are some key strategies to embrace them:

1. **Empowering Decision-Makers**: Decentralize decision-making and empower teams to make informed choices in their areas of expertise. This increases agility and the ability to adapt quickly to changing circumstances.

2. **Dynamic Planning**: Move away from rigid, long-term plans to dynamic planning processes. Agile organizations engage in short-term planning cycles that allow them to adjust their strategies in response to real-time feedback and emerging opportunities.

3. **Change-Ready Leadership**: Leadership must exemplify adaptability and support a culture where change is embraced. Leadership teams need to model agility, openness to experimentation, and the ability to pivot in response to new information.

4. **Agile Mindset Across All Levels**: Encourage, train, and coach all members of the organization to adopt an agile mindset. This means being open to change, willing to learn from both successes and setbacks and actively seeking opportunities for improvement.

Promoting a Culture of Experimentation

Risk-taking and experimentation embody the belief that growth and discovery come from challenging the status quo, accepting uncertainty, and embracing failure as a necessary part of success. Just as in life, where we learn and grow through trial and error, organizations thrive when they are willing to step into the unknown and take calculated risks.

A culture of experimentation encourages organizations to be innovative and adaptive by allowing employees to test new ideas, take risks, and learn from their failures. It has now become essential in the fast-changing business environment where agility and innovation are key to staying competitive.

You can build this culture by following the steps below.

1. Encourage Experimentation

Organizations must openly support innovation and risk-taking to promote experimentation. This means encouraging employees to explore new ideas and not being afraid of failure. During high-performance team building efforts, let teams know that experimentation is of great value in the organization and celebrate those who take the initiative to try something new, even if it doesn't work out.

For example, companies like Google allow employees to dedicate a portion of their time to personal projects, a policy famously known as the "20% Time" rule. This initiative has led to innovative solutions, such as the development of Google News, a platform that aggregates news stories from various sources. By giving employees the space to explore their own creative ideas, Google promotes a culture of experimentation and innovation. This empowerment encourages employees to pursue projects that might not directly align with their core work but often result in groundbreaking products and features.

2. Create Safe Spaces for Failure

Failure is an inevitable part of experimentation, but it shouldn't be seen as a negative outcome. Instead, create a safe space where failure is viewed as a learning opportunity. When employees know that failing doesn't come with harsh consequences, they are more likely to take risks and innovate.

One way to do this is by promoting a "fail fast, learn faster" approach. Encourage teams to run small and low-risk experiments that allow them to quickly gather feedback, learn from the outcome, and adjust their strategies as needed. This way, failures happen on a smaller scale and provide valuable lessons without significant risk.

3. Provide Resources for Experimentation

For experimentation to thrive, employees need access to the right resources. This could include time, tools, or even training. Allocate budget or resources specifically for innovation projects. By giving teams the support they need, you signal that experimentation is not only allowed but actively supported.

At Amazon, experimentation is a core part of how the company operates. Teams are encouraged to explore new ideas and test innovative solutions, even when those ideas might challenge or disrupt existing products and services. This approach allows Amazon to evolve and remain at the forefront of innovation. By giving employees the freedom to take risks and pursue bold projects, Amazon has been able to develop groundbreaking initiatives like Amazon Web Services (AWS) and Amazon Prime. This willingness to invest in experimentation helps the company stay agile and responsive to changing market needs.

4. Promote Continuous Learning

Encourage a mindset of continuous learning by encouraging that there's always something to be gained, even from failed experiments. Teams should be debriefed after every experiment, focusing on what went well, what didn't, and what can be improved in future attempts. This process helps employees grow and improve over time.

By promoting this learning mindset, organizations like Pixar have been able to maintain their creative edge, where teams regularly review and critique each other's work to ensure the highest standards of quality and innovation.

5. Reward Innovation and Risk-Taking

Recognize and reward employees who take smart risks and innovate, even if their experiments don't result in immediate success. Offering rewards such as public acknowledgment, promotions, or bonuses reinforces the message that experimentation is a valued behavior within the company.

This could be as simple as hosting an "Innovation Day" where employees present their experiments, successes, or lessons learned. Recognizing these efforts publicly fosters a culture where others feel inspired to take the initiative.

6. Lead by Example

Leadership plays a huge role in promoting this culture. When leaders are willing to experiment, admit their failures, and demonstrate resilience, they set a strong example for the rest of the organization. Leaders who take risks and speak openly about their failures help normalize experimentation as part of the business process.

Building a culture of experimentation is about embracing the unknown and encouraging your team to test new ideas, even if they fail. Organizations can stay ahead of the curve by creating safe spaces for failure, promoting continuous learning, and rewarding innovation. When employees feel supported in taking risks and trying new things, they are more likely to create solutions that drive the business forward.

Agile Beyond IT

While agile methodologies originally emerged in software development, their principles can be effectively applied to many other business areas, including marketing, HR, and product development. Agile focuses on flexibility, collaboration, and delivering value quickly, which are essential across all departments.

Agile in Marketing

Agile allows marketing teams to adapt quickly to customer feedback and market trends. Instead of waiting for a big annual campaign, agile marketing teams work in short cycles (sprints) to test and refine strategies. For example, a company could launch a small social media campaign, gather insights, and adjust the next round based on real-time data.

Marketing teams can use agile frameworks like Scrum or Kanban, break their campaigns into smaller tasks, and hold regular meetings to review progress and adjust strategies. This ensures they remain flexible and aligned with customer needs while speeding up delivery.

Agile in HR

Agile methodologies are also transforming HR by promoting more dynamic, people-focused processes. In recruitment, for instance, agile allows HR teams to quickly adjust hiring practices based on feedback from candidates and hiring managers. Agile HR can also make performance reviews more continuous, with regular check-ins instead of annual reviews.

HR teams can use agile practices like daily stand-ups and sprints to keep projects like employee onboarding or training flexible and iterative. These practices help HR departments stay responsive to employees' changing needs, facilitating a more engaged workforce.

Agile in Product Development

Agile is particularly effective in product development, where teams need to quickly adapt to changes in technology and consumer demand. By using agile methodologies, product teams can release new features faster, gather feedback, and refine their products continuously.

Product development teams can work in cross-functional squads (like at Spotify), where designers, engineers, and marketers collaborate on small pieces of a product. They deliver these increments quickly, assess customer reactions, and then improve the product based on what works and what doesn't.

Here are some notable examples of companies that successfully implemented agile transformation, showcasing how they adapted to new methodologies and gained significant advantages:

1. **Spotify**: The music streaming giant adopted agile methodologies, specifically a customized "Squad" model, where small, autonomous teams (called squads) work cross-functionally on specific features. This model promoted flexibility, innovation, and independence within teams, allowing Spotify to scale rapidly and maintain its position as an industry leader. Their approach is widely recognized as an innovative way to organize and manage work in fast-changing environments.[19]

2. **Zappos**: Zappos, an online retailer known for its unique corporate culture, embraced agile transformation by moving to a "holacracy" model. Holacracy is a management system where traditional hierarchy is removed, and decision-making is spread across self-organized teams called **circles**. Each team is responsible for making decisions in their specific area without needing approval from higher-ups.

This transition from a traditional hierarchy to self-organized teams enabled employees to make more decisions independently, fostering adaptability and improving responsiveness to customer needs. Zappos' transformation

---

[19]https://www.pragmaticinstitute.com/resources/articles/data/case-study-how-spotify-prioritizes-data-projects-for-a-personalized-music-experience/

enhanced its flexibility and allowed it to stay competitive in the e-commerce market.[20]

3.   General Electric (GE): GE, particularly within its software division, implemented **Scrum** practices to improve project delivery times. GE's use of agile methodologies, such as Scrum, demonstrated that agile principles can be applied beyond the tech sector. By adopting these practices, GE improved efficiency and responsiveness, leading to faster project completions and better alignment with customer expectations.

These examples highlight the power of agile transformation across different industries. By adopting agile methodologies, these companies improved collaboration, innovation, and the ability to respond swiftly to changing market conditions, ultimately driving organizational success.

Implementing Agile Methodologies

Adopting agile methodologies transforms the way an organization functions. Listed below are key strategies to implement agile methodologies successfully:

1.   Education and Training: Begin by educating all employees on agile principles like Scrum (a structured framework where teams work in short cycles called *sprints* to deliver small, incremental improvements) and Kanban (a method focusing on visualizing work on a board, limiting

---

[20]https://www.scrummasterprep.com/blog/zappos-journey-to-agile

tasks in progress to improve flow and efficiency). Training programs should cover both the values behind agile and practical frameworks that employees can use daily.

2.   Cross-Functional Teams: Create diverse teams that bring together skills from different departments. These teams work collaboratively, encouraging innovation and problem-solving. Having a mix of perspectives fosters creativity and helps navigate complex challenges.

3.   Iterative Development: Break down projects into smaller, achievable goals. Instead of aiming for one big delivery, focus on incremental steps. This helps teams stay flexible and react quickly to changing market demands or project needs.

4.   Cultural Transformation: Agile is a mindset, not just a process. Organizations must encourage open communication, teamwork, and a willingness to learn from both successes and failures. Building a culture that rewards experimentation and learning fosters continuous improvement.

5.   Feedback Mechanisms: Regular feedback is essential for agile success. Establish clear loops for feedback from both customers and internal stakeholders. This ensures teams can adjust their approaches based on real-time insights, improving outcomes and staying aligned with business goals.

Agile methodologies provide a structured yet flexible framework for managing digital transformations. Agile strategies empower organizations to experiment, learn, and quickly adjust their course, ensuring they remain competitive in an era of rapid technological advancement.

Agile Leadership Principles

Agile leadership encourages a mindset that promotes flexibility, collaboration, and rapid adaptation to change. Leaders who support agile principles create an environment where teams can thrive and innovate. The following key principles are essential for agile leadership:

1. Servant Leadership

Agile leaders practice servant leadership, which flips the traditional power hierarchy. Instead of directing or controlling teams, servant leaders focus on supporting their teams by removing obstacles and empowering them to make decisions. This approach encourages autonomy and fosters a culture of trust.

In an agile environment, a servant leader ensures that teams have the resources they need to succeed while fostering a sense of ownership and responsibility among team members. This leadership style helps create an open, collaborative atmosphere where employees feel valued and motivated to perform at their best.

2. Decentralized Decision-Making

In agile leadership, decision-making is decentralized. Agile leaders empower teams to make decisions at the local level without waiting for approval from higher-ups. These speed up the decision-making process, reduce bottlenecks, and enable teams to respond more quickly to changes in the market or project requirements.

Decentralized decision-making promotes flexibility, as teams can pivot quickly when necessary. It also encourages accountability, as team members take full ownership of their projects. Leaders provide guidance and set clear goals but allow teams the freedom to determine how best to achieve those objectives.

3. Continuous Learning

Agile leaders promote a culture of continuous learning and improvement. In a rapidly changing business environment, staying competitive requires constant adaptation. Agile leadership supports teams by encouraging experimentation, learning from failures, and making ongoing adjustments.

Leaders should model this behavior by seeking feedback, staying open to new ideas, and being willing to change their approach. Continuous learning also involves investing in employee development, providing opportunities for training, and encouraging employees to take initiative in their growth.

Agile leadership is about empowering teams, decentralizing decision-making, and fostering a culture of continuous learning. These principles help create an environment where teams are more adaptable, innovative, and capable of delivering value quickly. By adopting these leadership approaches, organizations can stay competitive and thrive in an ever-changing market.

Measuring Agility

Measuring organizational agility is crucial for assessing a company's ability to adapt, innovate, and respond to market shifts. To gain meaningful insights into adaptability and performance, organizations need well-defined metrics that capture the essence of their agility. Specialized consulting firms like CDiGlobal are well-equipped to help develop and implement these metrics, providing expertise that enables organizations to track and enhance their agility effectively.

Here are some key methods for measuring agility:

1. Adaptability Index

The adaptability index measures how quickly and efficiently an organization can adjust to changes, whether in market trends, technology, or customer needs. This index looks at several factors, including how fast a company can reallocate resources, adopt new tools, and change business strategies.

To measure it, track how long it takes for teams to respond to new challenges, implement changes, and complete tasks once new information or obstacles arise. Assess how frequently your organization is rethinking and adapting its strategy in response to shifts in the industry.

2. Time-to-Market

Time-to-market refers to the speed at which a company can develop and deliver new products or services. Reducing time-to-market is a clear sign of agility, as it shows that teams can quickly respond to customer needs or market opportunities. This metric is critical in industries where rapid innovation can determine market leadership.

To do this, you can track the amount of time it takes to go from idea generation to product launch. If teams are delivering faster with fewer delays, it suggests that the organization is working in an agile manner. It's also helpful to compare the time-to-market of competitors to gauge your organization's relative agility.

3. Customer Feedback Loops

Agile organizations actively seek feedback and quickly incorporate it into their processes. Customer feedback loops measure how effectively and frequently customer input is gathered and used to improve products or services.

Evaluate how often teams collect customer feedback (through surveys, user testing, etc.) and how quickly that feedback is turned into actionable changes. The shorter the loop between receiving feedback and implementing changes, the more agile the organization is.

4. Cycle Time

Cycle time is the amount of time it takes to complete one iteration or cycle of a process, whether that's developing a feature, producing a product, or completing a marketing campaign. Reducing cycle times shows that teams are working efficiently and responding rapidly to changes or new information.

Track how long it takes to complete tasks from start to finish. A lower cycle time indicates that teams are working in a more streamlined and agile way, continuously delivering value.

5. Employee Engagement and Collaboration

Agile organizations rely on highly engaged and collaborative teams. Measuring employee engagement and collaboration provides insight into how well the organization is promoting a culture of agility. Engaged employees are more likely to adapt quickly and work collaboratively to solve problems.

Use surveys or assessments to measure employee satisfaction, collaboration across teams, and participation in decision-making. Regularly check in on how engaged and motivated teams are, as higher engagement levels often translate to greater agility.

These metrics offer valuable insights into how quickly and effectively teams can adapt to changing conditions and deliver value to the market. Regularly reviewing these measurements helps ensure that agility is maintained and continuously improved across all levels of the organization.

Agile Tools and Techniques

Agile tools and techniques help organizations implement and manage agile methodologies effectively. These approaches promote flexibility, collaboration, and rapid delivery of value. Below is an overview of some key agile tools and techniques that can be applied across various departments:

1. Scrum

Scrum is one of the most widely used agile frameworks, particularly in software development, but it can also be adapted for other business functions. It breaks down projects into sprints, which are short, time-boxed iterations (usually 2–4 weeks) during which teams deliver small, functional components of the project.

Key Elements:

- **Product Owner**: Responsible for defining what the team should be working on, focusing on customer needs.

- **Scrum Master**: Facilitates the process, ensures the team adheres to Scrum principles, and removes obstacles.

- **Daily Stand-ups**: Short, daily meetings where team members discuss progress, potential roadblocks, and next steps.

Scrum can be applied in marketing for content creation, in HR for hiring processes, or in product development to deliver iterative product features.

2. Kanban

Kanban is another popular agile tool that focuses on visualizing workflows and improving efficiency. It uses a Kanban board to track the status of tasks as they move through different stages (e.g., "To Do," "In Progress," "Done"). Kanban emphasizes continuous delivery and helps teams manage workflow by limiting the number of tasks in progress at any given time.

Key Elements:

- **Kanban Board**: A visual representation of tasks in different stages of completion.

- **Work-in-Progress (WIP) Limits**: Limits the number of tasks a team can work on simultaneously, reducing bottlenecks.

Kanban is highly effective in environments where there's a steady flow of tasks, such as customer service, software maintenance, or operations.

3. Design Thinking

Design Thinking is a user-centered approach to problem-solving that focuses on understanding the needs of end users before developing solutions. It encourages teams to empathize with users, define the problem, ideate possible solutions, prototype, and then test those solutions.

Key Elements:

- **Empathize**: Understand the user's needs and challenges.

- **Ideate**: Brainstorm creative solutions based on user insights.

- **Prototype and Test**: Quickly develop and test solutions, refining them based on feedback.

Design Thinking is highly adaptable and can be used in product development, marketing, and customer service to create solutions that better meet user needs.

4. Lean

Lean methodology, closely related to agile, focuses on delivering value by eliminating waste, improving processes, and focusing on customer needs. Lean uses principles like just-in-time production, continuous improvement (Kaizen), and delivering value as efficiently as possible.

Key Elements:

- **Value Stream Mapping**: Identifying and analyzing the steps in a process to eliminate unnecessary steps and maximize efficiency.

- **Kaizen (Continuous Improvement)**: A process of constantly refining operations and workflows to enhance productivity and quality.

Lean is often applied in manufacturing, but its principles can be adapted to other areas like marketing or logistics to streamline processes.

5. Extreme Programming (XP)

Extreme Programming (XP) is a software development technique that emphasizes customer satisfaction, continuous feedback, and frequent releases. It encourages small, frequent releases of software to ensure continuous delivery of value and quick feedback loops.

Key Elements:

- **Pair Programming**: Two programmers work together on the same code to ensure higher quality and faster problem-solving.

- **Test-Driven Development (TDD)**: Writing tests before the code to ensure that the solution meets the required standards.

Although commonly used in tech, XP principles can be applied to any process where continuous feedback and rapid iteration are important.

Agile tools and techniques like Scrum, Kanban, Design Thinking, Lean, and Extreme Programming enable organizations to be more flexible, responsive and customer-focused. These tools can be applied across different business functions, helping organizations stay competitive and adaptable in fast-changing environments.

Overcoming Resistance to Agility

Adopting an agile mindset often meets resistance within organizations, especially those with long-standing practices and established hierarchies.

Kodak, once a global leader in photography, serves as a powerful example of a company that failed to adapt to technological change. Despite pioneering the digital camera in the 1970s, Kodak's strong attachment to its traditional film-based business caused it to delay fully embracing digital photography. This cultural inertia—resistance to changing established practices—became a major barrier to transformation. Leadership was reluctant to pivot away from its profitable film products, fearing it would hurt its core business. As a result, Kodak invested heavily in film and failed to leverage its valuable digital patents. This allowed competitors like Canon and Sony to dominate the digital market.

By the time Kodak tried to shift focus to digital products, it was too late. Its slow response to technological advancements, combined with inconsistent leadership and strategic missteps, led to the company's decline. In 2012, Kodak filed for bankruptcy, marking a dramatic fall from its once-dominant position. Although it restructured and shifted focus to commercial printing, Kodak missed the chance to lead the digital revolution in photography.[21]

Resistance can stem from several factors, including entrenched hierarchies, fear of change, and short-term performance pressures. Addressing these obstacles requires thoughtful strategies and a commitment to fostering a culture of adaptability.

1. Entrenched Hierarchies

A major barrier to adopting agility is the presence of entrenched hierarchies. Traditional organizations, especially governments, are often structured around rigid frameworks where decision-making is centralized and information flows from the top down. This results in a slow, bureaucratic environment that finds it challenging to adapt to change. In contrast, agile organizations rely on decentralized decision-making, cross-functional collaboration, and flatter structures to remain responsive and adaptable.

To overcome hierarchical resistance, leadership must play an active role in driving change. Leaders should

---

[21]https://cdotimes.com/2023/09/27/case-study-kodaks-downfall-a-lesson-in-failed-digital-transformation-and-missed-opportunities/

communicate the benefits of agility and emphasize the importance of collaborative decision-making. Additionally, organizations can gradually introduce cross-functional teams, allowing employees from different departments to work together and make decisions without waiting for approval from higher-ups. This not only breaks down silos but also empowers teams to take ownership of their work.

2. Fear of Change

Fear of change is another significant barrier. Employees who are comfortable with the current way of doing things may be reluctant to adopt new practices, especially if they fear that these changes could make their roles less relevant or more demanding. Agile methodologies often require a shift in mindset, where employees need to embrace continuous learning, experimentation, and adaptability.

To address the fear of change, organizations should cultivate a supportive environment that promotes learning and experimentation. Building a culture that embraces change requires serious intervention strategies, which can be professionalized through expert guidance from consulting firms like CDiGlobal. These specialists can design and implement tailored change interventions that empower teams, foster resilience, and enhance adaptability.

3. Short-Term Performance Pressures

In many organizations, particularly in the financial services sector, where I worked full-time for over 18 years before transitioning to consulting, there is significant pressure from shareholders to deliver immediate results. Agile's focus on iterative development and continuous improvement can sometimes be perceived as too slow or uncertain, especially in environments driven by quarterly targets. The emphasis on long-term value often clashes with the demand for short-term gains, creating a tension between sustainable growth and rapid returns.

To balance agility with short-term performance pressures, it's essential to set clear, measurable goals for each agile iteration. By breaking projects into smaller, manageable pieces, teams can show progress more frequently, providing the organization with a sense of momentum. This helps demonstrate the value of agility, even in the short term. Moreover, leadership should clearly communicate how agile practices align with long-term strategic goals, reinforcing the idea that agility is not about moving quickly at all times but about making better, more informed decisions.

In conclusion, overcoming resistance to agility requires a combination of clear communication, leadership buy-in, and a commitment to building a culture of collaboration and adaptability. By addressing the root causes of resistance— entrenched hierarchies, fear of change, and performance pressures—organizations can create an environment that supports the successful adoption of an agile mindset.

Agile Mindset and AI Adoption

The agile mindset is essential for effectively adopting and integrating AI into an organization. Agile emphasizes adaptability, collaboration, and iterative progress, all of which are crucial when working with emerging technologies like AI. By fostering an agile mindset, organizations can ensure that they are prepared to navigate the complexities of AI adoption and fully leverage the potential of these technologies.

1. Adapting to New Technologies

AI adoption often involves significant changes to how an organization operates, from automating routine tasks to analyzing huge amounts of data for decision-making. These changes require a mindset that embraces adaptability and continuous learning, both of which are central to agile practices.

Agile's iterative approach aligns perfectly with the continuous nature of AI development. By working in short cycles (such as Scrum sprints), teams can test AI models, gather feedback, and refine their solutions incrementally. This not only reduces the risk of large-scale failure but also ensures that the AI system evolves in response to real-world conditions. In addition, cross-functional collaboration—another key element of agile—ensures that AI is integrated into different aspects of the business, not just isolated in the IT department.

2. Collaboration Across Teams

AI projects often involve multiple departments, including data scientists, engineers, product managers, and business analysts. Agile promotes cross-functional collaboration, breaking down silos and ensuring that all teams work together toward a common goal. This is especially important for AI adoption, where technical expertise must align with business objectives.

Implementing agile practices like regular stand-up meetings, sprint reviews, and retrospectives ensures that teams stay aligned and can address challenges as they arise. This collaborative environment allows for quicker problem-solving and a more holistic approach to AI integration.

3. Continuous Improvement and Learning

AI systems improve over time through continuous learning and refinement. Agile's focus on iterative development and regular feedback loops ensures that AI models are continually optimized based on new data and insights. This ongoing process of improvement is crucial for making AI systems more accurate, efficient, and valuable to the organization.

Agile encourages teams to embrace failure as a learning opportunity. In the context of AI, this means testing different models, experimenting with various approaches, and using feedback to make improvements. By fostering a culture of continuous improvement, organizations can ensure that their AI systems remain cutting-edge and effective.

In summary, an agile mindset is critical for successful AI adoption. Agile's adaptability, collaboration, and focus on continuous improvement align perfectly with the dynamic nature of AI, allowing organizations to fully harness the power of this transformative technology.

Future of Agile Organizations

As technology continues to evolve and market dynamics shift, agile organizations are well-positioned to thrive in the face of disruption. The principles of agility—adaptability, collaboration, and continuous improvement—are becoming increasingly important as businesses navigate new challenges. Looking ahead, several key trends are likely to shape the future of agile organizations.

1. Increased Integration of AI and Automation

As AI and automation become more prevalent, agile organizations will need to find ways to integrate these technologies into their workflows. AI can enhance agile practices by automating routine tasks, providing data-driven insights, and enabling faster decision-making. For example, AI-powered analytics can help agile teams prioritize tasks, identify potential risks, and make more informed decisions.

In the future, we can expect to see more agile organizations using AI to augment their processes, particularly in areas like project management, customer service, and product development. AI won't replace human teams but will work alongside them to enhance efficiency and drive innovation. This perspective is central to my book, which emphasizes a balanced approach to AI. I'm neither for nor against AI in itself; rather, I advocate for understanding how to leverage it effectively for organizational development. I stand against uninformed criticism, naivety, and ignorance surrounding AI, as these hinder meaningful progress and innovation.

2. Remote and Distributed Teams

The rise of remote work, accelerated by the COVID-19 pandemic, has reshaped how organizations operate. Agile organizations, with their focus on collaboration and flexibility, are well-suited to managing remote and distributed teams. Agile tools like Scrum and Kanban can be adapted to virtual environments, allowing teams to stay connected and productive no matter where they are located.

More agile organizations will embrace hybrid work models, where teams work both remotely and in the office. Agile methodologies will continue to evolve to support these distributed teams, with an increased emphasis on digital collaboration tools and virtual communication platforms.

3. Continuous Learning and Development

Agile organizations prioritize continuous learning and improvement. As industries become more technology-driven, the need for ongoing skill development will only increase. Agile organizations will need to invest in training and development programs that equip employees with the skills they need to adapt to new technologies and market changes.

Agile organizations will place even greater emphasis on upskilling and reskilling their workforce. This will include providing opportunities for employees to learn new technologies, such as AI and automation, and fostering a culture of experimentation and innovation.

In conclusion, the future of agile organizations is bright. As technology continues to disrupt industries, agile organizations will be better equipped to adapt, innovate, and thrive in an ever-changing market. By embracing AI, supporting remote teams, and prioritizing continuous learning, agile organizations will remain at the forefront of innovation and success.

Homo Magister and Agility

The Homo Magister concept, which emphasizes the dual role of leaders as both teachers and visionaries, aligns closely with the principles of agility. In an agile organization, leaders are not just decision-makers; they are mentors who guide their teams through uncertainty and promote a culture of learning and adaptability.

1. Teaching and Mentorship

Homo Magister leaders prioritize teaching and mentorship, which are essential for cultivating an agile mindset. In an agile organization, teams must be able to adapt quickly, learn from their mistakes, and continuously improve. Leaders who embody the Homo Magister ideal support this by creating a safe space for experimentation and by actively coaching their teams through challenges.

2. Visionary Leadership

Agility requires leaders who can see the bigger picture and guide their teams toward long-term goals while allowing flexibility in the short term. Homo Magister leaders are visionary in that they set a clear direction for the organization but are open to adjusting strategies as needed. This aligns with the agile principle of embracing change and being responsive to new information.

3. Fostering a Learning Culture

Agile organizations thrive on continuous learning, and Homo Magister leaders are instrumental in fostering this culture. By encouraging curiosity, openness to new ideas, and a willingness to learn from failure, these leaders create an environment where teams feel empowered to innovate and adapt.

The Homo Magister concept supports the development of an agile mindset by emphasizing leadership qualities that promote learning, adaptability, and vision. In an ever-changing world, these qualities are essential for guiding organizations through uncertainty and ensuring long-term success.

Scaling Agility Across the Organization

Promoting an agile mindset within an organization requires thoughtful planning and a step-by-step approach. Below is a guide to help organizations begin building and implementing agility, starting from assessment through to continuous improvement.

1. Initial Assessment

To start implementing agile practices, begin with a comprehensive assessment of your organization. Engaging experts like CDiGlobal Consulting can help evaluate your current processes, identify areas of improvement, and pinpoint potential challenges. This initial assessment lays the groundwork for a tailored agile transformation strategy, ensuring that changes align with your organizational goals and capabilities.

- **Assess current processes**: Examine workflows, decision-making speed, and how well your teams respond to changes. Are processes rigid and slow to adapt? Are teams siloed?

- **Evaluate team culture**: Don't underplay the culture phenomena. Does your organization encourage collaboration, open communication, and innovation? Understanding your company's culture helps identify where shifts need to happen to foster an agile mindset.

- **Identify key stakeholders**: Pinpoint the key individuals who will drive the transformation, including leadership, department heads, and agile champions. Engaging these stakeholders in the early stages is essential for fostering a co-creation approach, where each contributor plays an active role in shaping the agile journey. This collaborative effort helps build alignment, ensures commitment, and accelerates the overall transformation process.

2. Set Clear Goals and Objectives

Setting clear goals will help keep the organization focused on the purpose behind the shift to agile practices.

- **Define what agility means for your organization**: Agility may look different depending on your company's structure and industry. Is the goal to increase customer responsiveness, streamline project management, or improve time-to-market?

- **Align agility with business objectives**: Ensure that agile practices will support overall business goals. For instance, if the goal is faster product development, agility should focus on iterative product releases and cross-functional collaboration.

3. Pilot Agile Practices in a Small Team

Starting with a small pilot project allows teams to experiment with agile methodologies on a smaller scale. This helps to gather insights on what works, identify challenges, and make adjustments before rolling out agile across the entire organization.

- **Choose a manageable project**: Select a project that can be completed in a few weeks and will benefit from agile principles, such as rapid iteration and continuous feedback.

- **Introduce agile frameworks**: Implement agile tools like **Scrum** or **Kanban** to manage workflows and track progress. For example, Scrum can be useful for organizing sprints, while Kanban helps visualize work and manage priorities.

- **Provide training**: Equip your team with the necessary agile knowledge by employing expert-led training. Ensure that everyone understands core agile values and how to apply key tools like Scrum and Kanban. This training aligns team members on expectations and processes, building a shared foundation that supports consistent, effective application of agile principles across the organization.

4. Collaborate and Learn

Agile is a team-oriented approach, and collaboration is essential. Encouraging open communication and creating an environment where teams can learn from mistakes without fear of failure is critical.

- **Promote cross-functional collaboration**: Break down silos by forming teams with diverse skill sets, including members from different departments like marketing, engineering, and product management.

- **Encourage feedback loops**: Regularly gather feedback from customers as well as team members. Continuous feedback enables constant improvement.

- **Support a growth mindset**: Encourage employees to embrace challenges and learn from setbacks. Leaders should model this behavior by sharing their own experiences and demonstrating openness to learning.

5. Decentralize Decision-Making

In traditional organizations, decision-making is often slow due to hierarchical layers of approval. Agile requires faster decision-making, which means empowering teams to make decisions on their own.

- **Empower teams**: Allow teams to make decisions that directly affect their work. This not only increases efficiency but also instills a sense of ownership and accountability.

- **Limit top-down control**: Leadership should focus on setting clear objectives and providing guidance but avoid micromanaging teams. Instead, trust teams to self-organize and deliver results.

6. Iterate and Adapt

Agility is not a one-time transformation; it involves consistent iteration and improvement. As your organization adopts agile practices, you'll need to constantly evaluate progress and make adjustments as needed.

- **Review progress regularly**: Hold regular retrospectives to assess what's working and what's not. This helps identify areas for improvement and fine-tune agile practices.

- **Adapt based on feedback**: Be open to changing workflows, tools, or strategies based on feedback. Agility requires flexibility, and the ability to pivot when necessary is a core part of agile principles.

7. Scale Agile Across the Organization

After a successful pilot project, the next step is to expand agile practices across other teams and departments. Integrate this expansion into the organization's broader strategic plan to ensure alignment with overall business objectives. Scaling agile in this way fosters cross-departmental consistency, enhances collaboration, and embeds agile as a foundational approach within the organization's long-term vision.

Extend agile to other functions: Apply agile methods to areas beyond IT and product development, such as marketing, HR, or operations.

- **Standardize agile practices**: While flexibility is important, creating standard agile practices across teams will ensure consistency. For example, establish regular sprint planning sessions, daily stand-ups, and feedback loops.

- **Continuously improve**: Agility doesn't have an end date. It requires an ongoing commitment to improvement, learning, and adapting to new challenges.

8. Measure Success and Adjust

In line with your performance management strategy, it is essential to track progress using clear, tangible metrics to evaluate the success of your agile transformation. Set benchmarks that allow you to assess whether agile practices are delivering the desired impact. Regularly review these metrics and make adjustments as needed to ensure continuous improvement and alignment with your organizational goals.

- **Track key performance indicators (KPIs)**: These might include metrics like time-to-market, customer satisfaction, employee engagement, and team efficiency. Agile organizations should regularly check how well they are meeting these KPIs.

- **Use feedback for continuous improvement**: Based on your KPIs and regular feedback from employees, customers, and stakeholders, refine your agile processes. This ensures that agility is truly embedded in the organization.

Building an agile mindset in an organization starts with assessing the current state, setting clear goals, and fostering collaboration and continuous learning. With careful implementation, starting with small pilot projects and expanding over time, organizations can adopt agile principles and continuously improve their ability to respond to changes and challenges. By following these steps, organizations can lay the foundation for lasting agility and resilience in an ever-changing business environment.

Reflections:

As you consider applying the agile mindset within your organization, here are some thought-provoking questions to help guide you:

1. Does your organization have the flexibility to pivot quickly when faced with new challenges or opportunities? What barriers exist that may prevent agility, and how can you overcome them?

2. In what areas of your business can teams be given more autonomy to make decisions? How can you empower your employees to take ownership and responsibility for their projects?

3. Does your organization view failure as a learning opportunity? How can you foster a culture where employees feel safe experimenting and innovating, even if the results are not immediately successful?

4. Are there silos within your organization that hinder communication and collaboration? What steps can you take to break down these silos and promote cross-functional teamwork?

5. Are your leaders demonstrating flexibility, openness to feedback, and continuous learning? How can you encourage leadership at all levels to embrace and promote agility within the organization?

By reflecting on these questions, you can assess how agile principles align with your organization's current state and identify opportunities for facilitating a more agile mindset.

Agility enables businesses to quickly respond to changes, pivot when necessary, and continuously improve. We explored key elements of agility, such as flexibility, decentralized decision-making, cross-functional collaboration, and a focus on continuous learning and adaptation. These principles empower organizations to stay competitive in a rapidly evolving market.

An agile mindset allows for skillful pivots—the ability to change direction when needed without losing momentum. This is crucial in the AI era, where technological advancements require constant adaptation. Leaders play a pivotal role in fostering this mindset, acting as both visionaries and mentors who empower their teams to take risks and innovate.

Chapter 5: Making Data-Informed Choices

A few years ago, a large retail chain faced constant cash flow challenges emanating from inventory management. Shelves were either overstocked with items that didn't sell or empty due to misjudged demand. This imbalance led to wasted resources, customer dissatisfaction, and missed sales opportunities. After a careful analysis, I highlighted the need for urgent change before motivating AI-powered predictive analytics, and that's when it turned to AI-powered predictive analytics.

The retail chain implemented an AI system that used historical data, customer purchasing patterns, and external factors like weather and local events. The system helped forecast demand with much more precision. The chain could now predict which products would be in high demand at specific times and specific locations. This change drastically improved their inventory management, reducing both overstock and stockouts.

Beyond managing inventory, the company also transformed its customer experience. The AI analyzed data to recommend personalized product suggestions, boosting customer engagement. It also allowed the company to create targeted marketing campaigns tailored to individual preferences, which resulted in increased customer loyalty and higher sales.

This AI-driven transformation highlighted the immense value of data-driven decision-making. By leveraging predictive analytics, the retail chain optimized its operations and enhanced the overall shopping experience, positioning itself as a forward-thinking leader in its industry. The ability to use data to guide decisions allowed the company to anticipate customer needs, manage inventory more effectively, and improve overall efficiency. Building on this, adopting a data-centric culture is crucial for organizations looking to thrive in the AI era.

Data-Centric Culture

A data-centric culture refers to an organizational environment where decisions are driven primarily by data rather than intuition, gut feelings, or past experiences. Data is considered a critical asset in this culture, and teams rely on it to make informed decisions at every level. The move from intuition-based to evidence-based decision-making is becoming essential, especially in the AI era, where the ability to process and analyze large amounts of data provides a significant competitive advantage.

In a data-centric organization, data flows freely and is accessible to everyone who needs it. Employees are encouraged to use data in their day-to-day tasks, whether it's for making strategic decisions or improving operational efficiency. A few years ago, I worked for a merchant bank that was transitioning to a commercial bank. Each morning, we would gather to review our performance, examining comparative statistics and seeing where we stood. This included a daily breakdown of revenue versus all costs. The organization invested in tools, technologies, and training to ensure that employees can easily access, analyze, and act on data insights. For example, a marketing team might use customer behavior data to personalize campaigns, while a logistics team relies on real-time data to optimize supply chains.

The core principle of a data-centric culture is that decisions are grounded in facts rather than assumptions. Leaders and employees are expected to back up their strategies and recommendations with data. This reduces the risk of biased or misguided decisions and ensures that the company is taking the most informed path forward.

Building a data-centric culture also involves breaking down silos. In many traditional organizations, data is fragmented and restricted to specific departments. A data-centric organization, however, promotes cross-functional collaboration, making data available across teams so that it can be leveraged in various contexts. For example, data from customer service can inform product development or marketing strategies.

Companies should adopt this culture since it is crucial in the AI era because AI technologies thrive on data. Without a strong foundation of clean, accessible, and well-managed data, organizations cannot fully realize the potential of AI. Predictive analytics, machine learning models, and other AI technologies require data to function effectively.

Predictive Analytics as a Key AI Technology

Predictive analytics is one of the most powerful AI technologies enabling data-driven decision-making. It involves using historical data, statistical algorithms, and machine-learning techniques to identify patterns and predict future outcomes. Predictive analytics gives organizations the ability to foresee trends, anticipate customer behaviors, and make proactive decisions, making it an essential tool in many industries.

Predictive analytics works by analyzing past data to forecast future results. It starts with data collection, where an organization gathers relevant data—this can include customer purchase histories, website behavior, or operational metrics. Next, the data is cleaned and prepared to ensure it is accurate and consistent. Afterward, machine learning algorithms analyze this data to detect patterns and relationships. These patterns are then used to predict what will happen in the future. For example, a retail company might use predictive analytics to forecast which products will sell more during the holiday season based on historical sales data.

Applications of Predictive Analytics

Predictive analytics has emerged as a powerful tool across a variety of industries. It has helped businesses make informed decisions by analyzing past data to forecast future outcomes. By leveraging machine learning algorithms and statistical models, companies can anticipate customer behaviors, market trends, and operational needs with greater accuracy. From healthcare to finance, marketing to supply chain management, predictive analytics is revolutionizing how organizations operate, enabling them to improve efficiency, personalize customer experiences, and reduce risks. Mentioned below are a few areas where it has been helpful.

1. **Marketing**: Predictive analytics helps companies understand customer preferences and tailor personalized marketing campaigns. This enhances targeting, leading to more effective campaigns and higher customer engagement.

2. **Finance**: In finance, predictive analytics is crucial for forecasting market trends, assessing credit risks, and optimizing investment decisions. This helps financial institutions manage risks more effectively and allocate resources where they are most needed.

3. **Healthcare**: Predictive analytics is used to anticipate patient outcomes, helping doctors personalize treatment plans, predict disease outbreaks, or optimize hospital resource allocation. This leads to better patient care and more efficient healthcare services.

4. **Supply Chain Management**: By predicting demand, predictive analytics helps companies manage their inventory levels, avoiding overstock or stockouts. This is especially useful in industries

where demand fluctuates due to seasonality or market changes.

According to research by EY published in 2023. The organizations that have embraced digital supply chain management systems, including AI-powered predictive analytics, have increased supply chain resilience by 35%. This research underscores the critical role of technology in mitigating disruptions and ensuring the continuity of operations in an increasingly interconnected world.[22]

One of the most notable impacts of predictive analytics is the improvement of operational efficiency. Companies can optimize inventory management, reduce costs, and streamline processes by predicting demand. For example, an airline might use predictive analytics to forecast flight bookings, adjusting ticket prices accordingly to maximize revenue.

Moreover, predictive analytics provides a competitive edge by enabling companies to personalize customer experiences. Using data to predict what individual customers might need or want allows organizations to deliver more targeted products, services, and recommendations. This personalization improves customer satisfaction and increases loyalty, which, in turn, boosts profitability.

The key challenge in implementing predictive analytics lies in data quality and quantity. The accuracy of predictions depends on the quality of the data being analyzed, hence the

---

[22]https://www.ey.com/en_us/insights/operations/digital-supply-chain-become-resilient-and-agile

need to adopt good data governance principles. Therefore, organizations must invest in proper data management practices to ensure clean and relevant data is available for analysis.

Predictive analytics is a critical AI technology that enables businesses to make data-driven decisions, improving operational efficiency, personalization, and overall strategy. Its applications span multiple industries, and organizations that embrace it can make smarter, more informed decisions.

Championing Data-Centric Culture: The Homo Magister Approach

A Homo Magister leader sees the value in integrating data and technology into everyday decision-making. She/He actively champions this transformation by promoting the use of analytics, AI, and predictive tools across departments, ensuring that teams understand the strategic advantages these technologies offer. These leaders promote an organizational culture that treats data as a vital asset, ensuring employees have access to data tools and training to make informed choices based on evidence rather than gut feelings.

However, Homo Magister leaders don't just implement these systems and walk away. They serve as guides and educators and help their teams interpret data, question its implications, and balance it with human intuition. They understand that while technology can provide insights, human judgment is crucial in making the best decisions. For instance, while AI might predict customer behavior trends, the leader's human insight frames these predictions within the larger company vision.

Balancing Technology and Human Insight

What sets Homo Magister leaders apart is their ability to balance technological capabilities with human understanding. They recognize that data is a powerful tool, but it must be complemented by the wisdom that comes from experience, creativity, and emotional intelligence. These leaders help employees navigate the complexities of data, teaching them to ask the right questions, challenge assumptions, and consider the broader impact of decisions on people, culture, and society.

For example, while AI can optimize operations or forecast sales, it is the Homo Magister leader who ensures that ethical considerations, customer needs, and long-term goals are integrated into the decision-making process. They teach their teams to view data not just as numbers but as a story that, when combined with human insight, can lead to truly innovative solutions.

Homo Magister leaders are also committed to continuous learning. They recognize that technology and human skills must evolve to stay competitive in the AI era. These leaders actively encourage ongoing education and experimentation, ensuring that their teams are up-to-date with the latest tools and equipped with the critical thinking skills needed to interpret and apply those tools effectively.

In this way, the Homo Magister leader not only facilitates the technical transition to data-driven decision-making but also ensures that their team develops the mindset needed to thrive in a world where technology and human insight work in tandem.

Responsible AI Adoption Framework

Implementing AI-driven decision-making systems requires not only technical expertise but also a strong focus on ethics. As AI becomes more integrated into business processes, organizations need to develop a Responsible AI Adoption Framework that ensures ethical practices. Below is a step-by-step guide for ethically implementing AI, with careful consideration of issues like data privacy, algorithmic bias, and transparency.

1. Understand and Define AI's Role

Before implementing any AI system, it's important to clearly define its purpose. Start by identifying the specific areas where AI will be used and the type of decisions it will assist. For example, will AI handle customer service, manage supply chains, or make hiring recommendations? This step sets the foundation for how data will be used and what ethical considerations need to be taken into account.

2. Ensure Data Privacy

Data privacy is critical when adopting AI, as these systems often rely on large amounts of personal data. Organizations need to implement strict data protection protocols to ensure sensitive information is handled securely. Follow these practices:

- **Data anonymization**: Remove personally identifiable information (PII) from datasets so individual identities are protected.

- **Comply with regulations**: Ensure compliance with regulations such as the **General Data Protection Regulation (GDPR)** or **California Consumer Privacy Act (CCPA)** to protect user data and avoid legal issues.

- **Transparent data collection**: Inform users about how their data will be collected, stored, and used. Always seek consent before collecting sensitive data.

3. Address Algorithmic Bias

AI systems can inadvertently develop biases based on the data they are trained on. This can lead to unfair outcomes, especially in areas like hiring or credit scoring. To ensure fairness:

- **Diverse datasets**: Use datasets that represent a wide variety of people, backgrounds, and behaviors to reduce bias.

- **Regular audits**: Continuously monitor AI systems for biased behavior. Regularly review how AI systems make decisions, checking if specific groups are being disproportionately affected.

- **Bias mitigation**: Implement corrective measures, such as re-training models with more balanced data or adjusting algorithms, to reduce bias in decision-making.

4. Build Transparency into AI Systems

Transparency is key to ensuring ethical AI adoption. AI systems should be understandable so users can see how decisions are made. To maintain transparency:

- **Explainability**: Ensure that AI models are interpretable and can provide explanations for the decisions they make. Users should understand why certain outcomes were reached.

- **Open communication**: Be clear about the limitations of AI systems. Inform stakeholders that AI is not perfect, and its recommendations should be reviewed in context.

- **Human oversight**: Incorporate human checks on critical decisions made by AI, especially in sensitive areas like healthcare, finance, or criminal justice.

5. Prioritize Accountability

AI systems should not operate without accountability. Ensure that people are responsible for overseeing the AI systems and are held accountable for their decisions:

- **Assign AI accountability**: Designate specific roles or teams responsible for overseeing AI ethics, data management, and AI performance within the organization.

- **Ethical committees**: Establish internal committees that regularly evaluate the ethical implications of the AI systems and suggest improvements.

- **Regular reviews**: Conduct frequent audits of AI systems and assess whether the AI still aligns with the organization's ethical guidelines.

6. Foster a Culture of Continuous Learning

Ethical AI adoption requires an organization to stay up-to-date on new developments in AI ethics, privacy laws, and emerging technologies. Encourage continuous learning and improvement through:

- **Employee training**: Provide ongoing training for employees on the ethical use of AI and the potential risks involved in data privacy and bias.

- **Collaborate with experts**: Work with AI ethics experts or partner with academic institutions to stay ahead of the latest trends and ensure best practices.

Implementing AI ethically is more than just a technical task; it's about making decisions that protect user privacy, prevent bias, and ensure transparency. By following this Responsible AI Adoption Framework, organizations can balance the power of AI technology with human insight and ethics, building trust and accountability while delivering data-driven results. The framework creates a solid foundation to responsibly leverage AI's potential while safeguarding the interests of individuals and society.

Tech Mastery Strategies

For organizations aiming to excel in data analytics and AI-driven decision-making, developing technical expertise is critical. Below are several approaches to ensure successful mastery of these technologies:

1. **Training Programs**: One of the most effective ways to develop tech mastery is through well-structured training programs. Organizations should offer regular workshops, courses, and certifications for employees. This includes hands-on training in data analytics tools, AI platforms, and machine learning frameworks like TensorFlow or Python. Online courses, such as those offered by Coursera, Udemy, or DataCamp, are also beneficial for upskilling employees at their own pace. Creating internal knowledge-sharing initiatives, like lunch-and-learns or hackathons, helps foster a culture of continuous learning.

2. **Hiring Strategies**: To build strong capabilities in AI and analytics, organizations need to recruit talent with

specialized skills in data science, machine learning, and AI. This can be done by targeting top universities, participating in tech conferences, or using platforms like LinkedIn to identify skilled professionals. Organizations should also focus on cross-functional talent—individuals who can bridge the gap between technical and business teams.

3. Partnerships with Tech Providers: Partnering with **tech providers** is a valuable strategy for gaining expertise in AI. Collaborations with AI vendors, cloud providers, or data analytics firms allow organizations to access the latest technologies and expert consulting. Strategic partnerships with companies like **Google Cloud**, **AWS**, or **Microsoft Azure** help businesses implement advanced tools without having to build everything in-house.

Change Management for AI Integration

Integrating AI into an organization often brings significant changes to workflows, decision-making processes, and employee roles. Managing these transitions smoothly requires effective change management strategies:

1. Communicating the Benefits: Employees and stakeholders must understand the value of AI-driven decision-making. Leadership should clearly explain how AI will improve efficiency, enable better decision-making, and enhance job roles rather than replace them. This can alleviate concerns about job displacement.

2. Engaging Stakeholders Early: Involve key stakeholders early in the AI integration process to gain their buy-in. Cross-functional teams can offer feedback and identify challenges that need to be addressed upfront. Including employees in the process increases transparency and ensures they feel a part of the transition.

3.   **Addressing Concerns**: One of the most common concerns when implementing AI is fear of job loss or feeling obsolete. Leaders should address these concerns directly by showing how AI will augment, rather than replace, human work. **Reskilling programs** should be made available to ensure employees can adapt to new roles and responsibilities.

4.   **Fostering a Culture of Adaptability**: Organizations should encourage employees to embrace **continuous learning** and adaptability. This can be done through offering training in AI tools, promoting a growth mindset, and celebrating early wins from AI projects to build confidence in the technology.

AI Ethics and Governance

As organizations increasingly rely on AI and data-driven decision-making, they must establish strong ethical guidelines and governance structures to ensure responsible use of these technologies.

1.   **Data Privacy and Security**: Data is the fuel for AI, but it comes with significant privacy concerns. Organizations must implement strict data protection measures, including encryption and anonymization of sensitive data, to protect user privacy. Compliance with

regulations like **GDPR** and **CCPA** is also essential to avoid legal and reputational risks.

2. Algorithmic Bias: One of the most critical ethical concerns in AI is **bias** in algorithms. AI systems can unintentionally perpetuate discrimination if they are trained on biased datasets. Regular audits of AI models should be conducted to detect and mitigate bias, ensuring fairness and transparency in decision-making. Implementing **bias correction techniques** and involving diverse teams in model development can help address this issue.

3. Transparent AI: For AI systems to be trusted, they need to be transparent. Organizations should ensure that AI models can explain how decisions are made. This means creating explainable AI (XAI) systems where humans can understand and review outcomes. This is particularly important in high-stakes areas like healthcare, finance, or criminal justice.

4. AI Governance Committees: Setting up dedicated AI governance committees helps maintain oversight of AI projects. These committees should consist of data scientists, ethicists, legal experts, and business leaders who can review AI applications, ensure they align with ethical standards, and address any concerns related to data use or algorithm performance.

5. Accountability and Audits: Organizations must establish clear accountability for AI outcomes. This involves assigning specific teams or leaders to oversee AI ethics and performance. Regular audits of AI systems ensure that they are functioning as intended and in accordance with ethical guidelines. If errors occur, organizations should be prepared to correct them and take responsibility for any unintended consequences.

These strategies for tech mastery, change management, and AI ethics provide a solid foundation for organizations to responsibly integrate AI into their operations, ensuring both innovation and ethical integrity.

Netflix provides an excellent example of how data-driven decision-making can lead to groundbreaking innovations. Once a DVD rental service, Netflix transformed into a global streaming giant by leveraging vast amounts of user data to drive personalized recommendations and inform content creation decisions. The company uses data from user behaviors, including viewing patterns, search histories, ratings, and interactions with the platform, to craft a personalized experience for every viewer. This level of personalization has played a huge role in Netflix's success, with 80% of content streamed on the platform coming from these tailored recommendations.

Netflix doesn't stop at recommendations; it also uses data analytics to inform content production. Before greenlighting original shows or films, Netflix searches its data to predict the success of potential projects. One of its early triumphs was **House of Cards**, a show that was commissioned based on data insights revealing a strong interest in political dramas and actor Kevin Spacey among its users. This decision proved a major success, helping Netflix establish itself as a serious player in original content production.

However, Netflix faced challenges along the way. One major hurdle was managing the enormous volume of data generated by millions of users in real-time. To handle this, Netflix invested in scalable cloud infrastructure, particularly through its partnership with **Amazon Web Services (AWS)**. This allowed the company to process and analyze massive datasets quickly and provide real-time insights that fuel its decision-making processes.

Balancing data with creativity was another challenge. While data informs many of Netflix's decisions, the company knew it couldn't rely solely on numbers for storytelling. Instead, data insights guide what audiences might enjoy, but creative professionals are given the freedom to innovate, ensuring that original content remains fresh and engaging.

The impact of Netflix's data-driven approach has been profound. Not only has it enhanced the user experience by making it easier for viewers to discover content they love, but it has also helped the company make more informed, efficient investments in original programming. This has allowed Netflix to stay ahead of competitors in the streaming space. Additionally, Netflix's success has influenced the broader entertainment industry, pushing traditional media companies to adopt similar data-driven strategies for content creation and distribution.

Overcoming Data Silos

Breaking down data silos is essential for organizations looking to promote cross-functional collaboration, improve decision-making, and leverage data analytics more effectively. Data silos occur when different departments or teams within an organization keep their data isolated from one another, limiting access and preventing the full benefits of data integration. Addressing this issue requires both **technical solutions** and **cultural changes** to promote collaboration and ensure that data is accessible across the organization.

1. Technical Approaches
Centralized Data Platforms:

A common technical strategy for breaking down silos is implementing a **centralized data platform** where all teams can store and access data. By using data lakes, cloud storage solutions, or integrated platforms such as **Amazon Web Services (AWS)**, **Google Cloud**, or **Microsoft Azure**, organizations can create a shared environment where data from different departments is housed together. These platforms provide scalability and ensure that data is available to those who need it, regardless of department boundaries. Centralized systems also simplify data management and enable **real-time analytics**.

Data Integration Tools:

Another solution is to use **data integration tools** that bring together data from different silos without needing a single centralized location. These tools, like **Apache Kafka**, **Talend**, or **Informatica**, allow different systems to communicate with one another, ensuring smooth data flow across the organization. **APIs** (Application Programming Interfaces) also play a key role, as they enable different software systems to share data without requiring a complete system overhaul.

Implementing Data Governance:

Technical solutions are incomplete without proper data governance policies that define who can access, share, and modify data. Establishing data stewardship roles ensures that data is well-managed, clean, and usable across different departments. Clear guidelines around data usage also promote accountability and trust, encouraging more open data sharing.

2. Cultural Approaches
Fostering a Collaborative Culture:

Even with the best technical tools, overcoming data silos requires a cultural shift. Leaders must encourage a collaborative **mindset** across departments, emphasizing the value of shared data in driving better organizational outcomes. This can be done through cross-functional teams, where employees from different departments collaborate on projects and share data. Leaders should actively promote open communication, break down departmental barriers, and create incentives for employees who contribute to data-sharing initiatives.

Breaking Departmental Mindsets:

In many organizations, data silos form due to entrenched mindsets where departments view their data as their own proprietary resource. Leaders must address this by educating **teams** on the benefits of data sharing for the entire organization. Demonstrating how shared data can lead to better decision-making, faster problem-solving, and innovative solutions helps reduce resistance. Recognizing and celebrating successful data-sharing initiatives can also reinforce the message.

Regular Training and Skill Development:

Providing training programs focused on data literacy and analytics is another way to foster cross-functional collaboration. Employees should be trained not only on technical tools but also on how data from different departments can be combined to drive valuable insights. When teams understand the bigger picture, they are more likely to see the value in sharing their data and collaborating with others.

Leadership Buy-In:

Finally, leadership must lead by example. When executives actively promote data transparency and make decisions based on integrated data, it sets a strong precedent. Regularly sharing success stories of how cross-departmental data collaboration has led to significant improvements can further inspire teams to work together.

Breaking down data silos requires a combination of technical solutions—such as centralized platforms, data integration tools, and governance frameworks—and cultural changes to foster collaboration. By addressing both aspects, organizations can create an environment where data flows freely, and cross-functional teams can leverage it for better decision-making, innovation, and overall business success.

AI-Human Collaboration Models

As AI continues to be integrated into business processes, the collaboration between AI systems and human decision-makers is evolving into a critical factor for success. AI-human collaboration models are designed to leverage the strengths of both humans and AI, allowing organizations to make better decisions, enhance productivity, and innovate faster. The key to these models is recognizing that AI excels in areas like data processing, pattern recognition, and automating routine tasks, while humans bring creativity, contextual understanding, and ethical judgment.

1. Decision-Support Systems: In this model, AI systems provide data-driven insights, but humans remain responsible for the final decisions. AI analyzes large datasets and identifies patterns that might be missed by human decision-makers. For example, AI can suggest strategies for optimizing inventory or personalizing marketing campaigns, but a human decides how to apply those insights in the broader context of the company's goals and values. This model is common in areas like finance, where AI can analyze market trends, but financial advisors offer personalized guidance based on the client's needs.

2. Collaborative Intelligence: This framework emphasizes a true partnership where both AI and humans work together to solve problems. AI handles repetitive, data-intensive tasks, while humans tackle creative or strategic elements. For instance, in healthcare, AI systems can assist doctors by analyzing medical records and suggesting treatment options based on patterns from previous cases. The doctor then uses their expertise to select the most appropriate course of action for the individual patient. This model improves efficiency without replacing the human's critical role.

3. Human-in-the-Loop Systems: In this model, AI performs tasks but requires human intervention to verify and refine results. This is especially useful in areas like fraud detection, where AI systems can flag potentially fraudulent activities based on established patterns. However, a human analyst reviews the flagged cases to ensure that the AI has not made errors or produced false positives. Human-in-the-loop systems ensure that AI's speed and data-processing abilities are complemented by human judgment.

In all these models, the goal is to balance the data-processing capabilities of AI with the creativity and emotional intelligence of human beings, ensuring that decisions are both data-driven and ethically sound.

Future of Work Projections

The shift toward data-driven decision-making and the integration of AI into the workplace is reshaping job roles and workforce structures. As automation and AI take over routine tasks, new roles are emerging, while existing ones are evolving to focus more on tasks that require human intuition, creativity, and ethical judgment.

1. Emergence of New Roles: One of the most significant impacts of AI on the future of work is the creation of new roles that focus on developing, managing, and maintaining AI systems. Positions such as AI specialists, machine learning engineers, and data scientists are in high demand as organizations strive to build and refine their AI-driven tools. Additionally, new roles like AI ethicists and data governance officers are emerging to ensure that AI systems are used responsibly and ethically.

2. Evolution of Existing Roles: As AI automates repetitive tasks, many traditional roles are evolving. For example, in industries like finance and healthcare, routine data entry and administrative tasks are being automated. This has allowed professionals to focus more on strategic decision-making and customer interaction. Marketing professionals are using AI to gather insights about customer behavior, but their role is shifting to developing creative campaigns and building stronger customer relationships. Similarly, in logistics, while AI optimizes delivery routes and inventory management, human workers focus on more complex problem-solving and relationship management with suppliers and customers.

3. Focus on Human Skills: As more tasks become automated, the demand for skills like critical thinking, problem-solving, emotional intelligence, and creativity will increase. While AI excels at processing data and identifying patterns, it cannot replace the human ability to think outside the box, understand complex social dynamics, or apply ethical reasoning in nuanced situations. This shift suggests that future jobs will prioritize soft skills alongside technical expertise, and employees who can combine both will be in high demand.

4. Continuous Learning: With the rapid pace of technological change, employees will need to commit to continuous learning and upskilling to stay relevant in the workforce. Organizations will need to invest in training programs that help workers adapt to new tools and technologies, especially in areas like data analytics and AI. This will also create opportunities for companies to partner with educational institutions to ensure their workforce is prepared for the evolving job market.

Thus, while AI and automation will undoubtedly transform the future of work, they will also open new opportunities for human-centric roles that emphasize creativity, leadership, and ethical decision-making. The workforce of the future will be a dynamic blend of AI-driven efficiency and human ingenuity, ensuring that organizations can adapt to changing market demands while maintaining ethical and strategic oversight.

Measuring Data-Driven Transformation

Adopting data-driven decision-making processes is a significant shift for many organizations, and it's essential to evaluate the impact of this transformation through specific Key Performance Indicators (KPIs) and metrics. Both quantitative and qualitative measures provide valuable insights into how data-driven approaches are influencing business outcomes, operational efficiency, and overall organizational culture. Here's how companies can effectively measure their data-driven transformation:

1. Quantitative Measures

These KPIs are numerical and provide concrete evidence of the results stemming from data-driven decision-making.

- **Revenue Growth**: A clear indicator of the effectiveness of data-driven decisions is the impact on revenue. Companies should track changes in sales and profitability after implementing data analytics tools. For example, using predictive analytics to optimize pricing strategies or customer targeting can directly result in higher revenues.

- **Cost Reduction**: By leveraging data for operational improvements, organizations can identify inefficiencies and reduce costs. Companies should measure reductions in waste, operational expenses, and inefficiencies. For example, supply chain optimizations driven by data analytics may lead to better inventory management, reducing excess stock and improving cash flow.

- **Time to Decision**: Data-driven decision-making tools, such as AI and analytics platforms, should speed up the decision-making process. Organizations can track how long it takes for key decisions to be made before and after implementing these tools. Shorter decision cycles often indicate more efficient use of data.

- **Customer Acquisition Cost (CAC)**: Data-driven marketing allows businesses to target the right customers more effectively. By tracking CAC, companies can see if the use of data analytics in marketing has led to lower costs in acquiring new customers.

- **Customer Retention Rate**: A well-implemented data strategy often results in better customer engagement and retention. By analyzing customer behaviors and preferences, companies can personalize experiences, which can lead to higher customer loyalty. Monitoring changes in customer retention rates can reveal the success of such data-driven personalization efforts.

- **Operational Efficiency**: Data-driven decision-making should also improve processes, leading to greater efficiency. This can be measured through metrics such as production time, error rates, or turnaround time for projects. For example, in manufacturing, tracking metrics like machine downtime or production bottlenecks can reveal improvements post-data integration.

2. Qualitative Measures

Qualitative metrics are more subjective but equally important, as they provide insight into how data-driven processes impact organizational culture and employee engagement.

- **Employee Adoption and Engagement**: It's crucial to assess how employees are interacting with data tools. Are they using analytics to inform their decisions? This can be measured through employee surveys, feedback sessions, or internal data usage reports. High adoption rates suggest that data-driven processes are being embraced, while low engagement may point to the need for additional training or culture shifts.

- **Data Literacy Across Teams**: The success of a data-driven transformation also depends on how well employees understand and use data in their roles. Companies can measure improvements in data literacy through skill assessments, training completion rates, and the quality of insights teams are generating. The more data-literate the workforce, the greater the value extracted from analytics tools.

- **Cross-Departmental Collaboration**: As organizations break down data silos, collaboration between departments should improve. Qualitative surveys and observations can reveal whether teams are sharing data more freely and working together more effectively. If marketing, product development, and customer service teams are increasingly collaborating based on shared data insights, it indicates a successful cultural shift toward data-driven operations.

- **Cultural Shifts Toward Data**: A truly data-driven organization fosters a culture where decisions are consistently backed by data rather than gut instincts. Measuring this cultural shift can be done through leadership feedback, internal surveys, and the frequency of data-centric discussions in decision-making meetings. Leaders should encourage employees to ask, "What does the data say?" as a natural part of discussions.

3. Tracking Progress Over Time

One of the best ways to ensure data-driven transformation is moving in the right direction is by tracking these KPIs over time. Organizations should implement dashboard reporting systems that regularly monitor the chosen KPIs. Regular assessments—monthly or quarterly—allow companies to identify trends and make adjustments if certain goals aren't being met.

- **Benchmarking**: It's also helpful to compare metrics with industry benchmarks to understand how the organization's data-driven efforts stack up against competitors.

- **ROI on Data Initiatives**: Tracking the return on investment (ROI) from data projects is a critical metric for understanding the financial impact of the transformation. This involves comparing the costs of implementing data-driven tools and systems to the financial gains they generate through improved efficiency, revenue growth, or customer satisfaction.

The successful adoption of data-driven decision-making requires not just the implementation of data tools but also a clear system for measuring impact. By tracking a mix of quantitative and qualitative KPIs—such as revenue growth, cost reductions, employee engagement, and cultural shifts—organizations can assess the effectiveness of their data-driven strategies and make adjustments where necessary. Measuring progress ensures that data-driven transformation is delivering real, measurable benefits, both in operational outcomes and in fostering a culture that values data-informed decisions.

Transitioning to a data-driven organization requires a well-structured action plan that balances strategy development, implementation, and continuous improvement. Below is a step-by-step guide that outlines practical steps for embedding data-centricity within your organization.

1. Define Your Data Strategy

The foundation of data-centricity starts with a clear data strategy. This should outline how data will be collected, managed, and used to support business objectives. To define this strategy:

- **Align data goals with business objectives**: Ensure that data initiatives directly contribute to broader business goals, such as improving customer experiences, optimizing operations, or driving revenue growth.

- **Identify key data sources**: Determine what internal and external data is needed. This could include customer behavior data, operational metrics, or market trends.

- **Data governance framework**: Establish guidelines for data quality, privacy, and security. It's critical to have policies in place for managing data ethically, particularly in compliance with regulations like GDPR or CCPA.

2. Assess Current Data Capabilities

Before making improvements, assess the current state of your data infrastructure. This includes:

- **Data audit**: Conduct a comprehensive audit of the data you currently have. Evaluate its quality, accessibility, and relevance to your business needs.

- **Technology assessment**: Review your existing data management tools, analytics platforms, and integration capabilities. Ensure your organization has the necessary technology to support data-driven decision-making or identify gaps that need to be addressed.

- **Data literacy evaluation**: Evaluate the data literacy of your workforce. Are employees equipped to interpret and act on data insights? Determine where skills gaps exist and address them through targeted training.

3. Create a Data-Driven Culture

Building a data-centric organization requires a cultural shift where data becomes integral to decision-making across all departments. Steps to foster this culture include:

- **Leadership buy-in**: Gain support from executives and senior leadership to prioritize data initiatives. Leaders must model data-driven decision-making behaviors, encouraging others to follow.

- **Promote data literacy**: Offer ongoing training to help employees at all levels become comfortable working with data. This could include workshops, online courses, or mentoring programs.

- **Cross-functional collaboration**: Encourage departments to share data and insights across teams, breaking down silos. Data should be seen as an organizational asset, not restricted to specific departments.

- **Data champions**: Designate data champions within different teams who promote the use of data in daily operations and decision-making.

4. Invest in Technology and Tools

Data-centricity requires investing in the right technology to capture, analyze, and act on data insights. Implement or upgrade the following tools:

- **Data analytics platforms**: Invest in user-friendly analytics platforms like **Tableau**, **Power BI**, or **Google Analytics** to make data insights accessible to employees across the organization.

- **AI and machine learning**: For advanced analytics, incorporate AI and machine learning tools to unlock predictive insights that help optimize operations, forecast trends, and drive innovation.

- **Data integration tools**: Ensure data flows seamlessly across systems and departments by implementing data integration solutions like **Zapier**, **Informatica**, or **Apache Kafka**.

- **Data visualization**: Equip teams with visualization tools to turn raw data into understandable insights that facilitate informed decision-making.

5. Implement Data-Driven Decision-Making Processes

Once the infrastructure and culture are in place, it's time to implement **data-driven processes** in everyday decision-making:

- **Set KPIs and metrics**: Identify the key performance indicators (KPIs) that will be used to measure success. Regularly track these metrics to monitor the impact of data-driven decisions.

- **Pilot projects**: Start with small pilot projects where teams can test data-driven approaches. Evaluate the outcomes and refine processes before scaling across the organization.

- **Real-time analytics**: Introduce real-time data analytics for faster, more agile decision-making. This allows teams to adapt strategies quickly in response to changing market conditions or operational needs.

6. Continuous Improvement

Data-centricity is not a one-time transformation—it requires ongoing refinement and improvement. To sustain your organization's data-driven journey:

- **Regularly review and refine**: Periodically assess the data strategy, tools, and processes to ensure they remain aligned with evolving business goals and market trends.

- **Collect feedback**: Encourage feedback from employees on the effectiveness of data-driven decision-making and where improvements can be made. Use this feedback to adjust training programs or update tools as necessary.

- **Monitor emerging technologies**: Keep an eye on new technologies that can further enhance your data capabilities, such as advanced AI algorithms, blockchain for secure data sharing, or quantum computing for faster analysis.

7. Track Success

Measuring the impact of data-driven transformation is key to understanding its success. Track the following metrics:

- **Business outcomes**: Compare performance metrics such as revenue, cost savings, customer retention, or operational efficiency before and after implementing data-driven practices.

- **Employee engagement with data**: Monitor the extent to which employees are using data tools and contributing to data-driven discussions and decisions.

- **Data quality improvements**: Track the improvements in data quality, accuracy, and accessibility over time.

By following this action plan, organizations can gradually transition toward becoming data-centric, unlocking the full potential of data to enhance decision-making, operational efficiency, and overall business success. The key is to develop a well-defined strategy, foster a data-driven culture, and invest in the necessary tools and technologies to support continuous improvement.

Reflections:

To help readers apply the concepts of data-driven decision-making within their own organizations and leadership strategies, consider the following reflection questions:

1. How are data currently used in your organization's decision-making process? Reflect on whether your decisions are primarily based on data or intuition. Are there gaps in data usage? Are teams empowered to use data, or is it siloed in specific departments?

2. Think about the cultural, technological, or skill-based obstacles your organization might be facing. What has been done to overcome these challenges? What more can be done?

3. Assess whether your data infrastructure (analytics tools, data storage, data quality) is sufficient to support the goals you're trying to achieve. Do you need to upgrade tools or platforms to better facilitate data-driven decisions?

4. In what ways can leadership play a more active role in promoting data-driven decision-making?

5. What opportunities could arise from breaking down data silos in your organization?

6. Think about your organization's current data governance policies. Are there clear protocols for managing data privacy and security? How can these processes be improved to ensure compliance and data integrity?

7. What KPIs or metrics are in place to assess the effectiveness of data-driven decision-making? Are these measurements giving you the insights needed to adjust strategies when necessary?

Transitioning to data-driven decision-making is a critical step for organizations aiming to stay competitive in the AI era. Businesses can unlock the full potential of data insights by developing a clear data strategy and investing in the right tools and talent. Measuring progress through clear KPIs and embracing continuous learning ensures that the organization remains agile despite rapid technological advancements. Most importantly, ethical governance and transparency in data usage will help build trust and ensure responsible AI adoption, positioning the organization for sustained success in an increasingly data-centric world.

Chapter 6: Aligning AI With Business Goals

A healthcare provider was facing a critical challenge. Patients often came in with advanced stages of diseases that could have been treated more effectively if detected earlier. However, despite having highly skilled medical staff and advanced diagnostic tools, identifying diseases at the earliest stages remained difficult.

Unfortunately, it led to delayed treatment and, in some cases, poorer outcomes. The provider knew that finding a way to catch diseases earlier could drastically improve patient health, but the existing tools and processes weren't enough.

I helped them realize the need for a transformative approach, and eventually, the provider decided to implement an AI system specifically designed for early disease detection. This AI system analyzed large amounts of patient data, from medical history to lifestyle factors and genetic predispositions. The goal was to identify subtle patterns and signs that might indicate the onset of diseases like cancer, heart conditions, or diabetes, even before traditional methods would catch them.

The integration process was thorough. Medical staff and data experts worked together to ensure the AI system was trained accurately and focused on minimizing false positives and ensuring reliability. With the AI system in place, the provider could now detect early warning signs with remarkable accuracy. This allowed doctors to intervene sooner and create tailored treatment plans before a disease could further progress.

The results have been remarkable. Patients now benefit from earlier diagnoses, which has led to timely treatments that significantly boost recovery rates and improve overall health outcomes. This not only transformed the quality of care but also redefined the provider's approach to preventative medicine, showing how a carefully implemented AI strategy can become a game-changer in healthcare.

An AI strategy is a detailed plan that outlines how an organization can best leverage artificial intelligence to meet its goals. It is not only about adopting AI tools or automating tasks; it requires you to align AI projects with the broader vision of the company. An effective AI strategy considers the specific ways that AI can support an organization's objectives, whether it's improving customer experience, optimizing operations, or driving innovation.

A well-crafted AI strategy includes several key elements. First, it identifies specific areas where AI can add value. This could mean using predictive analytics to anticipate customer needs, employing natural language processing for better customer service, or automating repetitive tasks to free up employee time. Next, an AI strategy defines the data, technology, and skills needed to make these initiatives work. Since AI relies heavily on high-quality data, organizations need systems in place to manage and analyze this information effectively.

Additionally, a strong AI strategy emphasizes scalability and flexibility. As technology and market conditions evolve, organizations need an approach that allows for AI tools to adapt and grow with the business. Most importantly, it aligns all AI initiatives with the company's overall mission and goals, ensuring that the use of AI directly contributes to the company's success rather than operating as a standalone function.

With the rapid growth of digital technologies, having a solid AI strategy is now a necessity for any forward-thinking organization. It not only helps organizations stay competitive but also enables them to make better, data-driven decisions that enhance customer experiences and improve operational efficiency.

Machine Learning as a Foundational AI Technology

Machine learning (ML) is a foundational technology within artificial intelligence that enables computers to learn from data, identify patterns, and make decisions without human intervention. Machine learning fundamentally involves algorithms that adapt and improve as they process more data, allowing systems to refine their accuracy over time. ML is used in applications across various industries, from personalized product recommendations and fraud detection to predictive maintenance and medical diagnosis.

Functionality of Machine Learning

The functioning of machine learning begins with training data, a dataset that the ML model uses to identify patterns and make predictions. The model processes this data, adjusting its internal settings (often called weights) to minimize errors and improve predictive accuracy. This process is iterative; the more data the model processes, the better it can generalize and make accurate predictions. Machine learning generally falls into three types:

1. **Supervised Learning**: The model is trained on labeled data (input-output pairs) and learns to map inputs to outputs, allowing it to make predictions on new data. Common applications include fraud detection and image recognition.

2. **Unsupervised Learning**: The model learns from unlabeled data to find patterns or group data into clusters, often used in customer segmentation and anomaly detection.

3. **Reinforcement Learning**: The model learns through trial and error by interacting with an environment often used in autonomous systems like robotics and gaming.

Applications of Machine Learning

Machine learning has wide-reaching applications across multiple sectors. In **retail**, it powers recommendation engines that suggest products based on a customer's past behavior, driving sales and engagement. **Healthcare** benefits from ML in areas like diagnostics, where it analyzes medical images, patient histories, and genetic data to detect diseases early and recommend treatments. It also detects fraudulent transactions by analyzing spending patterns and transaction data in Finance. Similarly, in **manufacturing and logistics**, predictive maintenance models analyze sensor data to anticipate equipment failures, optimizing maintenance schedules and reducing downtime.

Machine learning is also used in **customer service** through natural language processing (NLP) models that power chatbots and virtual assistants. These models handle inquiries, classify issues, and even understand sentiment, allowing customer service teams to deliver quicker and more tailored responses. **Marketing** teams use ML to analyze customer data and predict behavior, which helps in personalizing campaigns and understanding customer needs more deeply.

Potential Impact on Business Processes

The potential impact of machine learning on business processes is transformative. By automating routine tasks and enhancing decision-making, machine learning allows businesses to operate more efficiently and make better use of resources. Here are some key areas where ML drives impact:

- **Enhanced Decision-Making**: Machine learning enables businesses to make data-driven decisions, reducing reliance on intuition and manual processes. Predictive analytics can predict trends, guide product development, and inform strategies based on detailed data insights.

- **Operational Efficiency**: Automation of repetitive tasks allows employees to focus on higher-value work. Predictive maintenance in manufacturing, for instance, reduces downtime and maintenance costs by identifying issues before they escalate.

- **Customer Personalization**: By analyzing customer behavior, ML allows businesses to deliver personalized experiences that improve customer satisfaction and loyalty. Personalized recommendations and targeted marketing campaigns help businesses engage customers on a more individual level.

- **Risk Management**: Machine learning plays a crucial role in identifying and mitigating risks, particularly in industries like finance and insurance. Models trained to detect anomalies can flag suspicious activity, prevent fraud, and assess risks more accurately.

Machine learning is a versatile tool that adapts to various contexts and applications, making it invaluable for businesses that want to stay competitive in a data-driven world. As companies continue to adopt and refine ML models, they can expect greater efficiencies, more accurate predictions, and customer insights. It positions them for success in a rapidly evolving technological world.

Organizational Impact Analysis

Implementing an AI strategy significantly reshapes an organization, influencing various aspects, from product development to customer service and internal workflows. Below are key areas where AI strategy impacts organizational structure and operations, each demonstrating the technology's potential to drive agility, efficiency, and customer-centricity.

1. Product Development

AI enhances the product development process by offering **insights into customer preferences and market trends** in real-time. This allows product teams to make more informed decisions when designing, testing, and launching new products.

- **Faster Iterations**: With AI-driven analytics, companies can shorten their product development cycles by quickly gathering and analyzing feedback from test groups or initial market reactions.

- **Personalization**: AI allows companies to tailor products to specific customer needs, making it easier to refine features or add capabilities that customers genuinely want, thereby increasing customer satisfaction and product success.

For example, Pharmaceutical giant Novartis uses AI in clinical trials to enhance patient recruitment and monitor real-time data from ongoing trials. AI helps identify suitable candidates for trials based on medical history, lifestyle, and genetic factors, which makes trials more targeted and efficient. This AI-powered process has helped Novartis reduce the time and cost of drug development, bringing medications to patients more quickly.

2. Customer Service

AI-driven solutions, including chatbots and virtual assistants, have transformed customer service by enabling **24/7 support** and improving the speed of issue resolution.

- **Automated Support**: Chatbots can handle routine queries, enabling customer service representatives to focus on more complex issues that require human interaction. This results in a faster, more efficient customer service experience.

- **Sentiment Analysis**: AI tools analyze customer emotions and feedback, allowing representatives to respond with empathy and personalized service. This enhances customer satisfaction and can help reduce churn rates.

For instance, financial institutions and retail brands use AI to improve the customer journey by analyzing past interactions and providing predictive recommendations, which improves the quality of service and builds stronger customer loyalty.

An example of a well-known company utilizing AI in customer service is **Bank of America** with its virtual assistant, **Erica**. Launched in 2018, Erica provides 24/7 customer support, handling routine queries and guiding users through banking processes. By using natural language processing and machine learning, Erica helps customers with tasks such as checking balances, paying bills, and locating nearby ATMs. Erica's capabilities also extend to offering proactive financial advice based on users' spending patterns, helping to personalize the customer experience.

3. Internal Processes and Operations

AI transforms internal operations by automating repetitive tasks, forecasting demand, and enhancing data management. From HR to the supply chain, AI improves efficiency and allows employees to focus on higher-value tasks.

- **Human Resources (HR)**: AI-driven systems streamline the recruitment process by scanning resumes, identifying qualified candidates, and even automating interview scheduling. Once hired, employees can benefit from AI-driven personalized learning programs that match their skill development needs.

- **Logistics and Inventory Management**: AI predicts demand patterns, optimizes inventory levels, and improves supply chain resilience. By forecasting potential disruptions, AI helps organizations adjust proactively, minimizing downtime and maximizing productivity.

For example, logistics companies like UPS and FedEx use AI to optimize delivery routes and manage fleet maintenance, reducing fuel costs and improving delivery efficiency.

4. Decision-Making and Strategy

An AI strategy changes day-to-day processes and also affects the **overall decision-making framework** within an organization. Data-driven insights enable leaders to make strategic choices based on real-time analytics, moving from reactive to proactive management.

- **Enhanced Decision-Making**: AI supports data-based strategies by offering predictive insights that can help organizations anticipate market shifts and customer needs.

- **Cross-Departmental Collaboration**: AI-driven data integration allows different departments to collaborate more effectively, as they have access to centralized data insights. For example, marketing and sales can work more closely with product development by sharing customer feedback and data trends.

This shift toward data-centric decision-making fosters a more agile organization, where departments align their strategies and work together seamlessly, making the organization more adaptable and competitive.

An AI strategy reshapes operational workflows and also impacts an organization's entire structure, making it more efficient, customer-focused, and agile. From product innovation to customer service and internal operations, AI equips organizations to solve complex challenges, promote collaboration, and make smarter decisions. This integrated approach helps companies respond quickly to market changes and maintain a competitive edge.

Guiding Ethical and Effective AI Strategy

The Homo Magister describes a leader who not only adopts technological advancements like AI but also guides their organization through these changes with a balanced focus on both **innovation and ethics**. Leaders embodying this ideal understand that implementing an AI strategy is not solely about using advanced tools but about ensuring these tools align with the organization's core values and mission.

1. Balancing Technological Opportunities with Human Insight

Leaders who embody the Homo Magister approach know that while AI offers powerful new capabilities, it should serve to enhance human work, not replace it entirely. In the development of an AI strategy, they ensure that AI solutions support employees' roles, improve efficiency, and foster collaboration rather than automate everything in a way that may hinder human creativity and insight. For instance, in decision-making processes, a Homo Magister leader uses AI to generate data-driven insights while valuing human judgment in the final decision. They view AI as a complementary tool that adds depth to the organization's ability to innovate and respond to complex challenges while ensuring human expertise remains central.

2. Prioritizing Ethical Considerations in AI Strategy

The Homo Magister leader ensures ethical considerations are incorporated throughout the AI development and implementation process. They proactively address issues like algorithmic bias, data privacy, and transparency to prevent unintended consequences that could arise from using AI. For instance, in areas like hiring, they ensure AI systems are thoroughly audited for potential biases and make adjustments to ensure fairness in recruitment decisions.

Additionally, Homo Magister leaders prioritize **data privacy**, recognizing that AI often relies on sensitive information. They implement strict data governance policies to protect user data and comply with relevant regulations, such as GDPR or CCPA. By balancing AI's data needs with ethical considerations, these leaders build trust among employees, customers, and stakeholders, reinforcing the organization's reputation.

3. Cultivating an Ethical and Data-Literate Workforce

A key component of the Homo Magister approach is building an organizational culture that values both data literacy and ethical awareness. Leaders encourage employees to become familiar with data insights and AI tools, but they also train them in the ethical use of technology. This can include regular training sessions on data ethics, transparency, and the responsible use of AI-driven systems. As a result, the Homo Magister leaders will be able to prepare their workforce to make thoughtful and ethical decisions when working with AI, ensuring that the technology aligns with the organization's goals and ethical standards.

4. Aligning AI Strategy with Organizational Goals

For a Homo Magister leader, an AI strategy must closely align with the organization's broader goals. Rather than pursuing AI for its novelty, they identify areas where AI can genuinely add value, such as improving customer service, optimizing supply chains, or supporting data-driven innovation. This alignment ensures that AI projects are meaningful and directly contribute to the company's success rather than becoming isolated tech experiments.

5. Ensuring Long-Term Accountability and Adaptability

Homo Magister leaders recognize that an effective AI strategy requires long-term accountability. They establish clear protocols for monitoring AI performance and ethical compliance over time, adjusting strategies as needed. This adaptability allows the organization to respond to new ethical challenges and technological advances, keeping AI use responsible and relevant.

In sum, leaders who adopt the Homo Magister perspective in AI strategy lead with a unique combination of **vision, ethical mindfulness, and adaptability**. They can drive their organization forward by carefully balancing the potential of AI with human-centered values responsibly and innovatively.

Responsible AI Adoption Framework

Creating a responsible AI adoption framework involves a well-defined, ethical approach to designing and implementing AI strategies. By prioritizing **transparency**, **fairness**, and **accountability**, organizations can ensure that their AI systems are not only effective but also trusted and ethically sound.

Mentioned below is the step-by-step guide to developing a responsible AI strategy:

Step 1: Define Clear Objectives Aligned with Ethical Standards

Start by outlining the goals of your AI initiatives. Rather than implementing AI for its novelty, ensure each project aligns with your organization's mission and serves a real purpose, such as improving customer experience, enhancing operational efficiency, or driving innovation. Each objective should also be evaluated for ethical considerations so it complements broader values like fairness and accountability.

Step 2: Prioritize Transparency in AI Design

Transparency is key to building trust in AI systems. Organizations should aim to make AI processes understandable to both employees and customers. Follow the mentioned strategy to prioritize transparency in AI Design:

- **Develop Explainable Models**: Use machine learning algorithms that provide clear insights into how decisions are made. For instance, in predictive models, clarify what factors are most influential in the outcomes.

- **Communicate Limitations**: Educate stakeholders about AI's strengths and limitations, and be upfront about areas where AI might fall short.

- **Enable User Control**: Allow users to access information about how their data is used and to have control over their data, which can enhance trust in AI applications.

Step 3: Ensure Fairness in Data and Algorithms

To avoid biased outcomes, organizations need to assess their data and algorithms for fairness:

- **Conduct Data Audits**: Review data sources for diversity and completeness to prevent biased representations. Ensure that data reflects the diversity of the population it serves, particularly in high-stakes areas like hiring or healthcare.

- **Bias Mitigation Techniques**: Implement methods like re-weighting data or introducing fairness constraints in algorithms. Regularly audit and adjust AI models to address any emerging biases.

- **Inclusive Team Involvement**: Engage diverse teams in the development of AI models. This helps to identify blind spots that may be overlooked if only one perspective is considered.

Step 4: Build Accountability and Ethical Oversight

Accountability structures ensure that ethical standards are maintained throughout the AI lifecycle:

- **Assign Responsibility**: Designate specific roles or committees to oversee AI ethics, with team members who regularly review AI projects for compliance with ethical guidelines.

- **Continuous Monitoring**: Develop protocols for ongoing monitoring of AI performance, especially in sensitive applications. Implement feedback loops that allow issues to be flagged and addressed in real-time.

- **Establish Audit Trails**: Maintain clear documentation of how AI models are developed, tested, and updated. This creates transparency and provides an audit trail if ethical concerns arise.

Step 5: Ensure Data Privacy and Security

Data privacy is a critical part of any responsible AI framework. Follow the below-mentioned steps to protect user data:

- **Data Anonymization**: Remove or obscure personally identifiable information (PII) in datasets, making it harder to trace data back to individuals.

- **Secure Data Storage**: Implement robust cybersecurity measures to protect data against breaches or unauthorized access.

- **Comply with Regulations**: Follow data protection laws like the General Data Protection Regulation (GDPR) and California Consumer Privacy Act (CCPA), ensuring AI applications meet privacy standards.

Step 6: Promote a Culture of Ethical AI Use

The success of responsible AI relies on cultivating an organizational culture that values ethical considerations in all AI applications:

- **Regular Training**: Provide ethics training for all employees involved with AI, helping them understand the implications of AI decisions.

- **Open Dialogue**: Encourage open discussions on the ethical impact of AI, creating an environment where employees feel comfortable raising concerns or suggesting improvements.

- **Ethics Review Boards**: Form internal committees or ethics review boards to evaluate AI projects and ensure alignment with the organization's ethical standards.

Step 7: Implement Feedback Loops for Continuous Improvement

Implementing feedback loops is a crucial part of ensuring that AI systems remain effective, ethical, and aligned with organizational goals.

- **Collect User Feedback**: Regularly gather end-user feedback to identify areas where AI can be improved or where ethical concerns may arise.

- **Adapt to Technological Changes**: AI technologies and ethical standards evolve, so it's essential to revisit your framework periodically to ensure it remains effective and relevant.

- **Re-Evaluate Goals**: As AI projects grow and develop, assess whether they still align with the original ethical standards and objectives.

Organizations can create AI systems that are both effective and ethically sound by following this responsible AI adoption framework. A well-structured approach not only maximizes the benefits of AI but also builds trust with users and sets a foundation for responsible innovation.

Tech Mastery Strategies

Building AI expertise within an organization is about more than just training employees on new technology; it's about establishing a forward-looking framework that empowers teams to use AI as a driver for innovation and growth. Developing tech mastery involves fostering an environment where skills continually evolve, solutions adapt to changing needs, and partnerships provide new perspectives and cutting-edge tools. Here's a breakdown of key strategies to master AI technology effectively.

1. Building Internal Capabilities

Building AI expertise within an organization requires investing in both internal talent and strategic partnerships. First, identifying and developing key AI skills internally is essential. This includes recruiting specialists like data scientists and machine learning engineers, as well as upskilling current employees in data literacy and AI fundamentals. Workshops, certification programs, and partnerships with educational institutions can provide valuable, specialized training. Cross-functional collaboration, through internal hackathons and project-based learning, further strengthens AI integration and ensures that AI projects support broader organizational goals.

2. Leveraging External Partnerships

External partnerships can complement these internal efforts, allowing organizations to access advanced AI tools without creating everything in-house. Collaborations with AI providers, academic institutions, or even competitors in certain sectors bring specialized expertise. Consulting firms also help design tailored AI strategies, and partnerships with companies like Microsoft or IBM offer scalable, cloud-based AI services.

3. Encouraging Continuous Learning and Adaptability

AI technology evolves rapidly, making continuous learning a critical component of tech mastery. Organizations should create a culture that encourages employees to stay updated with the latest advancements in AI. This includes promoting an agile mindset where employees are encouraged to experiment, take calculated risks, and learn from outcomes. Leaders should support this culture by allocating time and resources for employees to explore new AI technologies.

However, the journey doesn't stop with skill-building. Implementing AI often brings significant changes to workflows, roles, and the organization's culture itself. For this reason, robust change management practices are crucial for helping employees and stakeholders adapt to these transitions.

Change Management for AI Integration

Implementing AI can lead to significant changes in workflows, roles, and even organizational culture. Therefore, effective change management is essential to guide employees and stakeholders through the transition smoothly.

1. Communicate the Vision Clearly

One of the primary challenges in AI integration is resistance to change. Employees might fear job displacement or struggle to understand AI's value. Leaders should address these concerns by clearly communicating the AI strategy's goals, such as improving customer service, enhancing productivity, or enabling innovation. Explaining how AI can complement human work rather than replace it can reduce anxiety and foster enthusiasm.

For example, showing how AI reduced repetitive tasks for a particular team and allowed them to focus on creative problem-solving helps reinforce the positive impact of AI integration.

2. Training and Upskilling

Change management requires equipping employees with the skills needed to adapt to new technologies. Organizations should provide comprehensive training programs on how to work with AI tools, interpret data insights, and make data-driven decisions. This could include hands-on workshops, interactive learning sessions, or pairing employees with AI experts for mentorship.

Upskilling efforts should extend beyond technical roles. Employees in non-technical roles, such as marketing or customer service, should also be trained in data literacy to understand how AI insights can improve their work. By fostering a learning environment, organizations empower employees to see AI as a valuable tool rather than a threat.

3. Encourage Collaboration and Feedback

Involving employees in the AI integration process can enhance buy-in and make the transition smoother. Organizations should create cross-functional teams to lead AI projects, allowing employees from various departments to collaborate on implementation. Additionally, gathering regular feedback enables leaders to address challenges, refine strategies, and make improvements based on real-world feedback.

Finally, recognize and reward adaptability. Highlighting employees who embrace AI in their workflows sets a positive example and encourages others to be open to change.

Let's examine **Amazon** as a case study of a company that redefined its industry through strategic AI use, particularly in e-commerce, logistics, and cloud computing. Amazon's approach to integrating AI strategically has been a key driver of its success and industry dominance.

Amazon incorporated AI into its business operations, focusing on **customer experience** and **operational efficiency**. One of its earliest and most famous applications is its **recommendation engine**, which uses machine learning to suggest products based on user behavior, previous purchases, and browsing patterns. This personalization transformed the e-commerce experience, making it more tailored and engaging, which eventually increases sales and customer retention.

In logistics, Amazon uses **predictive analytics** and **automated warehousing** to streamline its supply chain. By forecasting demand and optimizing inventory levels across fulfillment centers, Amazon reduces delivery times and cuts costs, ensuring efficient logistics even with a vast product range. AI also powers **Amazon Robotics** within its warehouses, with robots handling tasks like item selection, packing, and inventory management, which enhances speed and accuracy in order fulfillment.

Moreover, Amazon's investment in **Amazon Web Services (AWS)** made cloud computing accessible and affordable for millions of businesses worldwide. Through AWS, Amazon offers AI-powered services like **Amazon Rekognition** for image recognition, **Amazon Lex** for building conversational interfaces, and **SageMaker** for machine learning model development, making advanced AI tools available to other companies. This strategic move transformed Amazon from an e-commerce platform into a leader in the tech industry, revolutionizing cloud computing.

Amazon's AI integration wasn't without challenges. The company faced the task of **processing massive volumes of data** generated by millions of daily transactions and interactions. To address this, Amazon developed a robust data infrastructure to store, analyze, and process data efficiently. Additionally, scaling AI across operations requires substantial investment in R&D, infrastructure, and skilled talent.[23]

Another challenge was managing **public and regulatory scrutiny** over data privacy and labor practices in AI-driven automation. Amazon invested in data protection measures and adapted its data privacy policies to meet compliance standards, though it continues to face challenges related to privacy and workforce automation.

Amazon's strategic use of AI has had transformative impacts on the industry and beyond. Through its recommendation engine, Amazon set the standard for personalization in e-commerce, pushing other retailers to adopt similar approaches. The efficiency in Amazon's logistics network enabled it to offer faster and more reliable delivery options, a significant competitive advantage that reshaped customer expectations around online shopping.

AWS's success in providing cloud-based AI solutions has also empowered businesses across sectors, enabling them to

---

[23]https://www.amazon.science/latest-news/solving-some-of-the-largest-most-complex-operations-problems

access advanced AI tools without needing in-house expertise. This democratization of AI has been a game-changer, fueling innovation in industries such as healthcare, finance, and education.

By prioritizing AI for personalization, operational efficiency, and scalability, Amazon created a sustainable competitive edge and set new industry standards. This case highlights the profound impact of a strategic AI approach in transforming both a company and its industry.[24]

Overcoming Resistance to AI

If an organization is facing resistance from employees due to fears of job replacement, concerns over data privacy, or skepticism about AI's reliability, it can address these issues by implementing strategies that prioritize transparency, trust-building, and proactive communication.

1. Transparent Communication

Open communication about AI's role and potential impacts can reduce fear and foster understanding. Leaders should provide employees with clear information about how AI will be used, emphasizing how it will support rather than replace their roles. Regular Q&A sessions, forums, and clear documentation about AI's functions, limitations, and goals can create a space for employees to express their concerns and get accurate answers.

---

[24]https://cdotimes.com/2024/08/23/case-study-amazons-ai-driven-supply-chain-a-blueprint-for-the-future-of-global-logistics/

2. Demonstrate Practical Benefits Early On

It's essential to showcase how AI can ease tasks rather than increase workloads or replace employees. Starting with small, manageable AI applications in specific departments can provide clear examples of how AI aids employees. For instance, implementing an AI-powered customer service tool can allow human agents to handle more complex inquiries, showing the value of AI without threatening their job roles. Sharing success stories from similar industries or showcasing pilot project results can also help illustrate AI's supportive role.

3. Offer Hands-On Training

Equipping employees with the knowledge to work alongside AI can help diminish fear and empower them to feel part of the change. Providing training sessions on AI basics, its specific functions within the company, and how to interpret AI-generated data makes AI feel less abstract and more approachable. Training also helps build data literacy, enabling employees to understand and utilize AI-driven insights confidently.

4. Establish Ethical Guidelines and Governance

Ethics play a significant role in overcoming skepticism around AI. By creating an ethics framework for AI applications, which includes data privacy standards, transparency in AI processes, and the assurance of fairness, companies can assure employees that AI adoption won't infringe on their rights or personal privacy. A designated AI ethics committee or board provides an additional layer of trust, as employees know that ethical considerations are overseen by a team dedicated to accountability.

5. Cultivate a Culture of Collaboration

Encourage a culture that sees AI as a partner rather than a replacement. This involves making it clear that AI is there to enhance human work by handling repetitive tasks or providing data insights, allowing employees to focus on creative, strategic, or complex problem-solving activities. Leaders should continually reinforce the message that AI supports people and that the organization values the unique contributions only humans can bring.

By prioritizing these strategies, organizations can shift perceptions around AI, transforming initial fears into enthusiasm and curiosity about how AI can enable more impactful, fulfilling work.

AI-Human Collaboration Models

Effective AI-human collaboration frameworks focus on augmenting human capabilities, using AI as a supportive tool that enhances human decision-making, productivity, and efficiency. The most effective collaboration models are rooted in the concept that AI should take over repetitive, data-intensive tasks, allowing humans to focus on areas requiring creativity, empathy, or strategic insight.

1. Decision-Support Systems

In decision-support systems, AI provides data-driven insights to assist humans, who then make the final decision. For instance, in finance, AI algorithms analyze market data to identify trends and make investment recommendations, but human analysts interpret these insights, considering external factors and applying judgment. This model is prevalent in industries like healthcare, where AI analyzes patient data to suggest possible diagnoses, but doctors determine the final treatment plan.[25]

2. Human-in-the-Loop (HITL) Systems

The Human-in-the-Loop model requires human interaction at various stages of AI processes, particularly when there is a need for validation or correction. For example, in content moderation on social media platforms, AI initially filters out content that may violate guidelines. However, human moderators review flagged content to ensure accuracy, providing final judgment to reduce errors in the AI's automated processes. This approach combines the speed of AI with the accuracy and empathy of human oversight.[26]

---

[25] https://arxiv.org/abs/2404.12056
[26]https://www.cambridge.org/core/journals/proceedings-of-the-design-society/article/humanai-collaboration-by-design/45BC30ADFF2FE3B204D4A29DD67F6353

3. Collaborative Intelligence

In collaborative intelligence models, humans and AI actively work together on tasks. In retail, for example, AI might analyze shopping behavior to identify potential upsell opportunities, while sales associates use these insights to engage with customers and personalize interactions. This model thrives on the synergy between AI's data-driven analysis and humans' ability to connect with and understand customers in real-time. It ensures that the technology enhances the customer experience without replacing the human touch.

4. Autonomous Intelligence with Human Oversight

In cases where AI operates autonomously, human oversight is still crucial. For example, in self-driving vehicles, AI controls navigation and responds to road conditions. However, human supervisors monitor the technology and are prepared to intervene when necessary. This oversight builds trust in autonomous systems, as there is a safety net of human control, ensuring that AI's actions remain aligned with broader human objectives.[27]

Implementing AI-human collaboration models benefits organizations by creating an environment where AI and human talents are utilized optimally. AI excels at processing vast amounts of data quickly and performing repetitive tasks,

---

[27]https://dirox.com/post/assisted-augmented-and-autonomous-intelligence-what-differences#:~:text=Finally%2C%20autonomous%20intelligence%20involves%20machines,but%20a%20fully%20independent%20agent.

while humans bring insight, empathy, and ethical judgment to complex scenarios. This synergy not only enhances productivity but also builds a workforce that sees AI as an asset, not a competitor.

In conclusion, successful AI-human collaboration frameworks allow organizations to harness the strengths of both technology and human intellect. By implementing these models, companies can foster a workplace where AI supports human efforts, enriches jobs, and enables employees to focus on the aspects of their work that require creativity, innovation, and empathy.

Future of Work Projections

As artificial intelligence (AI) becomes more integrated into workplaces, job roles and workforce structures are evolving. The implementation of an AI strategy is reshaping industries by introducing new roles, redefining existing positions, and creating a greater need for specialized skills. Understanding these changes is critical for businesses and workers as they adapt to the new dynamics AI brings.[28]

1. The Rise of New Roles and Skills

The adoption of AI in business settings creates demand for specialized roles in data science, machine learning, and AI ethics. Positions such as **data scientists, machine learning engineers, AI trainers**, and **AI ethicists** have

---

[28]https://www.sciencedirect.com/science/article/abs/pii/S0007681318300387

become essential as organizations seek professionals to build, manage, and evaluate AI systems. These new roles emphasize the importance of understanding data analytics, machine learning algorithms, and ethical considerations. With AI, jobs once associated only with tech companies are now required in fields like healthcare, finance, manufacturing, and logistics, prompting a re-evaluation of necessary skills within these industries.

Additionally, AI implementation drives the need for hybrid roles—those that combine traditional skill sets with tech-related knowledge. For example, marketers are increasingly expected to understand customer data analytics to tailor campaigns effectively, while HR managers are using AI tools to analyze recruitment patterns and employee engagement. This shift signifies that technical and data-related skills are becoming valuable across all fields, as AI touches almost every part of modern business.

2. Changes in Workforce Structure

AI is not just altering individual roles but reshaping entire organizational structures. Routine tasks that once required extensive human labor are now automated, allowing companies to build leaner teams that focus on strategic and creative work. **Process automation** in areas like data entry, report generation, and customer service allows employees to focus on high-level tasks that require human judgment, creativity, and interpersonal skills. This restructuring is creating a workforce that is more agile and adaptable, with individuals often required to handle a broader range of responsibilities.

Organizations are also moving toward a more project-based approach, where cross-functional teams collaborate on specific AI initiatives. This structure enables teams to be dynamic and responsive, bringing together experts from various departments to work on AI-driven projects. As AI reduces the need for repetitive tasks, the workforce becomes more focused on problem-solving, innovation, and customer engagement.

3. The Growing Importance of Continuous Learning

To remain competitive, organizations will need to prioritize **upskilling** their workforce. The rapid pace of AI advancements means that current skills can become outdated quickly. Companies are investing in **continuous learning platforms** and partnerships with educational institutions to provide employees with ongoing training in areas such as data science, machine learning, and AI ethics. This shift emphasizes **lifelong learning** as employees adapt to the changing demands of AI-driven environments.

AI's role in the workplace doesn't eliminate the need for human input; rather, it shifts the focus to roles that require decision-making, creativity, and empathy. Workers who embrace continuous learning and adapt to new technologies will find themselves well-positioned in the evolving job landscape.

4. Enhanced Focus on Soft Skills

As AI handles more technical and analytical tasks, there is a growing demand for soft skills such as critical thinking, communication, and adaptability. These skills become even more valuable in roles that require close collaboration with AI systems. Human qualities like ethical judgment, creativity, and emotional intelligence will remain indispensable as they cannot be replicated by AI, ensuring that humans maintain a central role in decision-making and strategy.

In summary, future work with AI integration will require a combination of technical and soft skills. As organizations adopt AI strategies, the workforce will see new roles emerge, existing roles evolve, and structures shift to focus more on creative, strategic, and human-centric tasks. Organizations that actively promote continuous learning and adaptability will be best prepared to succeed in an AI-driven world.

Leadership in the Age of AI

Leadership in the age of AI requires more than traditional management skills; it demands technological literacy, ethical reasoning, and the ability to guide teams through a rapidly evolving landscape. As AI transforms businesses, leaders must adapt their approaches to oversee its integration responsibly and effectively.[29]

---

[29]https://journals.econsciences.com/index.php/JEB/article/view/1436/1424

1. Technological Literacy

For leaders to make informed decisions about AI, they need a foundational understanding of the technology, including its potential and limitations. Technological literacy enables leaders to recognize where AI can add value to their organization, how it can streamline operations, and where it may pose risks. Leaders don't need to be AI experts, but they should understand key concepts like **machine learning, data analytics, and automation** to make strategic decisions about AI integration.

2. Ethical Reasoning

As AI takes on a greater role in decision-making processes, leaders must prioritize ethics to ensure AI use aligns with organizational values and public expectations. Ethical reasoning in AI involves considering data privacy, fairness, transparency, and accountability. Leaders should establish governance frameworks that monitor AI usage and prevent biases or unintended consequences.

3. Strategic Vision and Adaptability

Successful AI implementation requires a clear, strategic vision. Leaders need to define the role AI will play in their organization and set realistic goals that are aligned with business objectives. This vision allows teams to see the bigger picture and understand how AI contributes to long-term success. Adaptability is also essential as AI technologies evolve rapidly, often requiring organizations to pivot or adjust strategies to remain competitive.

4. Collaborative Approach

AI implementation requires cross-functional collaboration. Leaders need to foster a collaborative environment where departments work together to implement and manage AI projects. Leaders should create opportunities for teams to learn from each other, integrating insights from diverse fields such as IT, HR, and marketing to optimize AI's impact on various aspects of the organization. This approach strengthens the organization's ability to leverage AI across departments, from automating repetitive tasks in HR to using predictive analytics in sales and marketing.

In conclusion, effective leadership in the AI age combines technological knowledge, ethical foresight, and a commitment to learning and collaboration. Leaders who embrace these qualities can guide their organizations through AI integration responsibly, maximizing the benefits of AI while ensuring that it serves both organizational goals and ethical standards.

Measuring AI Strategy Success

Evaluating the success of an AI strategy requires carefully selected Key Performance Indicators (KPIs) and metrics that capture both **quantitative** and **qualitative** aspects. These measures give insight into how well AI initiatives meet organizational goals, improve operations, and align with employee expectations. Here's a breakdown of the critical KPIs and metrics for assessing the impact of AI strategies:

Quantitative Metrics

1. **Return on Investment (ROI)**: ROI is a fundamental measure of AI success and determines whether the AI initiative financially benefits the organization. Calculate ROI by comparing the financial gain from AI projects (e.g., cost savings, revenue increase) against the cost of implementation, including software, hardware, and labor expenses. A positive ROI signifies that the AI strategy is adding value.

2. **Cost Savings**: AI is often implemented to reduce costs in areas like labor, operational inefficiencies, and resource management. Track the extent to which AI solutions, such as automation and predictive maintenance, lower costs in various processes. For instance, if an AI-driven predictive maintenance model reduces machine downtime by 20%, this metric highlights a direct financial benefit.

3. **Time to Market**: In industries like retail and software, speed is crucial for competitive advantage. By implementing AI to streamline processes like product testing, development, and customer analysis, companies can track reductions in time to market for new products. This metric is particularly valuable in dynamic markets where rapid adaptation leads to a stronger market presence.

4. Process Efficiency: AI tools, like robotic process automation (RPA), optimize workflows by automating routine tasks. Metrics here can include improvements in order processing time, inventory management cycles, or customer service response times. Increased efficiency means the AI tools are helping achieve operational goals.

5. Revenue Growth from AI Initiatives: Calculate the increase in revenue directly attributable to AI applications. This could include AI-driven sales recommendations, personalized marketing, or upselling based on predictive analytics. Track revenue growth for a clear indicator of how AI contributes to the bottom line.

Qualitative Metrics

1. Employee Satisfaction and Adoption: Successful AI integration should not only improve workflows but also enhance job satisfaction by reducing repetitive tasks and supporting decision-making. Employee satisfaction surveys can gauge how well teams are adapting to AI, how AI impacts their job roles, and whether they feel AI enhances their work.

2. Customer Satisfaction and Retention: Many AI strategies focus on improving customer experience. Use metrics like Net Promoter Score (NPS), customer retention rate, and direct feedback from customer surveys to determine if AI is enhancing the customer journey. For example, AI-driven personalization and faster response times can positively impact customer loyalty.

3. Innovation and Agility: Assess whether AI fosters a more innovative and adaptable culture within the organization. For instance, are employees able to take more risks and experiment due to insights derived from AI? Is the organization more agile in adapting to market changes thanks to AI-driven predictions?

4. Alignment with Organizational Goals: Measure how well AI initiatives align with long-term goals. This can be qualitative and involve feedback from leadership and stakeholders. If AI projects align closely with the strategic direction of the company, it signals a well-integrated AI strategy.

By combining quantitative measures (e.g., ROI, cost savings) with qualitative assessments (e.g., employee satisfaction), organizations can comprehensively evaluate their AI strategy's impact, identify areas for improvement, and ensure AI initiatives remain aligned with business objectives.

Creating a successful AI strategy requires a structured approach, from initial assessment to implementation and ongoing refinement. Here's a step-by-step guide to help organizations develop and execute an effective AI strategy:

1. Conduct an Initial Assessment

To develop a successful AI strategy, organizations should start with an initial assessment to identify the business goals and needs that AI can address, such as customer satisfaction or operational efficiency. It's essential to align AI objectives with these larger goals to ensure that AI solutions add meaningful value. Assessing current capabilities is also key; this includes evaluating resources, technology infrastructure, and data quality, as AI relies on high-quality, accessible data. An initial assessment should also examine team skills to determine any gaps in AI and data expertise. Additionally, understanding legal and ethical requirements is crucial when handling sensitive data. This phase should involve reviewing data privacy regulations and ethical considerations and establishing a governance framework to oversee responsible AI practices.

2. Develop the AI Strategy

Once the initial assessment is complete, the next step is to create a well-defined AI strategy. This includes setting measurable objectives and KPIs that align with the organization's broader goals, whether they focus on improving efficiency, reducing costs, or boosting customer engagement. Selecting the right use cases is crucial—prioritize AI applications that have high potential for impact and alignment with business needs. For instance, a company focused on sales growth might start with an AI-driven recommendation engine. Begin with pilot projects to validate effectiveness before implementing AI at a larger scale. Establishing a timeline and budget is also essential. A clearly defined timeline, complete with realistic milestones and allocated resources for technology and training, helps keep the project on track.

3. Implement the AI Solution

When it's time to implement the AI solution, organizations must decide whether to build tools in-house or partner with external AI providers, depending on the available expertise and project complexity. Data preparation and integration are foundational in this phase; data should be cleaned, standardized, and made accessible across systems to ensure seamless functionality. Conducting a pilot program with a limited scope helps test the AI's effectiveness and provides insights for adjustments. Gathering performance feedback during this phase confirms whether the AI solution meets the predefined KPIs and is ready for broader application.

4. Training and Change Management

Employees need to be equipped with the skills to work with AI effectively, which involves technical training and understanding how to interpret AI-generated insights within their workflows. It's also important to address any resistance by clearly communicating AI's supportive role in enhancing, not replacing, human work. This open approach helps reduce fear and builds enthusiasm for AI's potential.

5. Monitor and Refine

AI integration is not a one-time effort; it requires continuous monitoring and refinement. Regularly updating AI models and algorithms ensures they remain relevant as data and business needs evolve. Consistent tracking of KPIs helps evaluate the AI's impact and allows for ongoing improvements. Collecting feedback from employees, customers, and other stakeholders is also essential, as it provides insights for refining the AI strategy to ensure it continues to align with and support organizational goals effectively.

Following these steps can set a strong foundation for developing and implementing a strategic AI approach, enabling organizations to harness AI's full potential and drive impactful transformation.

Reflections:

To help readers think through the application of AI strategy concepts within their own organizations, here are some reflection questions designed to spark ideas and guide initial planning:

1. Reflect on specific pain points and think about how AI could help streamline processes, improve decision-making, or offer new solutions.

2. How does AI align with your organization's broader mission and goals?

3. What data resources does your organization currently have, and what additional data might you need? Consider whether there's a need to improve data collection, quality, or integration before implementing AI.

4. What potential ethical challenges could AI adoption pose in your organization? Think about areas like data privacy, algorithmic bias, and transparency. What steps will your organization take to ensure ethical and responsible AI usage?

5. How will AI change the roles and responsibilities of employees in your organization? Consider how AI might alter workflows or require new skills and what measures will be necessary to help employees adapt to these changes.

6. What metrics will you use to assess the success of your AI initiatives? Define key performance indicators (KPIs) that reflect the intended outcomes of AI adoption. Consider both quantitative metrics, like ROI, and qualitative measures, such as employee satisfaction and process improvements.

By reflecting on these questions, organizations can begin to identify the foundational elements of an AI strategy that aligns with their unique needs, strengths, and values.

Creating a successful AI strategy today means keeping things practical and clear. It starts with defining your goals and considering where AI can have the biggest impact, whether improving efficiency, customer experience, or creating new opportunities. Set clear targets and measurable KPIs to track progress and keep the strategy on course. Then, look at what you already have in terms of resources, skills, and data. High-quality, accessible data is essential, as is a skilled team or access to external AI expertise. Choose specific use cases where AI can make a real difference, and consider starting with a pilot to test the waters before rolling out more broadly.

Employee training and change management are also critical. Make sure your team understands the value of AI and sees it as a tool to enhance their work, not replace it. Openness about AI's role can ease concerns and build enthusiasm. Finally, AI implementation isn't one-and-done; it requires continuous monitoring and refinement. Regularly update models, track KPIs, and gather feedback to keep your AI strategy effective and aligned with changing needs. Organizations can leverage AI to drive real value and stay competitive by approaching AI with this adaptable and clear-sighted plan.

Chapter 7: Optimizing Human-AI Partnerships

A financial services company in New York had built its reputation on a careful, detailed approach to risk assessment. The company relied on a team of skilled analysts who manually reviewed financial histories, market trends, and individual customer profiles. For years, this approach had worked well; their method was thorough, grounded in experience, and ensured accuracy. Yet, as the firm expanded and the industry began adopting more advanced technology, cracks started to appear in their process.

Other firms, many of them younger and tech-driven, were making decisions faster by using AI to speed up data analysis. As a result, clients began to notice delays. Requests for rapid assessments piled up, and it became clear to leadership that the traditional methods, while effective, could not keep up with the growing demand without impacting quality.

The firm's leadership team began discussing options to address this growing problem. They had heard about how other companies were using AI to accelerate processes, but the idea of handing over such a critical function to machines made many uneasy. Could a system really understand the complexities and nuances that their human analysts mastered? Would it complement their work or risk making it obsolete? Still, with the pressure increasing, they decided to explore the potential of AI to enhance—not replace—their analysts' work.

After months of research, the firm chose an AI-powered risk assessment system that promised to work alongside its human team. This system was designed to handle the heavy lifting of data analysis, processing huge volumes of financial data, and identifying potential risks based on complex patterns that could often escape even the most attentive human eye. The implementation began slowly, with the AI introduced in phases, allowing analysts time to adjust to the new tool and give input on how it could best support them.

The AI system quickly analyzed layers of data and identified trends and risks in real-time. It freed up the analysts from time-consuming data crunching and helped them to focus on the bigger picture and apply their judgment to nuanced cases. Decisions that once took days were now made in hours, with the AI providing preliminary findings that analysts could then interpret and act on. Over time, the AI became more effective, continuously learning from the feedback and insights provided by the analysts.

As the collaboration took root, the firm noticed a significant improvement both in speed and accuracy. Clients received faster, well-informed decisions that strengthened their trust in the firm. The analysts, initially skeptical, appreciated how the AI took care of repetitive tasks, giving them more room to apply strategic thinking. For the firm, this was a turning point; AI had not replaced their expertise but had empowered it, proving that a well-designed human-

AI partnership could turn a traditional challenge into a competitive advantage.

Human AI Collaboration

Human-AI collaboration involves creating a partnership where humans and artificial intelligence work together, each bringing unique strengths to achieve better outcomes. Rather than replacing human roles, this collaboration enhances tasks by combining AI's speed and data processing power with human insight, creativity, and judgment. For example, in fields like healthcare, finance, or customer service, AI can analyze large sets of data and provide recommendations, but humans make the final decisions, considering factors that go beyond data.

This approach allows organizations to harness the advantages of AI, such as processing huge amounts of information quickly and identifying patterns while keeping humans in control, especially in areas where ethical judgment, empathy, or complex decision-making is required. In customer service, AI chatbots handle common questions quickly, but humans step in for more complex issues. In medical fields, AI might analyze scans to detect patterns, but doctors interpret these findings in the context of the patient's overall health.

Human-AI collaboration is essential because it balances AI's capabilities with human oversight, ensuring that technology serves people's needs rather than replacing human insight. This partnership also allows teams to achieve more innovative solutions, as AI's data-driven insights open new possibilities, while humans bring adaptability and ethical awareness to guide decisions responsibly.

NLP Applications Across Industries

Natural Language Processing (NLP) is an area of artificial intelligence focused on enabling machines to understand, interpret, and respond to human language in a meaningful way. As a bridge between human and machine communication, NLP plays a vital role in enhancing human-AI collaboration by allowing AI systems to comprehend text, speech, and context in ways that approximate human understanding.

How NLP Works

NLP functions through a series of sophisticated techniques and algorithms that allow AI to break down and analyze human language. NLP involves multiple stages, including:

1. **Text Preprocessing:** The AI processes and cleans raw data, breaking down sentences into words (tokenization), standardizing language, and filtering out irrelevant words.

2. **Syntactic and Semantic Analysis:** Syntactic analysis checks the grammatical structure, while semantic analysis interprets meaning.

3. **Machine Learning and Deep Learning Models:** Using vast datasets, machine learning algorithms identify patterns in language to understand context, tone, and intent. Deep learning models, such as recurrent neural networks (RNNs) and transformers like BERT and GPT, further enhance understanding by retaining context over longer sentences or passages.

Through these stages, NLP enables AI to perform tasks such as recognizing named entities (like people or places), understanding intent, translating languages, summarizing text, and even generating human-like responses.

Applications of NLP in Business

NLP has a wide range of applications that transform various business processes by improving customer experience, streamlining internal operations, and aiding decision-making.

- **Customer Service:** NLP powers chatbots and virtual assistants, enabling 24/7 support by answering customer inquiries, guiding users, and escalating issues that require human intervention. This application enhances customer service efficiency and allows employees to focus on complex cases.

- **Sentiment Analysis:** Companies can use NLP to analyze customer feedback, reviews, and social media to gauge public opinion and understand customer sentiment. This helps tailor marketing strategies and improve product development.

- **Data Analysis and Insights:** NLP allows businesses to extract valuable insights from large volumes of unstructured data like customer reviews, emails, and documents. For example, law firms use NLP to analyze legal documents, identify key points, and summarize case information, saving time and reducing manual labor.

- **Human Resources:** NLP assists in screening resumes, matching candidate skills with job requirements, and even analyzing employee feedback. This speeds up the hiring process and improves talent management.

Potential Impact on Business Processes

The integration of NLP can greatly enhance productivity, accuracy, and responsiveness within organizations. NLP's ability to quickly interpret large volumes of unstructured data improves the speed and quality of decision-making, as seen in applications from finance to healthcare. For example, financial services firms can use NLP to analyze news feeds and market data in real-time, providing traders with timely information that impacts investment decisions.

Additionally, NLP facilitates human-AI collaboration by making AI interactions more natural and intuitive, which is particularly valuable for customer-facing roles. The capability of NLP systems to understand language nuances and respond appropriately allows businesses to maintain a human touch in customer interactions while benefiting from AI's scalability and speed.

NLP is continually advancing, with ongoing developments in deep learning and transformer models pushing the boundaries of what AI can understand and generate. As NLP technology improves, it will further close the gap between human and AI communication, driving even greater collaboration and efficiency across various business processes.

Organizational Impact Analysis

Human-AI collaboration is changing how organizations function at every level, impacting decision-making, job roles, and team dynamics. In decision-making, AI offers a new level of support by quickly analyzing huge sets of data and surfacing insights that humans alone might miss. This doesn't eliminate the need for human judgment—instead, it enhances it. For example, in financial services, AI might provide risk assessments based on market data, but human analysts use those insights to make decisions, adding their knowledge of market trends and client needs. The result is faster, more informed choices, which allow companies to be more agile and proactive.

Job roles, too, are evolving. As AI takes over repetitive and time-consuming tasks, people can focus on more strategic and creative parts of their jobs. Customer service is a good example: chatbots handle standard questions, leaving representatives free to solve more complex, nuanced problems. This shift doesn't only improve productivity but also makes jobs more engaging, as employees get to focus on areas where human touch and critical thinking matter most. In this setup, workers often feel more valued and integral to the organization's success, which can boost job satisfaction.

Team dynamics adapt as well. Human-AI collaboration requires cross-functional teams working together with data scientists, AI specialists, and experts from various departments. This setup promotes sharing knowledge across technical and non-technical areas, ensuring that AI projects are grounded in the organization's broader goals. Collaborative teams help bridge gaps, align AI solutions with real business needs, and keep ethical considerations in check.

Leaders who embody the Homo Magister ideal play a crucial role in guiding these shifts by balancing the strengths of AI with human expertise and insight. These leaders don't just push for AI adoption; they ensure it's done to support their team rather than sidelining it. They encourage their employees to view AI as a tool that enhances, not replaces, their skills. By promoting a learning culture, they ensure that people build up the technical and analytical skills needed to work effectively alongside AI, whether it's data literacy or understanding how AI makes decisions.

Ethics and transparency are also central to Homo Magister's leadership. Leaders with this mindset champion the responsible use of AI, ensuring that employees know how and why AI makes certain recommendations. In healthcare, for instance, this might mean making sure AI-powered diagnostics are used as supportive tools, with doctors making the final calls. Homo Magister leaders build trust by being open about AI's limitations and advocating for human judgment in high-stakes decisions.

These leaders also promote a workplace that values experimentation, where employees feel comfortable giving feedback on AI systems and suggesting improvements. When workers see that they can influence how AI is used, it strengthens collaboration and helps everyone feel more invested in the technology's success. In this way, Homo Magister leaders create an environment where human-AI partnerships thrive, blending the precision of technology with the creativity and ethical oversight only humans can provide.

Responsible AI Adoption Framework

Adopting AI responsibly means integrating it in ways that respect ethical standards, maintain transparency, and keep humans in control. To ethically implement human-AI collaboration, organizations can follow a structured and step-by-step framework.

1. Define Ethical Guidelines and Objectives: Start by clearly defining the ethical principles that will guide AI use. Organizations should establish priorities like fairness, transparency, and respect for privacy. It's essential to set objectives that ensure AI supports broader organizational goals without infringing on user rights. This includes assessing potential impacts on employees, customers, and other stakeholders.

2.   Ensure Transparency and Explainability: AI can sometimes be complex and hard to understand. Therefore, it's essential to make its functioning as transparent as possible. This involves selecting algorithms that allow explainability, meaning stakeholders can understand how AI arrived at specific recommendations or decisions. Transparency fosters trust, as employees and customers feel more comfortable with AI's role in decision-making when they understand its workings.

3.   Maintain Human Agency: Human agency is about ensuring that people, not machines, have the final say in decisions, especially in sensitive areas. This approach helps preserve human judgment and responsibility, especially in the healthcare and finance sectors, where AI can offer recommendations, but humans make the final decisions. To ensure that human agency remains central in AI collaboration, it's crucial to clearly define when AI should act on its own and when human input is necessary. For example, in areas like healthcare diagnostics or financial decision-making, AI might provide insights, but a person makes the final call.

4.   Set Up Continuous Monitoring and Evaluation: AI systems should be continuously monitored to ensure they are working ethically and effectively. This monitoring process involves assessing the outcomes of AI recommendations, especially when dealing with high-stakes data or sensitive information. Monitoring also allows organizations to catch and address any biases or inaccuracies that may arise over time, ensuring that AI's behavior aligns with ethical standards and remains relevant to the organization's goals.

5. Encourage Feedback and Adjustments: Involve employees, customers, and stakeholders by encouraging feedback on AI's impact and performance. Regular input from these groups can help refine AI systems and ensure they meet ethical guidelines while staying relevant.

Tech Mastery Strategies

To implement effective human-AI collaboration, organizations must build expertise across all levels. Developing this tech mastery involves both formal training programs and practical experience to equip employees with the skills they need to work alongside AI systems effectively.

1. Provide Foundational Training on AI Concepts: Start by ensuring employees understand the basics of AI, including what it is, how it works, and how it's applied in the organization. Offering workshops, online courses, and seminars on topics like machine learning, data analysis, and algorithm basics can make AI concepts more accessible to non-technical team members. This foundational knowledge reduces uncertainty and builds confidence, allowing employees to see AI as a supportive tool.

2. Develop Role-Specific Skills: Different roles interact with AI in unique ways, so training should be tailored to fit each position's needs. For example, customer service representatives might need to learn how to interpret data insights from AI-driven chatbots, while data analysts require more advanced skills in machine learning and predictive analytics. Tailoring training to specific roles ensures that each team member understands how AI can complement their tasks, making collaboration smoother and more effective.

3. Encourage Hands-On Experience and Project-Based Learning: Building tech mastery requires more than just classroom learning. Allowing employees to work on real-life projects with AI tools can help them gain practical experience. Internal hackathons, AI-driven projects, and cross-departmental teams provide hands-on opportunities to learn and experiment with AI. This approach enhances understanding and helps employees become more comfortable with integrating AI insights into their daily routines.

4. Promote a Culture of Continuous Learning: AI technology is constantly evolving, so fostering an organizational culture that values continuous learning is essential. Encourage employees to stay updated on the latest AI developments through platforms like Coursera, LinkedIn Learning, and Udacity. Regularly updating skills helps employees adapt to new AI capabilities, ensuring that their expertise remains relevant and that they can leverage AI tools effectively as they evolve.

By following these strategies, organizations can develop a workforce that not only understands AI but also sees it as a tool to enhance productivity, creativity, and decision-making.

Transitioning to a human-AI collaborative work environment requires thoughtful change management to address concerns, provide support, and build enthusiasm among employees. Here's how to guide teams through this shift effectively:

1. Address Employee Concerns

- **Acknowledge Fears and Misconceptions:** Many employees worry that AI will replace their jobs. Address these concerns openly and explain that AI is there to assist, not replace, their roles.

- **Highlight AI's Supportive Role:** Emphasize that AI takes over repetitive tasks, enabling employees to focus on higher-level work that involves creativity, strategy, and human interaction.

- **Share Real-Life Examples:** Use cases from other companies (e.g., chatbots in customer service managing FAQs) help illustrate that AI handles routine tasks while people handle more complex situations.

2. Offer Comprehensive Training

- **Build Foundational Knowledge:** Provide hands-on training to familiarize employees with AI tools and their functions.

- **Role-Specific Training:** Tailor training programs to different job roles so employees can understand how AI impacts their specific tasks.

- **Mentorship and Support:** Pair less tech-savvy employees with tech-experienced mentors to offer support and guidance throughout the transition.

3. Create Feedback Loops

- **Encourage Open Feedback:** Give employees a platform to discuss how AI impacts their work, voice concerns, and suggest improvements.

- **Iterate on AI Applications:** Use employee feedback to refine AI applications, making sure they support employees' needs and goals.

- **Celebrate Small Wins:** Share examples of AI improvements to demonstrate the positive impact on workflows and morale.

AI Ethics and Governance in AI-human Collaboration

Ethics and governance in human-AI collaboration ensure responsible AI use that aligns with organizational values and maintains human oversight. Consider these strategies for ethical implementation:

1. Define Boundaries for AI Decision-Making

- **Clarify AI's Role vs. Human Judgment:** Set specific guidelines for when AI can make autonomous decisions and when human oversight is required. For example, AI might provide risk assessments, but humans make final decisions in areas like finance or healthcare.

- **Prioritize Human Judgment:** Ensure that in critical decisions, human judgment remains central to prevent over-reliance on AI alone.

2. Enhance Transparency and Explainability

- **Choose Transparent AI Models:** Opt for AI models that are interpretable, allowing stakeholders to understand how decisions are made.

- **Communicate Limitations Clearly:** Be transparent about what AI can and cannot do, ensuring all stakeholders have realistic expectations.

- **Enable Audits:** Use AI systems that allow for audits to identify and correct any unintended biases or ethical concerns.

3. Set Up Ongoing Monitoring and Governance

- **Establish an Ethics Committee:** Appoint a team to monitor AI's use, ensuring it aligns with ethical standards and organizational values.

- **Implement Data Privacy Policies:** Regularly review data privacy policies to comply with regulations and maintain customer trust.

- **Adapt AI as Needed:** AI systems should be regularly assessed and adjusted to align with ethical standards, evolving business needs, and regulatory requirements.

By following these steps, organizations can responsibly manage the shift to human-AI collaboration, creating an environment that values technological innovation and ethical oversight.

For example, SepsisLab, an AI system designed for early sepsis detection, supports clinicians by predicting the likelihood of sepsis in patients. This tool provides actionable laboratory test recommendations that help medical professionals make timely and informed decisions in high-stakes situations. By collaborating with AI, clinicians can access a data-driven perspective that augments their expertise, leading to improved patient outcomes in critical scenarios. The SepsisLab case highlights the benefits of human-AI collaboration, where AI aids with rapid, data-intensive analysis, allowing clinicians to focus on patient care, ethical decision-making, and empathy, which are uniquely human contributions.

The collaboration model seen in SepsisLab exemplifies the "human-in-the-loop" framework. In this approach, AI provides initial predictions while humans validate, interpret, and apply these insights. The combination enhances diagnostic accuracy and efficiency, showing how AI can effectively supplement human decision-making without replacing it. This partnership also demonstrates the importance of ethical design in AI, as it emphasizes the role of transparency and accuracy in fostering trust among users and patients.

For more details on this study, you can explore the case studies provided by the Partnership on AI, which showcases diverse applications of human-AI collaboration in healthcare and other fields.[30]

Additionally, MIT Press offers extensive insights into real-world AI collaboration models that include healthcare applications and strategies for overcoming challenges in human-AI teamwork.[31]

---

[30]https://partnershiponai.org/paper/human-ai-collaboration-framework-case-studies/

[31] https://direct.mit.edu

Overcoming Resistance to AI Collaboration

Addressing resistance among team members is key to successfully implementing AI-human collaboration. Employees often view AI with caution, fearing it may replace their roles or disrupt established workflows.

1. **Education and Training**: The first step to reducing fear is to increase understanding. When employees are informed about how AI works, its limitations, and its specific role in the organization, they tend to feel more comfortable. CDiGlobal offers training that covers the basics of AI, its applications in their field, and how it will complement rather than replace human efforts to help bridge the knowledge gap. Training should be interactive and provide real-life examples that employees can relate to.

2. **Clear Communication on AI's Purpose**: To address concerns about job security, leaders should communicate the exact role of AI within the organization. AI's purpose is often to automate repetitive tasks, allowing employees to focus on more strategic, creative, or problem-solving work. For example, in customer service, chatbots can manage routine inquiries, freeing representatives to handle complex cases that require human empathy. This reassures employees that AI is a tool for assistance, not a replacement.

3. **Transparency in AI Decision-Making**: When employees understand how AI makes decisions, they are more likely to trust its outputs. Explainability features within AI systems allow users to see the factors influencing AI-

driven recommendations or predictions. For instance, if a risk assessment AI provides a score, breaking down the factors contributing to that score helps build trust. Transparency creates an environment where employees feel they are working alongside AI, not under it.

4. Highlight Success Stories: Share examples of how AI has positively impacted similar roles or industries. Real-life success stories provide concrete evidence that AI can improve workflow efficiency and job satisfaction. When employees see peers benefiting from AI, their own trust in the technology grows.

5. Create Feedback Loops: Engage employees in providing feedback on AI tools. Allowing them to voice concerns, make suggestions, and report issues not only improves AI systems but also gives employees a sense of ownership. Feedback loops show that the organization values employee input and is committed to improving the human-AI collaboration experience.

AI-Human Collaboration Models

Effective human-AI collaboration relies on structured frameworks that balance AI's analytical capabilities with human insight and judgment. Key models for structuring AI-human collaboration include task allocation, communication protocols, and performance evaluation processes.

1. Task Allocation: Determining which tasks are best suited for AI and which require human input is the foundation of effective collaboration. Routine, data-intensive tasks—like data analysis or pattern recognition—are typically assigned to AI, while humans handle tasks requiring judgment, creativity, or emotional intelligence. For instance, in healthcare, AI may assist in identifying patterns in patient data, but doctors make final diagnoses based on the AI's insights combined with their experience. This allocation not only increases efficiency but also ensures AI is used where it is most effective without overstepping into areas best managed by humans.

2. **Communication Protocols**: Clear communication between AI systems and human workers is essential for a smooth workflow. AI systems should deliver insights in an understandable, user-friendly format that employees can easily interpret. Additionally, AI tools should offer explainability features, allowing users to see why a specific recommendation or prediction was made. This enhances transparency and helps employees feel comfortable relying on AI outputs.

3. **Performance Evaluation**: Just as employees' work is evaluated, the effectiveness of AI systems should also be regularly assessed. Evaluating AI performance involves monitoring its accuracy, relevance, and impact on workflows. Regular checks ensure the AI system remains aligned with the organization's goals and that it continues to complement human roles effectively. Including employees in this evaluation process encourages continuous improvement and ensures that the AI system is genuinely helpful and not disruptive.

Overcoming resistance to AI requires building understanding, trust, and clear communication around its role in the organization. By implementing structured collaboration models with well-defined roles for both AI and human workers, organizations can create a balanced environment where AI enhances human performance, fostering a partnership that maximizes the strengths of both.

Future of Human-AI Collaboration

As AI continues to integrate into workplaces, it's reshaping job roles and transforming traditional workforce structures. Here's a look at what these changes might bring:

1. Emergence of New Job Roles

- **AI Trainers**: These professionals refine AI systems to ensure they perform effectively in specific business contexts. They guide AI learning to meet the unique requirements of the organization, making AI more accurate and relevant to real-world tasks.

- **AI Ethics Officers**: Ensuring AI operates ethically, these roles monitor fairness, transparency, and bias within AI systems. This is essential as more industries adopt AI, and ethical considerations have become a priority.

- **Algorithm Auditors and AI Quality Assurance Specialists**: These roles involve auditing and evaluating AI outputs to ensure they are consistent, fair, and reliable. They help maintain trust in AI systems, especially when these systems influence high-stakes decisions.

2. Shift to Agile, Project-Based Teams

- **Cross-Functional Collaboration**: AI will support leaner, project-based teams that bring together members from various departments, creating flexibility to adapt to changes quickly.

- **New Collaborative Roles**: Roles like "AI Collaboration Facilitators" may emerge to manage and optimize workflows between AI and human team members. This ensures smooth transitions and effective task allocation, maximizing AI's capabilities while complementing human skills.

For instance, Zuckerberg's leadership has led to the integration of technologies like virtual reality (VR) and augmented reality (AR) into Meta's products, breaking down silos between VR and social media teams.

3. Increasing Importance of Hybrid Skills

- **Data and Technical Literacy Across Roles**: As AI becomes essential in many fields, employees across various roles—such as marketing, customer service, and finance—will need skills in data analytics and machine learning basics.

- **Focus on Soft Skills**: As AI handles data-driven tasks, human roles will increasingly focus on creativity, problem-solving, and empathy, areas where AI cannot compete. This shift enhances job satisfaction and enables employees to engage in higher-level, strategic work.

Leadership in the Age of AI Collaboration

Leaders in AI-enhanced workplaces need to blend traditional leadership skills with a tech-savvy mindset to maximize AI's potential alongside human talents. Here's what effective leadership in AI collaboration requires:

1. Develop AI Literacy

- **Understanding AI's Role and Capabilities**: Leaders don't need to be AI experts, but they should grasp AI's strengths and limitations to guide their teams effectively.

- **Communicating AI's Value**: Leaders must address employee concerns by explaining how AI can enhance their roles rather than replace them, building trust and openness toward AI.

2. Embrace Adaptability and Continuous Learning

- **Encourage Lifelong Learning**: AI evolves rapidly, so leaders should prioritize continuous learning by offering courses, workshops, and opportunities for skills development.

- **Promote Adaptable Mindsets**: By modeling flexibility, leaders set an example for their teams, creating a culture that embraces change and sees it as a path to growth rather than a disruption.

3. Prioritize Ethics and Transparency

- **Clear Ethical Guidelines for AI**: Leaders should establish ethical standards, such as maintaining human oversight and clarifying the boundaries of AI decision-making.

- **Foster Transparency**: Implementing AI systems with explainability features allows employees and customers to understand AI processes. Leaders should communicate openly about AI's strengths and limitations.

4. Leverage Emotional Intelligence

- **Building Trust and Empathy**: AI may process data, but leaders bring the empathy needed to motivate teams.

- **Inspire Purpose and Creativity**: By balancing AI's efficiency with human creativity and insight, leaders can create a culture where technology supports—not undermines—the organization's values and goals.

Together, these strategies equip leaders to guide teams effectively in a collaborative AI environment, setting the stage for a more productive and fulfilling workplace where both AI and human capabilities are leveraged to their fullest.

Measuring Collaboration Success

To assess the success of human-AI collaboration, organizations need specific Key Performance Indicators (KPIs) that provide insights into productivity, accuracy, and employee engagement. Tracking these metrics can help evaluate how well AI supports human tasks and whether the collaboration is achieving its intended outcomes.

1. **Productivity Measures**: Productivity is a core metric used to determine if AI collaboration enhances work efficiency. KPIs like task completion time, output per employee, and project cycle time can reveal whether AI is enabling teams to work faster and more effectively. For instance, a customer service team using AI for automated responses might see an increase in the number of tickets resolved per day.

2. **Error Rates**: Error rates serve as an indicator of collaboration quality. AI-human collaboration should ideally lead to fewer mistakes in areas where AI provides support, such as data analysis or predictive modeling. By comparing pre- and post-AI implementation error rates, organizations can assess the AI's accuracy and reliability. For example, in healthcare diagnostics, reduced diagnostic errors through AI assistance can signify a successful collaboration.

3. Employee Satisfaction and Engagement: Employee satisfaction is essential for sustained human-AI collaboration. Metrics like employee feedback, turnover rates, and satisfaction surveys gauge how comfortable employees feel working alongside AI. High satisfaction often reflects confidence in AI tools, signaling that the collaboration enhances rather than disrupts their work.

Building effective human-AI collaboration requires a structured approach, from assessing readiness to continuous improvement. Here's a practical action plan:

1. Initial Assessment: Begin by evaluating the current technological infrastructure and workforce readiness for AI collaboration. Identify tasks suitable for AI assistance and areas where AI could complement human capabilities, such as data analysis or customer service automation.

2. Set Clear Objectives: Define what successful collaboration looks like. Establish measurable goals (like increased productivity, reduced error rates, and higher satisfaction) and outline how AI will specifically support team workflows. This clarity helps align the collaboration with business goals.

3. Training and Education: Invest in training programs to ensure that employees understand how to use AI tools effectively and feel confident with these technologies. Providing role-specific training for different departments also ensures employees can utilize AI features in a way that benefits their specific tasks.

4. Pilot Programs and Feedback: Start with a small pilot project to test the AI-human collaboration model. Gather feedback from participants, identify any bottlenecks, and refine the approach based on their insights. A pilot program helps fine-tune the integration before scaling it across the organization.

5. Continuous Improvement and Monitoring: Regularly review KPIs to track progress, adapt AI features based on user feedback, and stay updated on technological advancements that may enhance collaboration further.

Reflections:

Consider these questions to better prepare for implementing AI and optimizing it alongside human capabilities:

1. How does AI currently support or enhance your team's work? Think about the current AI tools in use and evaluate whether they genuinely add value. Are there areas where AI could provide more assistance or where additional training might improve its effectiveness?

2. What tasks could benefit from a human-AI partnership, and where should humans remain fully in control? Identifying tasks that AI could handle more efficiently, like data analysis or routine inquiries, can free up employees for more strategic roles. Are there decisions where human oversight remains crucial for ethical or contextual reasons?

3. How comfortable and equipped are your employees to collaborate with AI tools? Understanding employee perspectives can reveal gaps in comfort or capability. What training programs or resources would help them become more confident in using AI tools as collaborators?

4. How will you measure the success of human-AI collaboration within your organization? Consider what specific KPIs, such as productivity gains or employee satisfaction, you'll use to gauge whether the AI-human collaboration is beneficial.

5. What steps will you take to ensure that AI remains a trustworthy partner in your organization, especially regarding data privacy and decision-making?

Human-AI collaboration offers transformative potential as it enhances productivity and innovation by assigning routine, data-heavy tasks to AI while allowing humans to focus on strategic, ethical, and creative roles. This partnership enables more informed decisions, increases efficiency, and opens up new possibilities for innovation that neither humans nor AI could achieve alone. By working together, AI can help organizations in handling repetitive tasks, freeing people to focus on complex problem-solving and strategic work. This balanced approach boosts productivity and helps organizations stay adaptable and competitive in the business market.

Part III: Securing the AI-Enabled Future

Chapter 8: Cultivating Creative Solutions

In an age where staying relevant means staying innovative, one traditional manufacturing company decided it was time to do more than just keep up. They wanted to lead. Faced with a rapidly changing market challenge, they launched an internal startup incubator that sparked creativity and ambition within their workforce. But they didn't stop there. Recognizing the untapped potential around them, they forged partnerships with local universities and created a bridge between their seasoned engineers and bright, curious students eager to bring fresh ideas to the table.

This was a transformation of the company's culture more than it was a business strategy. By building this internal incubator, they turned their manufacturing floors and design labs into collaborative spaces. Employees who once followed rigid processes were now encouraged to think outside the box, tackling problems like entrepreneurs, not assembly-line workers. The results? Innovative solutions that wouldn't have come from traditional workflows alone, solutions that set them apart from competitors still stuck in the "we've-always-done-it-this-way" mindset.

Through this new ecosystem, seasoned engineers worked alongside student innovators, blending practical know-how with cutting-edge theories from university labs. Together, they experimented, failed, learned, and ultimately succeeded in crafting products that were as fresh as they were functional. This wasn't just about launching new products; it was about igniting a culture of continuous improvement, where the next big idea could come from anyone, at any level, and where risks were celebrated as learning steps, not mistakes.

This journey demonstrates how a well-structured innovation ecosystem can revive traditional businesses, demonstrating that even the oldest companies can be at the forefront of modern innovation.

The Role of Innovation Ecosystems in the AI Era

An innovation ecosystem is a community of people and organizations working together to develop and launch new ideas. It includes a variety of key players, including companies, startups, universities, government agencies, and investors. Each of these groups brings something different to the table. Startups offer fresh ideas and quick action, established companies provide resources and experience, universities contribute to research, governments set policies, and investors fund ideas. When these groups connect and collaborate, they create a supportive environment for innovation.

In the age of AI, having a strong innovation ecosystem is more important than ever. Technology is moving fast, and businesses need to keep up if they want to stay relevant. An innovation ecosystem helps companies stay ahead by connecting them with the latest research, new technology, and real-world solutions. It allows them to grow and change faster than they could on their own. When different groups share insights and work together, they can come up with ideas that wouldn't happen in isolation. One team's discovery can inspire another to create something even better, speeding up progress for everyone.

The interconnected nature of an innovation ecosystem also means that everyone involved benefits. For example, a tech company might team up with a university to test a new AI tool. The university gains hands-on experience, and the company learns from the latest research. This sharing of knowledge and resources spreads the risks and rewards across the ecosystem, making it stronger and more flexible.

Building an innovation ecosystem is essential for companies nowadays. Organizations that actively build and participate in these communities gain a major edge. They can bring ideas to market faster, adapt to changes more easily, and stay at the forefront of AI and technology. In short, a thriving innovation ecosystem is the key to future success in our rapidly changing world.

The Evolution of Innovation

Innovation has come a long way since the early days of closed research and development (R&D) departments. Traditionally, companies kept their innovation efforts strictly in-house and relied solely on internal R&D teams to create new products, solve problems, and maintain their competitive edge. This "closed innovation" model thrived during the early and mid-20th century, with companies such as Bell Labs and Xerox PARC standing out as examples of groundbreaking in-house research. However, these isolated R&D departments also had limitations; they were slow, costly, and often missed insights and advancements beyond company walls.

In the late 20th century, a shift began to take place as companies recognized the limitations of the closed model and saw the potential of opening up innovation. This shift gave rise to open innovation, a model where organizations look beyond their own R&D departments and collaborate with external partners—such as universities, startups, and even other companies—to share knowledge and develop new products. Open innovation recognized that great ideas could come from anywhere, not just within a company's four walls. This approach allowed businesses to bring products to market faster, reduce development costs, and leverage a wider pool of expertise.

Technological advancements have played a crucial role in enabling this shift. The rise of the internet and digital communication has made it easier than ever for organizations to collaborate across distances and industries. Technologies such as cloud computing, video conferencing, and digital data-sharing platforms have removed many of the barriers to collaboration, allowing teams to work together in real-time from virtually anywhere in the world. As a result, companies can now access diverse knowledge networks, tap into global talent, and build on ideas from across industries.

Today, innovation has further evolved into an ecosystem approach. Rather than isolated collaborations, companies now participate in a network of interconnected organizations, including universities, research institutions, government agencies, startups, and corporations, all working together to drive innovation forward. This ecosystem approach goes beyond one-on-one partnerships, creating a community where resources, insights, and skills are continuously shared. It's a model that's particularly well-suited to the rapid pace of technological change we see in fields like artificial intelligence, biotechnology, and renewable energy.

In short, the journey from closed R&D to open innovation and now to innovation ecosystems reflects an ongoing trend: companies increasingly recognize that collaboration and shared knowledge are essential for staying competitive and relevant in a rapidly changing world. Technological advancements have been a driving force behind these shifts, making it possible for organizations to tap into collective expertise and create value in ways that were once unimaginable.

Cross-Pollination Spaces

Creating cross-pollination spaces is essential for promoting creativity, collaboration, and innovation across departments, disciplines, and organizations for both physical and virtual spaces. These spaces encourage people from diverse backgrounds and expertise to share ideas, test solutions, and push beyond traditional boundaries. Whether it's through open office layouts, dedicated innovation hubs, or virtual collaboration tools, these environments stimulate "cross-pollination," where ideas spread across different fields to generate unique solutions. Below are some strategies and examples of successful cross-pollination spaces and their key features.

Strategies for Creating Cross-Pollination Spaces

1.   Open and Flexible Physical Layouts: One effective strategy for fostering collaboration is to design open and flexible physical spaces. These layouts allow for spontaneous interactions, with features like shared tables, communal lounges, and open meeting areas that bring people together naturally. Google's offices, for example, are known for their flexible layouts, which encourage employees to interact and discuss ideas informally. By eliminating physical barriers, organizations can create an environment that promotes idea exchange across departments.[32]

2.   Dedicated Innovation Hubs: Many companies and institutions establish dedicated innovation hubs where employees or external collaborators can come together to work on specific projects. Innovation hubs provide all the necessary resources and tools for experimentation, such as advanced technology, prototyping equipment, and comfortable collaborative spaces. One successful example is

---

[32]https://hbr.org/2003/04/the-era-of-open-innovation

MIT's Media Lab, which is known for bringing together people from diverse fields like engineering, design, and arts to develop breakthrough innovations. Key features include an open lab environment, frequent events for idea-sharing, and access to the latest technology.

3. Virtual Collaboration Platforms: With remote work and global collaboration on the rise, virtual platforms have become a vital strategy for creating cross-pollination spaces. Platforms like **Slack, Microsoft Teams**, and **Miro** offer tools for real-time communication, document sharing, and collaborative brainstorming, allowing team members from different locations to work together seamlessly. Virtual spaces allow cross-functional teams to meet regularly, regardless of location, to share updates, insights, and ideas.

4. Interdisciplinary Projects and Teams: Creating interdisciplinary teams that work on shared projects is another way to foster idea exchange. Organizations can assign employees from different departments, such as R&D, marketing, and operations, to tackle challenges together. **IBM's Watson** project, for example, combined experts in artificial intelligence, healthcare, and business strategy to develop advanced healthcare solutions. By working with people from various fields, team members are exposed to new perspectives and can generate innovative solutions.

5. Co-Working and Shared Office Spaces: For companies that want to tap into a broader ecosystem, co-working spaces offer an ideal solution. These spaces bring together people from different organizations, industries, and disciplines, creating opportunities for organic idea-sharing and collaboration. **WeWork** and **Impact Hub** are popular examples of co-working spaces that support startups, freelancers, and large organizations alike. Key features include shared resources, flexible office layouts, and frequent networking events.

Examples of Successful Innovation Hubs

1. Silicon Valley's Innovation Ecosystem: Silicon Valley remains one of the most famous examples of a successful innovation hub. Major companies like Apple, Google, and Facebook are based here, along with numerous startups and venture capital firms. Its success comes from a mix of physical proximity, talent concentration, and a culture that encourages networking and risk-taking. Frequent industry events, informal networking spaces, and open collaboration between companies, universities, and investors foster a vibrant cross-pollination environment.

2. The European Innovation Hub (EIT): The European Institute of Innovation and Technology (EIT) has established hubs across Europe focused on fields like climate, digital, and health innovation. These hubs create partnerships between academia, research institutions, and businesses to drive sustainable and competitive growth in Europe. Through physical and virtual platforms, EIT hubs facilitate workshops, training, and collaborative projects that enable participants from different backgrounds to exchange ideas and develop solutions for complex challenges.

3. Innovation Space at 1871 (Chicago) 1871 is a prominent tech hub in Chicago designed to support entrepreneurs, startups, and established companies. With over 400 companies and thousands of members, 1871 combines shared workspaces, mentorship programs, and networking events to foster collaboration across industries. Its physical layout includes open work areas, private meeting rooms, and prototyping labs. The hub also offers a virtual platform where members can connect, share resources, and discuss ideas.[33]

Key Features of Effective Cross-Pollination Spaces

- **Open and Flexible Layouts**: Layouts that encourage movement and interaction, such as open seating areas and communal tables.
- **Shared Resources**: Access to prototyping labs, digital tools, and industry mentors to facilitate experimentation.
- **Networking and Events**: Regular workshops, hackathons, and seminars to foster idea-sharing.
- **Interdisciplinary Focus**: Encouragement of cross-disciplinary projects and teams to introduce varied perspectives.
- **Virtual Collaboration Tools**: Platforms that support remote work and global collaboration, ensuring teams stay connected.

---

[33]https://www.researchgate.net/publication/311645709_Open_innovation_Current_status_and_research_opportunities

Tech startup Partnerships

Established companies can gain significant advantages by partnering with tech startups. These partnerships provide fresh perspectives, cutting-edge technologies, and agile development processes that larger companies may lack. In today's fast-paced tech landscape, collaboration with startups offers established businesses an opportunity to stay competitive, innovate faster, and explore new markets. Here's an analysis of some popular partnership models that established companies can use to leverage startup partnerships:

Investment Partnerships

Investment partnerships involve established companies investing directly in tech startups. Through these investments, large companies gain a stake in the startup's growth and often gain early access to its innovations. This approach allows established companies to strategically place themselves at the forefront of technological advancements without taking on the full risk of in-house development. Investments can range from minority stakes to significant ownership, depending on the company's goals. For instance, tech giants often invest in AI and blockchain startups to stay ahead in emerging fields. Investment partnerships also give companies insight into industry trends and access to new talent.

Acquisitions

Acquiring a tech startup is a more direct way for established companies to integrate new technologies, talent, and products into their portfolio. Acquisitions allow companies to fully control the startup's resources and strategic direction. For example, acquisitions are common in the tech industry, where large companies buy out smaller ones with innovative products or technologies they want to incorporate. This can provide immediate benefits, like new products or patents, and help build internal capabilities in areas the company wants to expand. However, acquisition requires careful integration to avoid culture clashes and ensure the startup's innovative edge isn't lost within the larger organization.

Co-Development Partnerships

In a co-development model, established companies and startups work together on specific projects or products. This approach combines the startup's innovation and agility with the established company's resources, experience, and market reach. Co-development allows both parties to share risks and rewards while working on mutually beneficial outcomes. For instance, a retail corporation may collaborate with a tech startup to develop advanced analytics or AI-driven customer service tools. Co-development is particularly effective in rapidly changing industries, as it enables faster product development and deployment.

Mentorship and Accelerator Programs

Some established companies create mentorship and accelerator programs for tech startups, often involving access to funding, workspaces, and guidance from industry experts. These programs allow established companies to support startup growth while gaining early exposure to emerging technologies and business models. For startups, access to seasoned business leaders, technical experts, and established networks is invaluable. Companies like Google and Microsoft run such programs, helping startups scale while aligning their innovations with larger corporate goals. These partnerships also foster long-term relationships that can lead to future collaborations or acquisitions.

Joint Ventures

In a joint venture, an established company and a startup form a new entity, pooling resources to tackle a particular project or market opportunity. Joint ventures work well when both companies bring unique strengths to the table. For instance, a traditional healthcare company might create a joint venture with a health-tech startup to develop digital health platforms. This approach allows both parties to share ownership of the venture, balancing control and reducing risk while enabling each to tap into each other's expertise and customer bases.

By partnering with tech startups, established companies can access new technologies, reach new audiences, and create innovations at a faster pace than they could alone.

Whether through investment, acquisition, co-development, mentorship, or joint ventures, these partnerships offer mutually beneficial opportunities for both sides. Startups gain access to resources and market reach, while larger companies gain agility, innovation, and insight into cutting-edge technologies. In an age where speed and adaptability are key, partnerships with tech startups have become a vital strategy for established companies looking to maintain their edge in a competitive market.

Research Institution Collaborations

Collaborations between businesses and research institutions are powerful partnerships that blend industry needs with academic expertise. These partnerships are increasingly recognized as vital drivers of innovation, allowing businesses to tap into cutting-edge research, gain access to specialized skills, and develop solutions that wouldn't be possible within the constraints of a traditional corporate environment. By combining resources, industry knowledge, and research capabilities, companies and research institutions can drive advancements in technology, product development, and problem-solving faster and more efficiently.

Benefits of Collaboration between Businesses and Research Institutions

Access to Advanced Research and Expertise

Research institutions are home to specialized knowledge, cutting-edge research facilities, and academic experts with deep expertise in various scientific and technological fields. When businesses partner with universities and research centers, they gain direct access to these resources. This enables companies to explore complex questions, run advanced experiments, and build upon the latest theories and discoveries in the field. For example, partnerships in areas like artificial intelligence, biotechnology, and renewable energy allow companies to stay at the forefront of scientific developments without needing to establish costly in-house research teams.

Accelerated Innovation and Development

Businesses often face pressure to innovate quickly to maintain a competitive edge. Collaborating with research institutions allows companies to accelerate their R&D processes, as these institutions have the capacity for long-term, exploratory research that companies may not be able to undertake on their own. By working with academic researchers who are free to explore novel ideas, companies can discover new opportunities for product development and improvement. For instance, pharmaceutical companies frequently partner with medical research institutions to speed up drug discovery and development, leading to faster advancements in treatments and therapies.

Access to Emerging Talent

Collaborating with research institutions also provides businesses with access to students and early-career researchers who are highly trained in specialized fields. Companies can gain a pipeline of fresh talent familiar with the latest scientific techniques and trends, which is especially valuable for technology and science-driven industries. Many companies even offer internships, scholarships, and research grants as part of these collaborations, ensuring a steady flow of skilled professionals who are already familiar with the company's industry and goals.

Shared Resources and Reduced Costs

Establishing R&D facilities and conducting in-depth research can be prohibitively expensive for many companies, especially in fields that require complex equipment or highly specialized materials. Collaborating with research institutions enables businesses to share these resources, significantly reducing costs. Research labs often possess the necessary infrastructure and technology, allowing companies to utilize them for testing, experimentation, and prototyping without the financial burden of setting up in-house labs. This cost-sharing approach makes innovation more accessible to a wider range of businesses, from large corporations to small startups.

Knowledge Transfer and Real-world Applications

Collaborations with research institutions allow for a beneficial exchange of knowledge. Researchers can learn about the practical challenges and needs of the industry, which helps them focus their work on applications that have real-world impact. Meanwhile, companies gain insight into academic research that might be applied to solve industry-specific problems. For example, IBM's partnerships with universities have allowed it to incorporate fundamental AI research into practical applications, including IBM Watson. This knowledge transfer accelerates the path from research to real-world implementation, making innovations commercially viable faster.

Examples of Successful Business-Research Institution Collaborations

1. **Google and Stanford University** Google has long collaborated with Stanford, gaining access to the latest in machine learning and AI research. In return, Stanford's researchers receive funding and the chance to test their ideas in real-world applications. This collaboration has been instrumental in advancing technologies that power Google's AI and search capabilities.

2. **MIT Media Lab and Multiple Corporations** The MIT Media Lab has partnered with companies like

Samsung, LEGO, and General Motors to develop innovations across sectors. These collaborations have produced groundbreaking technologies, from digital learning tools to advanced automotive systems, by combining industry needs with academic research.

3. Pfizer and University of California, San Francisco (UCSF) Pfizer's partnership with UCSF is a strong example in the pharmaceutical field, where the collaboration focuses on early-stage drug discovery. Pfizer gains access to UCSF's expertise and research facilities, while UCSF benefits from Pfizer's industry knowledge and resources, accelerating the development of potential new therapies.

Collaborations between businesses and research institutions are essential for driving innovation. These partnerships provide companies with access to advanced expertise, reduce research costs, and allow for the exchange of knowledge that brings academic discoveries to market faster. In a landscape where staying competitive depends on continuous innovation, these collaborations empower businesses to explore, experiment, and push the boundaries of what's possible. As industries continue to evolve, the partnership between research institutions and businesses will remain a cornerstone of technological and scientific progress.

Open Innovation Practices

Open innovation is a powerful strategy that encourages organizations to look beyond their own resources for fresh ideas and solutions. Instead of relying solely on internal R&D, companies invite external individuals, organizations, and communities to contribute insights, innovations, and expertise. This approach leverages the creativity and knowledge of a broader audience, allowing companies to solve complex problems, accelerate product development, and keep up with rapidly changing markets. Below are some common open innovation strategies—crowdsourcing, hackathons, and innovation challenges—along with examples of successful initiatives and their outcomes.

1. Crowdsourcing

Crowdsourcing involves tapping into the ideas and expertise of a large group of people, typically through an online platform. Organizations use crowdsourcing to gather insights, solve problems, and generate innovative concepts by inviting input from anyone interested, be it customers, employees, or the general public. This strategy is particularly effective for gathering a large volume of ideas quickly and efficiently.

Take LEGO's crowdsourcing platform, for instance. LEGO Ideas invites fans to submit ideas for new LEGO sets. The platform allows users to vote on submissions, and LEGO reviews the top-voted ideas. Winning designs are turned into official LEGO sets, with the creator receiving a percentage of the sales. This initiative not only fosters fan engagement but also helps LEGO identify products that are likely to be popular. Sets like the LEGO Women of NASA and the LEGO Ship in a Bottle originated from this platform, showcasing the value of crowdsourcing in product innovation.

LEGO Ideas has led to the development of numerous fan-inspired products, boosting customer engagement and broadening LEGO's product line based on direct fan input.

2. Hackathons

Hackathons are time-bound events, often lasting 24-48 hours, where participants come together to solve specific challenges, develop prototypes, and create innovative solutions. Companies use hackathons to quickly generate new ideas, test them, and identify talented individuals who may become valuable collaborators or employees.

For instance, Facebook has a long history of hosting internal hackathons where employees from various departments work together to create new features. Many of Facebook's popular products, including the Like button, Timeline, and Facebook Chat, originated from hackathons. These events encourage employees to experiment with new ideas in a relaxed and collaborative environment, leading to breakthroughs that might not have happened within routine work structures.

Facebook's hackathons have fostered a culture of innovation, resulting in key product developments and features that keep the platform engaging and responsive to user needs.

Another example is NASA's Space Apps Challenge. NASA's Space Apps Challenge is an annual global hackathon that invites participants worldwide to create solutions for Earth and space issues. Challenges range from space exploration to environmental protection, and participants include programmers, engineers, and enthusiasts. Solutions developed during the hackathon have been used by NASA for real-world applications, such as data analysis and climate research.

The Space Apps Challenge brings fresh perspectives and innovative approaches to complex space-related issues, driving progress and expanding NASA's innovation network.

3. Innovation Challenges

Innovation challenges are competitions where companies pose specific problems and invite participants to propose solutions. These challenges are usually open to anyone and often come with monetary rewards, partnerships, or potential for product development. This approach helps organizations crowdsource solutions for complex issues while attracting creative minds from outside their usual talent pool.

For instance, the XPRIZE Foundation is known for hosting large-scale innovation challenges across a range of fields, from space travel to healthcare. One notable example is the **Ansari XPRIZE** for suborbital spaceflight, which offered $10 million to the first privately funded team to launch a reusable spacecraft into space twice within two weeks. This challenge drove significant advancements in the private space industry, eventually leading to the development of commercial space companies like SpaceX and Virgin Galactic.

The Ansari XPRIZE and subsequent XPRIZE competitions have spurred technological advancements, leading to major breakthroughs in fields such as space travel, AI, and environmental sustainability.

Benefits of Open Innovation

Open innovation strategies bring several benefits. They enable companies to:

- **Access Diverse Ideas and Perspectives**: Open innovation brings in fresh ideas from people with different backgrounds, skills, and experiences.

- **Reduce R&D Costs and Risks**: Instead of dedicating extensive resources to in-house R&D, companies can leverage external talent and ideas.

- **Increase Speed to Market**: Solutions sourced from open innovation can be developed and implemented faster than in traditional R&D processes.

- **Strengthen Customer and Community Engagement**: By involving customers or the public, companies foster brand loyalty and build stronger relationships with their audience.

Open innovation practices, such as crowdsourcing, hackathons, and innovation challenges, are proving to be powerful strategies for fostering creativity and driving growth. Through these strategies, companies gain access to a vast pool of ideas, talent, and solutions that might otherwise remain untapped. Successful open innovation initiatives like LEGO Ideas, Facebook's hackathons, and the XPRIZE Foundation demonstrate that inviting external collaborators into the innovation process can lead to groundbreaking outcomes.

***

Siemens, a global leader in industrial manufacturing, technology, and engineering, is an exemplary case of a company that has successfully built a thriving innovation ecosystem. Faced with rapid technological advancements, Siemens recognized the need to adapt and foster a culture of continuous innovation. Over the years, the company has implemented an open, collaborative approach to innovation, drawing from internal resources and external partnerships to build a comprehensive ecosystem that spans multiple countries, industries, and fields of research.

Siemens began by transforming its internal structure, encouraging cross-departmental collaboration, and creating spaces for innovation. Siemens established **Siemens Innovation Ecosystem** (SIE), a global network connecting research institutions, startups, universities, and companies. This ecosystem supports initiatives across industries like energy, healthcare, infrastructure, and manufacturing, allowing Siemens to tap into diverse expertise and new ideas. Key components of Siemens' approach include:

1. Siemens Innovation Centers

Siemens established several innovation centers worldwide, such as the **Siemens Corporate Technology (CT)** center in Princeton, New Jersey. These centers work on fundamental research, partnering with universities and startups to develop technologies in fields such as artificial intelligence, robotics, and energy efficiency. The centers create an environment where researchers, engineers, and business experts collaborate closely on projects that will meet future market demands.

2. Open Innovation and Co-Creation Platforms

Siemens launched platforms like **Siemens Connect**, which brings customers, startups, and technology partners into the innovation process. This platform allows Siemens to gather customer insights early in the development phase, co-create solutions with partners, and shorten the path to market. For instance, through Siemens Connect, the company has developed solutions for smart grids and industrial automation that incorporate direct input from users, improving adoption rates and usability.

3. Investment in Startups

Siemens actively invests in startups through **Next47**, an independent venture firm founded by Siemens. Next47 identifies startups working in emerging technology areas, such as autonomous machines, distributed energy systems, and cybersecurity, and provides them with funding and resources. By investing in and mentoring these startups, Siemens gains early access to breakthrough innovations and the ability to integrate them into its products and services.

4. Cross-Disciplinary Teams and Interdepartmental Collaboration

Siemens promotes cross-disciplinary teamwork by bringing together experts from different departments to work on shared projects. This approach ensures that various perspectives are considered, resulting in well-rounded, innovative solutions. For example, Siemens' healthcare and industrial automation teams collaborated to develop automation solutions for medical device manufacturing, leading to faster production and improved product quality.

Siemens faced several challenges in building its innovation ecosystem. Some of these included:

• **Cultural Resistance to Change**: Transitioning from a traditional R&D model to an open innovation approach required a cultural shift. Siemens addressed this by promoting a mindset of openness and collaboration across the company, encouraging employees to think beyond their departments and embrace new partnerships.

• **Integrating Startups**: Working with startups often presents a challenge in terms of aligning goals, processes, and timelines. Siemens overcame this by establishing Next47 as an independent entity, allowing startups to maintain their agility while benefiting from Siemens' resources and industry expertise.

- **Balancing Innovation and Standardization**: Siemens operates in industries with strict standards, such as energy and healthcare. Developing innovative solutions while adhering to regulatory standards required careful project management. Siemens created specialized teams that focused on regulatory compliance while collaborating with innovators, ensuring all solutions were market-ready.

However, Siemens' thriving innovation ecosystem has significantly impacted its ability to remain competitive and relevant in a fast-paced technological landscape. Here are some of the major impacts of Siemens' ecosystem:

- **Accelerated Product Development**: Through its collaborative approach, Siemens has reduced the time to market for new products, allowing it to respond faster to customer demands and industry trends. Innovations developed through Siemens' ecosystem, such as smart building technologies and advanced manufacturing solutions, have given the company a competitive edge.

- **Increased Revenue from New Products**: Siemens reports that a growing portion of its revenue comes from new products developed through its ecosystem. This includes digital solutions, AI-driven diagnostics, and renewable energy technologies, which are gaining popularity across global markets.

- **Advancements in Digitalization and Sustainability**: Siemens' innovation ecosystem has driven advancements in key areas like digitalization and sustainability. By working with external partners, Siemens has developed smart grid technology and energy management systems that support the transition to renewable energy. These technologies help Siemens' customers optimize energy usage and reduce emissions, aligning with the company's commitment to sustainability.

• **Strengthened Industry Positioning**: By establishing itself as a leader in open innovation, Siemens has strengthened its industry reputation and attracted top-tier partners and talent. Its commitment to collaboration and co-creation has built trust with customers and partners, solidifying Siemens' position as a forward-thinking, innovative company.

Siemens' success in building a thriving innovation ecosystem highlights the value of open innovation, collaborative platforms, and strategic investments in emerging technologies. By creating an interconnected network of partners, innovation centers, and cross-disciplinary teams, Siemens has harnessed the power of collective expertise and achieved breakthroughs that would have been difficult to accomplish in isolation. Siemens' journey showcases the importance of adaptability, cultural openness, and strategic partnerships in building a resilient and dynamic innovation ecosystem capable of thriving in the modern world.[34]

***

---

[34]https://www.siemens.com/global/en/company/innovation/collaborations-partnerships/research-and-innovation-ecosystem.html

Challenges and Obstacles in Building an Innovation Ecosystem

Building an innovation ecosystem is complex and often met with a range of challenges. **Cultural resistance** is one of the primary obstacles. Established organizations may have traditional structures and mindsets that hinder collaborative innovation. Employees may resist new ways of working, preferring familiar routines over cross-functional teamwork and open knowledge-sharing. Overcoming this requires a shift in organizational culture. Leaders can address this by actively promoting a culture of openness, encouraging employees to embrace new ideas, and celebrating small innovation successes to build momentum.

Another challenge lies in **intellectual property (IP) concerns**. When companies collaborate with external partners, they often worry about losing control over valuable intellectual assets. This fear can lead to hesitancy in sharing information or collaborating on projects that might be groundbreaking. To manage this, organizations can implement clear IP agreements at the outset, defining ownership and usage rights for all parties involved. This transparency provides a foundation for trust and can help alleviate concerns over IP security.

Managing diverse stakeholder interests is also a key challenge in building a successful innovation ecosystem. Ecosystems often include startups, established companies, universities, and government agencies, each with different objectives and timelines. Startups may push for rapid development, while academic institutions focus on long-term research, and governments prioritize public impact. Balancing these interests requires a structured approach, such as setting shared goals and creating a roadmap that aligns with all stakeholders' timelines. Regular check-ins and open communication channels ensure alignment and help address any emerging conflicts.

Homo Magister Perspective

Leaders who embody the **Homo Magister** ideal are particularly adept at fostering and guiding innovation ecosystems. These leaders don't just manage; they cultivate an environment where collaboration flourishes while keeping sight of strategic objectives. This balance of openness with intentional focus is crucial in innovation ecosystems because this is where diverse ideas and stakeholders converge.

One of the key ways Homo Magisters contribute to ecosystem growth is by **creating a culture of openness** that encourages participants to freely share ideas and expertise. They prioritize transparency, build trust among ecosystem members, and actively remove barriers to collaboration. Homo Magister leaders ensure that every member—whether a startup, university, or corporate partner—feels valued and motivated to contribute, knowing that their ideas are both heard and respected by encouraging an inclusive environment. This openness invites diverse perspectives, sparking innovation that might not arise in a more closed or competitive setting.

However, Homo Magisters recognize that openness must be balanced with a **clear, strategic vision** to ensure the ecosystem doesn't lose its focus. They define overarching goals that align with the organization's mission while allowing flexibility within those boundaries. For instance, if the ecosystem's goal is to advance sustainable technology, a Homo Magister leader ensures that projects and collaborations contribute to this vision, filtering out ideas that may veer off course. The Homo magisters can guide the participants toward purposeful innovation, giving structure to the ecosystem without stifling creativity by setting these parameters.

These leaders also play a pivotal role in **nurturing talent and providing mentorship** to ecosystem members. Rather than just delegating tasks, they guide and develop individuals and teams, helping them grow professionally and within the ecosystem. By sharing their experience and insights, Homo Magisters empower emerging leaders to think strategically and understand how their work fits into the bigger picture. This mentorship helps sustain the ecosystem, ensuring that the next generation of innovators is equipped with the skills and perspectives needed to continue advancing its goals.

In addition, Homo Magister leaders are **champions of ethical collaboration**, ensuring that knowledge sharing and intellectual property rights are managed respectfully. They establish frameworks for fair data usage, transparent IP agreements, and shared responsibilities. This ethical approach reinforces trust, fostering a sustainable ecosystem where participants are encouraged to collaborate without fear of exploitation.

Ultimately, Homo Magisters enable innovation ecosystems to thrive by balancing the freedom for exploration with the discipline of a shared mission. They cultivate environments that are both adaptive and grounded, allowing innovation to unfold in ways that are both visionary and impactful. Through this balance of openness and strategic focus, they guide ecosystems toward meaningful, sustainable progress.

While effective leadership sets the foundation for a thriving ecosystem, **artificial intelligence (AI)** plays a pivotal role in accelerating and enhancing innovation within these networks.

AI's Role in Enhancing Innovation Ecosystems

Artificial intelligence (AI) has become a transformative force within innovation ecosystems, enhancing collaboration, accelerating decision-making, and revealing insights that drive growth. By integrating AI into innovation ecosystems, organizations can leverage data-driven insights, predict trends, and streamline the exchange of ideas across departments and partner organizations. AI technologies offer several unique capabilities, from predictive analytics for spotting emerging trends to collaboration tools that break down barriers across global teams.

Predictive Analytics for Trend Spotting

AI-powered predictive analytics play a crucial role in helping organizations identify and anticipate market trends, technological shifts, and evolving consumer needs. Within an innovation ecosystem, this capability allows companies and their partners to stay ahead of the curve, making proactive adjustments rather than reactive responses. By analyzing vast datasets from various sources—including social media, market reports, and user feedback—AI can uncover patterns and forecast trends more accurately than human analysis alone.

For instance, an automotive innovation ecosystem might use AI to track shifts in consumer preferences toward electric vehicles or autonomous driving. By understanding these patterns early, companies within the ecosystem can align their research and development efforts, prioritize resource allocation, and capitalize on emerging opportunities before competitors. Predictive analytics enable the ecosystem as a whole to make informed, forward-thinking decisions, ensuring that new products or services meet real-world demand.

AI-Powered Collaboration Tools

Innovation ecosystems often include diverse stakeholders from multiple industries, locations, and areas of expertise.

AI-powered collaboration tools help streamline communication and coordination across these varied groups, allowing them to work seamlessly together despite geographical or organizational barriers. Tools like AI-driven project management platforms, automated meeting schedulers, and real-time language translation applications enable cross-functional teams to collaborate more effectively.

For example, large-scale innovation projects may involve experts from engineering, marketing, and design who need to share updates and coordinate their contributions in real-time. AI-based platforms like Microsoft Teams or Slack, enhanced with AI scheduling and task automation, make this coordination more efficient. These tools ensure that all members have visibility into project status, reducing the delays that often arise from miscommunication or logistical issues. Additionally, AI-powered translation tools enable seamless communication between global teams, making it easier to exchange ideas and insights across language barriers.

Enhanced R&D and Experimentation

AI also significantly boosts research and development (R&D) efforts within innovation ecosystems. By analyzing historical data and experimenting with different variables, AI can simulate outcomes and test hypotheses, accelerating the R&D process. In pharmaceuticals, for instance, AI can speed up the drug discovery process by identifying potential compounds, predicting their efficacy, and analyzing possible side effects before human trials begin. This efficiency enables pharmaceutical companies and their research partners to bring drugs to market faster, benefiting patients and enhancing the ecosystem's impact on public health.

Moreover, AI can streamline iterative design processes in sectors like manufacturing or consumer products. By using AI-driven design tools, companies can create digital prototypes, test different design parameters, and improve functionality at a fraction of the time and cost of traditional methods. This allows companies within the ecosystem to innovate rapidly and produce high-quality solutions that address current challenges.

AI as a Knowledge Management Tool

Knowledge sharing is fundamental to any innovation ecosystem, but managing and retrieving valuable insights from large amounts of data can be challenging. AI-powered knowledge management systems, such as natural language processing (NLP) search engines and recommendation algorithms, enable organizations to categorize, retrieve, and disseminate information effectively. For instance, an AI-based knowledge management system can scan research papers, patents, and internal reports to find relevant insights for a specific project, allowing teams to build on existing knowledge without starting from scratch.

This kind of AI-driven knowledge sharing ensures that all ecosystem participants benefit from collective expertise, reducing duplication of efforts and enabling faster progress. Additionally, as AI continuously learns and improves, it can identify and suggest relevant information to teams based on their needs, helping them make decisions grounded in comprehensive knowledge and past experiences.

AI's role in innovation ecosystems is transformative, acting as both a tool and a catalyst for accelerated growth and collaboration. From predictive analytics that highlight emerging trends to AI-powered collaboration tools that unify teams, AI technologies bring agility and insight to every stage of innovation. As organizations continue to harness AI within their ecosystems, they gain a competitive edge, allowing them to innovate at a pace that aligns with market demands and technological advances. By fostering a culture of data-driven decision-making and seamless collaboration, AI enables innovation ecosystems to achieve their full potential in today's fast-evolving landscape.

Measuring Ecosystem Success

Measuring the success of an innovation ecosystem is essential to understanding its health, productivity, and impact on the organization and its stakeholders. To evaluate the effectiveness of an innovation ecosystem, it's important to establish clear metrics that capture not only the volume of activity but also the quality of collaboration and the outcomes generated. Here are key indicators for assessing ecosystem success:

1. Collaboration Metrics: Collaboration is the backbone of a successful ecosystem, so measuring how effectively ecosystem members work together is critical. Indicators include the frequency of cross-functional meetings, the diversity of participants in projects, and the number of partnerships formed both internally and externally. Additionally, collaboration metrics can assess the level of engagement across departments and between the organization and its external partners. Higher rates of collaboration and participation can indicate a healthy, connected ecosystem.

2. Idea Generation and Implementation: A productive innovation ecosystem should not only generate a high volume of ideas but also ensure that those ideas are valuable and actionable. Metrics such as the number of new ideas submitted, the percentage of ideas that progress to the development phase, and the success rate of implemented ideas can provide insights into the ecosystem's productivity. Tracking the journey of ideas from conception to implementation helps measure how effectively the ecosystem converts ideas into impactful outcomes.

3. Success of Innovations: Ultimately, the ecosystem's success is measured by the impact of its innovations. Key performance indicators (KPIs) include the revenue generated by new products or services, customer satisfaction scores, and the time-to-market for new solutions. Additionally, tracking the ecosystem's contribution to achieving strategic goals—such as reducing costs, improving efficiency, or entering new markets—provides a holistic view of its success. These metrics enable ecosystem leaders to identify areas for improvement and ensure that the ecosystem remains aligned with business objectives.[35]

Measuring the success of an innovation ecosystem requires a well-rounded approach that captures both the quantity and quality of collaborative efforts, the effectiveness of idea generation, and the tangible impact of innovations. Collaboration metrics reveal the strength of connections within the ecosystem while tracking idea generation and implementation, which offers insight into the ecosystem's creativity and productivity. Ultimately, evaluating the success of innovations through key performance indicators ensures alignment with strategic objectives and highlights the ecosystem's real-world value. By consistently monitoring these metrics, leaders can identify areas for growth and make data-informed adjustments to sustain a dynamic, effective innovation ecosystem.

Future of Innovation Ecosystems

The future of innovation ecosystems is set to be shaped by ongoing technological advancements and shifts in the business landscape. As organizations adapt to rapid changes in technology, customer expectations, and market

---

[35]https://hbr.org/2006/04/match-your-innovation-strategy-to-your-innovation-ecosystem

competition, innovation ecosystems will likely evolve in several significant ways:

1.   Increased Integration of AI and Automation: As artificial intelligence (AI) and automation technologies advance, they will play an even larger role in driving ecosystem efficiency and insight generation. AI will enable real-time data analysis, helping ecosystem members spot trends faster, make decisions more accurately, and automate routine tasks. This will not only speed up the innovation process but also empower ecosystem members to focus on higher-level strategic work. Automated collaboration tools will allow teams to work seamlessly across regions and time zones, further enhancing productivity.

2.   Rise of Decentralized and Flexible Ecosystems: With the shift toward remote work and digital transformation, ecosystems are likely to become more decentralized and flexible. Innovations in virtual and augmented reality could facilitate immersive, remote collaboration, making it easier for global teams to share ideas and resources. Moreover, blockchain technology might enable more secure and transparent transactions, allowing organizations to establish partnerships and share intellectual property with greater confidence. These technologies will help organizations develop ecosystems that are adaptable, scalable, and inclusive of a wider variety of participants, from small startups to individual innovators.

3.   Increased Focus on Sustainable and Purpose-Driven Innovation: As societal and environmental concerns become more pressing, innovation ecosystems will increasingly focus on sustainable and purpose-driven goals. Companies are likely to seek out ecosystem partners who share their values and commitment to ethical practices. This shift will push ecosystems to create innovations that are not only profitable but also socially and environmentally responsible. Purpose-driven ecosystems will attract talent and partners who are passionate about creating positive change, leading to innovations that benefit both businesses and society.

4. Stronger Focus on Ecosystem Metrics and Impact: With more mature ecosystems and better metrics, organizations will become more strategic in evaluating their ecosystems' effectiveness. Data-driven metrics will guide decision-making, helping leaders optimize their ecosystem structure, partnerships, and processes. As ecosystems evolve, real-time dashboards, AI analytics, and machine learning models will play an increasingly central role in measuring and managing ecosystem performance, enabling organizations to make data-informed adjustments that maximize impact.

Innovation ecosystems are poised to become increasingly sophisticated, agile, and purpose-driven. As AI and automation advance, ecosystems will benefit from faster, more accurate insights, enabling seamless global collaboration. Decentralized and flexible structures will make it easier for diverse participants to contribute, creating a network of shared knowledge and innovation. The focus on sustainability and social responsibility will attract like-minded partners committed to creating positive change, while real-time metrics and data analytics will ensure ecosystems stay adaptable and effective. Organizations that embrace these trends and proactively refine their ecosystems will be well-equipped to drive impactful, long-lasting innovation in an evolving world.

Building an innovation ecosystem requires a thoughtful, step-by-step approach that aligns with your organization's goals and culture. Here's a guide to help you develop your own ecosystem:

1.   Initial Assessment: Begin by assessing your organization's current strengths, resources, and potential partners. Identify areas where innovation can have the greatest impact and the gaps in expertise or technology that external partnerships could fill. Conduct interviews, surveys, or workshops to gather insights from internal stakeholders about needs and opportunities.

2.   Define Your Strategy: Set clear objectives for your ecosystem. Define what success looks like and identify the types of partners—such as startups, universities, or industry groups—that align with these goals. Consider whether your focus will be on developing new products, advancing research, or creating sustainable solutions. Ensure your strategy incorporates both short-term and long-term goals to keep your ecosystem flexible and responsive.

3.   Identify and Engage Partners: Build a list of potential collaborators based on your strategy. Reach out to organizations that can bring complementary expertise and resources. Host introductory meetings to explore mutual interests and discuss expectations for collaboration. It's essential to establish trust and set clear terms for intellectual property sharing and data use.

4.   Create Collaboration Spaces: Design both physical and virtual spaces that encourage interaction among ecosystem members. Physical spaces might include innovation hubs or shared labs, while virtual platforms like collaborative software enable seamless communication and project tracking. These spaces should foster an environment where participants can easily share ideas, track progress, and access resources.

5.   Launch Pilot Projects: Start with pilot initiatives to test the ecosystem's effectiveness. Select projects that address high-priority needs and involve a manageable number of partners. Use this stage to assess the flow of communication, collaboration quality, and the initial outcomes of working together.

6.   Monitor and Measure Success: Develop metrics to track progress and measure ecosystem health. Monitor collaboration frequency, idea generation, and project outcomes. Collect feedback from ecosystem participants to understand any barriers and continually refine processes to ensure alignment with your goals.

7.   Continuous Improvement: Based on collected data and feedback, refine your ecosystem processes and partnerships. Stay flexible and open to adding new partners or adjusting goals as your organization and industry evolve. Establish regular review periods to ensure the ecosystem remains productive and aligned with organizational objectives.

Reflections:

To help you apply these steps to your organization, consider the following questions:

1. What specific goals does your organization have that could benefit from an innovation ecosystem?

2. Which external partners, such as academic institutions or startups, could provide valuable expertise or resources?

3. How can you create a culture of openness and collaboration that encourages knowledge sharing?

4. What metrics would best reflect success in your ecosystem?

5. How will you ensure continuous alignment between ecosystem activities and organizational goals?

These questions will help you understand your organization's needs and guide you in crafting a customized innovation ecosystem plan.

By understanding and applying these steps, organizations can create ecosystems that encourage open collaboration, leverage external expertise, and drive meaningful innovation. As we move further into the AI era, the importance of such ecosystems cannot be overstated; they are essential for adapting to rapid technological advancements and maintaining competitive advantage. Thoughtfully developed innovation ecosystems can transform organizations, positioning them to thrive in a dynamic, interconnected world.

Chapter 9: Steering Through Transformation

When Alex Morgan took over as CEO of a century-old manufacturing company, they brought along years of experience helping traditional businesses embrace digital change. Alex had spent their career right where technology meets old-school industry, making them a natural fit for a company with traditional roots but a need for fresh direction. People knew Alex as a leader who didn't just understand the latest tech but also valued the people behind it. They had this rare knack for moving companies forward while respecting what made them special in the first place.

Yet, this new role was one of their biggest challenges. The company was steeped in legacy systems and traditional methods, and although it had a solid reputation, it was beginning to feel the strain of a rapidly changing marketplace. Competitors were adopting AI and other advanced technologies, threatening the company's position if it didn't evolve. Alex knew that transforming this organization would require more than just implementing new technology; it would need a shift in mindset across the entire workforce.

From day one, Alex took a thoughtful approach. Rather than making sweeping changes, they started by introducing the workforce to AI through practical, accessible training sessions. Alex wanted employees at every level to understand and feel comfortable with the technology. They launched workshops and AI literacy programs. He invited everyone from floor operators to senior managers to explore AI's potential and how it could enhance their work. This grassroots approach sparked curiosity and, more importantly, helped employees see AI as an empowering tool rather than a threat.

Beyond training, Alex concentrated on breaking down departmental silos to foster greater collaboration. They formed cross-functional teams to work on AI-driven initiatives like predictive maintenance and enhanced customer service tools, ensuring that expertise from various areas could contribute to each project's success. Alex introduced physical and virtual workspaces where employees could easily connect, exchange ideas, and access resources to support this collaborative approach. This openness developed a more dynamic and interconnected environment.

At every stage, Alex balanced innovation with the company's long-term goals. They chose AI projects that aligned with core business needs, like improving supply chain efficiency and product quality. By keeping AI applications focused and purposeful, Alex ensured that technology served the company's mission, not just trends.

Through steady guidance, Alex transformed a legacy company into a forward-looking, AI-powered organization, proving that with the right leadership, even the most traditional businesses can evolve and thrive in a technology-driven world.

Alex's story gives a real glimpse into the Homo Magister style of leadership, where leaders go beyond directing from the top. They act as mentors and guides, fully invested in nurturing growth at every level.

This kind of leadership is more important than ever in today's AI-driven world, where new technologies and rapid changes are the norm. Instead of the old top-down, command-and-control style, the Homo Magister approach is all about guiding and empowering teams, promoting a culture of learning, and building an environment where innovation can really take off.

A Homo Magister leader understands that in a world driven by AI, success depends not only on adopting new tools but on cultivating a culture that embraces curiosity and collaboration. They lead by example, show openness to new ideas, and help their teams see AI as a tool that enhances, rather than replaces, human skills. This leader balances strategic vision with hands-on involvement, ensuring that the company's technological advancements align with its values and goals.

This leadership paradigm is distinct from traditional approaches, as it emphasizes mentorship over control. A Homo Magister leader invests in their team's growth and takes an active role in their development, promoting a workplace where people feel valued and inspired to contribute. This approach enables organizations to adapt more fluidly as teams are empowered to think critically and respond creatively to new challenges. By championing both human-centered leadership and strategic innovation, Homo Magister leaders are setting a new standard for what it means to lead in the modern world.

Essential AI-Era Skills for Modern Leaders

As the AI era reshapes industries and workplaces, leaders need a unique set of skills to guide their organizations through rapid technological change. It's no longer enough to rely solely on traditional management techniques; today's leaders must be agile, ethically grounded, and technologically savvy. Below are some of the most critical skills leaders need to thrive in an AI-driven world, along with examples of how these skills play out in real-life leadership situations.

1. Technological Literacy

In the AI era, leaders don't need to be programmers, but they do need to understand the basics of how AI works, its capabilities, and its limitations. This knowledge helps leaders make informed decisions about how and when to integrate AI tools and fosters trust among tech-savvy teams. For instance, a leader overseeing a customer service team could leverage their understanding of AI-driven chatbots and analytics to improve response times while still ensuring human agents are available for complex cases. By understanding AI's potential, they can strike the right balance between automation and human interaction.

2. Ethical Reasoning

As AI becomes more integrated into decision-making, leaders face complex ethical considerations, especially concerning data privacy, algorithmic bias, and transparency. Ethical reasoning allows leaders to think critically about these issues, ensuring that AI applications align with the company's values and societal expectations. For example, a retail executive implementing AI for personalized marketing needs to consider privacy issues and ensure customers' data is handled responsibly. By fostering a culture of transparency and fairness, they can build trust with consumers and avoid potential ethical pitfalls, positioning the company as a responsible innovator.

3. Adaptive Thinking

The AI landscape is constantly evolving, and leaders must be flexible and open to change. Adaptive thinking enables leaders to pivot quickly, embrace new ideas, and stay ahead of industry shifts. This skill is particularly valuable in sectors such as healthcare or finance, where technology is evolving at lightning speed. For instance, a leader in the banking sector may find that AI is changing how customers manage finances, from virtual assistants to fraud detection. By remaining adaptive, they can quickly assess which tools best serve their customers' needs, fostering innovation without overly committing to any single solution.

4. Cross-Cultural Competence

AI-driven tools and global collaboration go hand in hand, making cross-cultural competence essential. Leaders must be able to work effectively with diverse teams, understand different perspectives, and adapt communication styles as needed. In a company expanding globally, for example, a leader who understands local market nuances and respects cultural differences can better guide AI implementations that resonate with each audience. If AI is in multiple countries, they might adjust algorithms to reflect cultural sensitivities, creating personalized and respectful products in each region.

Consider a CEO of a multinational manufacturing company who's guiding an AI transformation. With strong technological literacy, they can evaluate which AI tools will streamline supply chain operations. They apply ethical reasoning to ensure that any automation in hiring processes doesn't lead to biased decision-making. They use adaptive thinking to quickly integrate AI-driven solutions as needs evolve, perhaps shifting from predictive maintenance to real-time monitoring when new technologies emerge. Finally, with cross-cultural competence, they ensure that AI applications respect the cultural dynamics of each regional market, fostering a global approach to innovation that respects local nuances.

By mastering these competencies, leaders position themselves—and their teams—to thrive in a world where AI is a powerful partner in growth and success. Leaders who cultivate these skills will drive their organizations forward and create ethical, innovative, and globally inclusive workplaces.

Technological Literacy

Technological literacy has become a fundamental skill for leaders as it helps them understand the basics of AI, data analytics, and machine learning concepts. It helps them ask the right questions, assess the potential of AI applications, and make informed decisions that align with their organization's goals and ethics.

What Technological Literacy Means for Leaders

Technological literacy for leaders involves a grasp of how AI tools work, their potential applications, and their limitations. Leaders need to understand concepts like machine learning algorithms, data privacy concerns, and the differences between supervised and unsupervised learning. This knowledge helps them see where AI can truly add value and where it may not be suitable.

For example, a leader with strong technological literacy would recognize the difference between an AI tool capable of automating customer service responses and one designed for complex data analysis. They would understand the implications of each and make decisions that balance efficiency with the customer experience.

Technological Literacy in Decision-Making

Technological literacy enables leaders to make decisions rooted in a realistic understanding of AI capabilities and risks. Without this understanding, they may adopt AI tools without fully recognizing their potential impact, leading to unintended consequences. For instance, in HR, an uninformed leader might adopt a recruitment AI system without understanding that it could reinforce biases, harming diversity efforts. In contrast, a tech-literate leader would evaluate the AI's training data and biases, ensuring it aligns with the organization's values.

Moreover, tech-literate leaders are better equipped to address team concerns and create an inclusive culture around AI adoption. When leaders understand the basics, they can engage in meaningful conversations with tech teams, offer informed guidance, and address skepticism from employees who may worry about AI replacing jobs or infringing on privacy.

Strategies for Developing Technological Literacy
1. Engage in Ongoing Learning

Leaders can build technological literacy through continuous learning. This might involve attending industry conferences, enrolling in AI-related workshops, or participating in online courses that cover essential AI concepts. Many platforms, such as Coursera, offer short courses on AI fundamentals tailored for business leaders. Leaders can stay updated on AI developments and gain insight into emerging technologies by investing time in these learning opportunities.

2. Collaborate with Technical Experts

Building close relationships with technical experts within the organization is invaluable. Leaders can create a culture of open communication with their AI and data teams, where they regularly discuss projects, tools, and the reasoning behind technological choices. This direct engagement not only helps leaders understand AI in practical terms but also builds trust and collaboration between tech teams and management.

3. Experiment with Small-Scale AI Projects

Leaders can develop knowledge by piloting small, manageable AI projects. These pilot initiatives allow leaders to see how AI functions in real-time, providing insights into the technology's capabilities and challenges. For example, a sales team leader might experiment with AI-driven predictive analytics for customer trends. By understanding how the technology works on a smaller scale, they can make better decisions when expanding AI use.

4. Read and Stay Informed on AI Trends

Staying informed on industry trends is another way to boost technological literacy. Regularly reading about AI advancements through tech publications, case studies, or industry reports helps leaders understand the subject and identify opportunities that could benefit their organization.

Consider a chief operating officer (COO) aiming to implement AI to optimize warehouse management at a logistics company. With a solid foundation in technological literacy, the COO recognizes which AI tools are most appropriate, understands the data quality requirements, and anticipates potential challenges. They consult closely with the data science team to select an AI system that aligns with the company's operational goals without overburdening the team. Being well-informed enables them to address concerns, make confident investment decisions, and clearly communicate the project's purpose to employees.

For leaders in the AI era, technological literacy isn't a luxury; it's a necessity. By understanding the fundamentals of AI, they're equipped to make decisions that balance innovation with practical needs. Developing technological literacy is a powerful step in becoming a leader who keeps up with change and actively shapes it for lasting impact.

Ethical Leadership in AI

In today's AI-driven world, leaders face complex ethical challenges, including safeguarding data privacy, addressing algorithmic bias, and ensuring transparency in decision-making processes. As AI takes on a more central role in decision-making, leaders are confronted with complex issues that often lack straightforward solutions. Ethical reasoning becomes essential in these situations, guiding leaders to make choices that comply with legal standards and reflect the organization's core values, uphold broader societal principles, and maintain public trust.

Key Ethical Challenges

Some of the main ethical challenges in AI include:

Data Privacy and Security

With AI relying on vast amounts of data, protecting personal and sensitive information is a significant concern. Leaders must ensure that data collection and usage policies are transparent and secure and that AI systems are designed with privacy as a priority.

Algorithmic Bias

AI systems can inadvertently reinforce or even amplify biases present in their training data, leading to unfair treatment or discrimination. For example, hiring algorithms may favor certain demographics over others, resulting in biased hiring practices. Leaders need to recognize and address these biases to ensure fair and equitable AI applications.

Transparency and Accountability

Transparency in AI decision-making processes is crucial, especially in areas directly impacting individuals, like healthcare, finance, or criminal justice. Leaders must ensure that AI systems are explainable so users understand how decisions are made and can hold the organization accountable.

Frameworks for Ethical Decision-Making in AI

To guide ethical leadership in AI, leaders can use frameworks that encourage structured, thoughtful decision-making:

The Fairness, Accountability, and Transparency (FAT) Framework

This framework encourages leaders to consider fairness, accountability, and transparency at each stage of AI development and deployment. Leaders can make more ethical choices by assessing whether AI applications treat all users fairly, whether there are accountability mechanisms in place, and whether the system operates transparently.

The Principle-Based Approach

This approach relies on core ethical principles, such as respect, honesty, and responsibility, to guide AI-related decisions. Leaders can assess whether AI initiatives align with these principles, ensuring that ethical considerations remain a priority throughout the lifecycle of AI projects.

Stakeholder Impact Analysis

Leaders can also assess the impact of AI systems on various stakeholders, from customers to employees and society at large. By identifying potential positive and negative outcomes for each group, leaders can weigh the broader social impact of AI and make decisions that balance organizational goals with ethical considerations.

Inspiring Through Change

Leading teams through AI-driven transformation requires strategic vision along with the ability to inspire and motivate. Change can often be met with resistance, especially when it involves new technologies. Leaders can guide their teams through the transformation with enthusiasm and buy-in by creating a compelling vision, fostering a culture of innovation, and promoting continuous learning.

Creating a Compelling Vision

A clear and compelling vision is essential for inspiring teams through change. Leaders should articulate how AI will enhance the organization, improve outcomes, or make daily tasks easier, emphasizing the benefits to both the organization and individuals. For example, a leader might share stories of how AI can automate repetitive tasks, allowing employees to focus on more creative, fulfilling work. This vision gives teams a reason to embrace AI, seeing it not as a threat but as a tool for growth.

Promoting a Culture of Innovation

Leaders must cultivate a culture that values experimentation, creativity, and innovation. This involves creating an environment where employees feel supported in exploring AI applications, testing new ideas, and learning from successes and setbacks. Leaders can promote this culture by recognizing and rewarding innovative thinking, celebrating incremental achievements, and providing support as teams engage with AI solutions. This approach boosts morale and embeds a forward-looking mindset within the organization, positioning it for sustained growth and adaptability.

Encouraging Continuous Learning

AI technologies evolve quickly, and employees need to feel equipped to keep up. Leaders can inspire confidence by providing resources, workshops, and training opportunities that allow employees to build AI literacy and understand the tools they're working with. By promoting a mindset of continuous learning, leaders empower employees to adapt, grow, and embrace the technology. This sense of mastery can reduce fear and uncertainty, making the transition to an AI-driven organization smoother and more successful.

Consider a healthcare leader implementing AI-driven diagnostics. By emphasizing the vision of improved patient care, creating an environment where healthcare professionals can experiment with AI tools without fear of judgment, and offering ongoing training, the leader can inspire teams to adopt these technologies with enthusiasm. Instead of seeing AI as a disruptive force, the team views it as a powerful aid in providing high-quality patient care.

In summary, ethical leadership and inspirational change management are essential to understanding AI transformations successfully. Leaders who prioritize ethical decision-making and foster a culture of vision, innovation, and continuous learning form an organization that not only adapts to AI but thrives with it, positioning itself as a responsible, forward-looking leader in the AI era.

Storytelling in the Digital Age

In today's digital world, storytelling has become a powerful tool for leaders, especially when guiding their organizations through transformative changes like adopting AI. Leaders who can clearly communicate the potential of AI through relatable, compelling stories often have a much easier time rallying their teams around new ideas and easing any fears about change. By painting a vision of what's possible and showing the real impact of AI, leaders can help employees see AI not just as a technology but as an exciting, valuable part of their work.

Using Storytelling to Make AI Real

One of the biggest hurdles leaders face with AI adoption is that it can feel abstract or intimidating to employees. Stories bring AI down to earth. By sharing real-world examples—whether from within the company or from other businesses—leaders can show how AI tools improve day-to-day tasks, support strategic goals, or even lead to breakthroughs. For example, instead of just announcing a new AI-driven customer service tool, a leader might share a story about how a similar tool reduced wait times and boosted customer satisfaction at another company. This makes the idea of adopting AI tangible and relatable, sparking interest rather than resistance.

Vision-Casting to Build Excitement and Trust

Beyond just explaining what AI can do, vision-casting allows leaders to connect these possibilities with the company's mission and future goals. This is where leaders can be aspirational, casting a vision that taps into the team's shared purpose. For instance, a healthcare executive implementing AI might paint a picture of a future where AI enables faster diagnostics, improving patient outcomes and making healthcare more accessible. By linking AI to a purpose the team already cares about, the leader makes the change feel meaningful and exciting.

Take Microsoft's CEO, Satya Nadella, as an example. Nadella frequently uses storytelling to illustrate how AI can empower users. He shares examples of how AI has helped businesses of all kinds, from small startups to global corporations, achieve things they couldn't before. By sharing these stories, he shows employees and customers the positive, human side of AI, making it feel accessible and beneficial.

Another example comes from Netflix. When Netflix began integrating AI-driven recommendation algorithms, leaders emphasized how this technology would enhance the viewer experience by making content discovery more personal and intuitive. Instead of focusing on the technical side, they shared a vision of giving customers a more enjoyable and tailored experience.

Creating a Storytelling Culture Around AI

For leaders aiming to embed storytelling in their AI strategy, it's helpful to create an open dialogue about AI's role in the company. Encouraging teams to share their experiences with AI, celebrate wins, and discuss challenges can create a storytelling culture that brings AI to life. When employees see the positive effects of AI firsthand and hear real examples from their colleagues, trust in the transformation journey is built.

Ultimately, storytelling and vision-casting serve to connect technological innovation with the human experience. Leaders who use these tools make AI feel less like a foreign technology and more like a powerful ally in achieving shared goals. With a compelling narrative, they guide their organizations through change, inspire excitement, and build a sense of shared purpose that can make the AI journey successful.

One remarkable example of a leader who embodies the **Homo Magister** ideal is Arvind Krishna, CEO of IBM. Leading one of the oldest tech companies in the world, Krishna has been instrumental in guiding IBM through a period of AI-driven transformation while staying true to its values and legacy. His approach illustrates the Homo

Magister model—a leader who combines mentorship with strategic foresight to drive meaningful change.

When Krishna became CEO, IBM was already known for its AI innovation, but he took on the task of embedding AI even deeper into the company's core operations and culture. Rather than simply imposing AI across the board, Krishna worked to make the transition both thoughtful and inclusive. He began by emphasizing continuous learning and upskilling, ensuring that employees had the knowledge and confidence to engage with AI tools and concepts. Krishna didn't just focus on technical training; he encouraged a shift in mindset, helping employees see AI as a tool to enhance their skills rather than a threat to their roles.

Krishna also prioritized open communication and collaboration. He encouraged teams to share their experiences and ideas, creating a feedback loop where employees could voice concerns and celebrate wins. By listening closely to feedback, he was able to adjust AI initiatives as they unfolded, making the process feel organic rather than forced. He championed transparency about AI's potential impact on jobs and productivity, showing a genuine commitment to aligning AI with employee and organizational well-being.

One of Krishna's biggest challenges was addressing the fear of job displacement. AI transformations often bring uncertainty, and employees naturally worry about whether automation might render their roles obsolete. Krishna tackled this by clearly communicating IBM's vision for AI as a supportive technology—one that would automate repetitive tasks, freeing up employees to focus on higher-value work. By framing AI as a tool to augment rather than replace, he was able to ease fears and build trust in the transformation.

Another challenge was promoting cross-functional **collaboration** in a company as large and established as IBM. Silos are common in big organizations, and they can stifle innovation. Krishna worked to bring different departments together, encouraging them to collaborate on AI initiatives that touched various business areas, from customer service to product development. Through this integrated approach, he enabled departments to share insights and tackle AI projects with a unified perspective.

Under Krishna's leadership, IBM has become a pioneer in AI and cloud computing, solidifying its position as a major player in enterprise technology. The shift toward AI-enhanced operations has streamlined IBM's internal processes and led to the development of groundbreaking products, such as IBM Watson for Healthcare, which supports faster, more accurate diagnostics.

Krishna's approach has had a lasting impact on IBM's culture, too. By embodying the Homo Magister ideal, he has reshaped IBM into a more adaptive, learning-focused organization. Employees at IBM now engage with AI not as an imposed technology but as a tool they helped to shape, making them more invested in the company's success.

Arvind Krishna's journey as CEO of IBM showcases the power of Homo Magister leadership in an AI-driven world. By balancing strategic vision with mentorship, he has guided IBM through a transformative period with empathy and purpose and created an organization that embraces AI and thrives with it.[36]

Developing Homo Magister Capabilities

Becoming a Homo Magister leader requires knowledge, empathy, and hands-on experience. In the AI era, this approach is especially valuable, as it empowers leaders to understand complex technology while supporting their teams' growth. Mentioned below are detailed strategies to develop the capabilities needed to embody Homo Magister leadership.

Commit to Continuous Learning

In a rapidly evolving field like AI, continuous learning is essential. Leaders can't rely solely on what they've learned in the past; they need to stay updated on emerging trends, tools, and strategies. Developing technological literacy through online courses, industry seminars, and workshops is a strong starting point.

However, continuous learning goes beyond taking courses. Engaging in thoughtful reading, including industry articles, research papers, and case studies, helps leaders understand AI trends and gain insight into how other

---

[36]https://newsroom.ibm.com/Arvind-Krishna

organizations are applying these tools. Leaders who make time for reading and discussion groups on these topics foster a habit of lifelong learning that is critical for staying relevant and informed.

Engage in Mentorship and Reverse Mentorship Programs

Mentorship is a two-way street. To truly embody the Homo Magister ideal, leaders should both mentor others and engage in reverse mentorship, where they learn from team members who are more familiar with specific technologies or methodologies. Mentoring team members on business and leadership skills helps leaders build trust, while reverse mentorship on emerging technologies allows them to understand AI's practical applications from those actively working with it.

Setting up a formal mentorship program within the organization is beneficial. Leaders can regularly meet with promising team members and offer guidance on career development and professional growth. Through these sessions, they can also gain fresh perspectives on the challenges and opportunities the company faces. This helps leaders stay connected to all levels of the organization, creating a culture of learning and growth.

Seek Immersive Experiences in AI and Emerging Technologies

For leaders, gaining hands-on experience with AI and emerging technologies can make a significant difference in their understanding. Participating in immersive learning experiences such as hackathons, AI boot camps, or innovation labs would give leaders a firsthand look at how these technologies work. Even if they aren't coding, observing AI applications in action enables leaders to understand the technology's capabilities and limitations.

For example, some companies host internal "AI days" where teams work on AI-related projects together. Leaders can join these sessions to observe and even participate in discussions on AI's potential applications within the organization. This direct exposure not only helps leaders understand how their teams interact with AI tools but also allows them to make better decisions about AI investments and strategies.

Emphasize Ethical Training and Decision-Making Skills

Developing ethical reasoning skills is crucial for making decisions that align with organizational values and social responsibilities. Leaders can participate in workshops and courses focused on AI ethics, data privacy, and responsible use of technology to sharpen their ethical decision-making skills. For instance, programs like MIT's "Ethics of AI" can provide leaders with frameworks for considering fairness, accountability, and transparency in AI.

In addition, establishing an ethics committee or an advisory board can provide leaders with valuable support and feedback on AI projects, which would allow them to approach technology decisions from multiple perspectives.

Foster a Culture of Experimentation and Innovation

A Homo Magister leader doesn't shy away from experimentation. Instead, they encourage their teams to test new ideas, learn from failures, and innovate freely. Leaders can foster this culture by setting up innovation hubs or dedicated experimentation budgets, allowing teams to explore AI solutions with minimal risk. This builds confidence within the team and encourages creative thinking.

Moreover, leaders can lead by example by sharing their own learning experiences and challenges, showing that they, too, are constantly evolving. Celebrating small successes and openly discussing what went wrong reinforces a growth mindset across the organization.

Build Cross-Disciplinary Knowledge

Homo Magister leaders understand that AI-driven transformation impacts every area of a business. To develop a well-rounded perspective, leaders should seek to build cross-disciplinary knowledge. This involves understanding the basics of finance, marketing, operations, and human resources, as these areas often intersect with AI applications. For instance, a leader aware of supply chain operations can better appreciate how AI-driven analytics could improve logistics.

Cross-functional projects or job rotations within the company can provide valuable exposure to different departments, allowing leaders to see how AI could be used in each area. This holistic understanding enables leaders to connect AI strategies with business needs and empowers them to lead more effectively.

Becoming a Homo Magister leader in the AI era requires more than just technical skills. It demands a mindset of continuous learning, ethical grounding, and a commitment to mentorship. These strategies don't just prepare leaders for the current technological landscape; they equip them to guide their organizations through an ever-evolving future, balancing innovation with values and purpose.

Overcoming Leadership Challenges in AI-Driven Transformation

Guiding an organization through an AI-driven transformation is no small task, and leaders often encounter a range of challenges. From resistance to change and skill gaps to ethical dilemmas, these obstacles can slow down progress if not carefully managed. However, with the right strategies, leaders can face these challenges effectively and promote a culture that embraces AI as an opportunity rather than a threat.

Addressing Resistance to Change

Resistance to change is one of the most common hurdles in any transformation, and AI adoption is no exception. Employees may feel apprehensive about how AI will impact their jobs, worry about learning new skills, or simply be uncomfortable with the shift in processes. Leaders must take a proactive approach to build trust and foster an open mindset toward AI.

Strategies to Overcome Resistance

- **Communicate a Clear Vision**: Leaders should articulate a clear and compelling vision of how AI will benefit the organization and its people. By sharing specific examples of how AI can make tasks easier, improve decision-making, or support growth, leaders can help employees see the potential value in the change.

- **Involve Employees Early**: Involving employees in the early stages of AI initiatives can help ease resistance. Leaders can create task forces or focus groups that allow employees to voice their concerns, suggest ideas, and feel a sense of ownership in the transformation. When employees feel included, they're more likely to support the change.

- **Provide Support and Training**: Offering AI literacy programs or hands-on training sessions can build confidence and make the transition smoother.

When employees feel supported in learning new skills, they are less likely to resist AI-driven changes.

Closing Skill Gaps

As AI tools become integrated into more roles, skill gaps within the workforce can pose a significant challenge. Employees may lack the technical knowledge needed to work with AI systems effectively, or they may feel overwhelmed by the rapid pace of technological change. Leaders must address these gaps to ensure their teams can fully engage with AI.

Strategies to Overcome Skill Gaps

- **Invest in Upskilling and Reskilling**: Leaders can introduce programs to help employees gain the skills needed to work with AI. Online courses, internal workshops, and partnerships with educational platforms are effective ways to build technical literacy across the organization.

- **Create Mentorship Opportunities**: By pairing employees with more tech-savvy colleagues or mentors, leaders can foster a collaborative learning environment. Reverse mentorship programs, where junior employees with technical knowledge mentor more senior staff, can be particularly effective.

- **Promote a Growth Mindset**: Leaders should emphasize that learning AI-related skills is a gradual, ongoing process. By creating a culture that celebrates continuous learning and values improvement over perfection, leaders can reduce employees' fear of failure and motivate them to embrace new skills.

Ethical Dilemmas

AI introduces complex ethical considerations, such as data privacy, algorithmic bias, and transparency. Leaders must be prepared to address these issues thoughtfully to ensure the responsible and fair use of AI. Ethical dilemmas can create uncertainty among employees and stakeholders, making it essential for leaders to take a strong, clear stance on ethical standards.

Strategies to Overcome Ethical Challenges

Several strategies are essential to address ethical challenges effectively, particularly in AI. Organizations can strengthen their ethical framework by incorporating a code of ethics and supporting responsible AI practices. This approach guides ethical decisions, ensuring that technology serves organizational and societal goals responsibly.

1. Establish a Clear Code of Ethics for AI: Creating a specific AI ethics code helps outline acceptable AI practices, protecting against potential misuse. Leaders can involve cross-functional teams in defining ethical standards tailored to the unique AI needs within the organization. This helps foster a culture where every team member understands their ethical responsibilities in AI development and deployment.

2. Integrate Responsible AI into Corporate Strategy: CDiGlobal Consulting offers services designed to implement a comprehensive responsible AI strategy. This strategy is crafted to align with an organization's broader goals, ensuring ethical AI use supports overall business objectives and respects stakeholder interests. By embedding responsible AI within the grand corporate strategy, companies can ensure that their AI initiatives align with both business priorities and ethical standards.

3. Prioritize Transparency and Accountability: Implementing transparency practices like explainable AI (XAI) allows stakeholders to understand AI decisions, fostering trust. Additionally, establishing clear accountability measures helps ensure responsible AI use across all levels of the organization.

4. Conduct Regular Audits and Updates: To stay ahead of evolving ethical challenges, regular audits of AI systems are essential. CDiGlobal's responsible AI strategy includes periodic reviews to identify potential ethical risks, monitor compliance, and update practices as technology and regulations change. This continuous improvement cycle ensures AI ethics remain relevant and effective.

5. Provide Ethics Training: Training employees on responsible AI practices is crucial for maintaining high ethical standards. This training helps teams understand potential ethical dilemmas in AI and equips them to handle these responsibly, supporting the organization's commitment to ethical integrity.

These strategies, reinforced by the responsible AI initiatives from CDiGlobal Consulting, enable organizations to implement AI in a way that aligns with both ethical expectations and business goals. This approach helps mitigate risks, safeguard trust, and promote responsible, ethical AI practices.

Balancing Short-Term Goals with Long-Term Vision

AI can bring rapid, short-term benefits to efficiency and cost savings, but focusing only on these can undermine the organization's long-term goals. Leaders need to balance the immediate gains of AI with a strategic vision for the future, ensuring that AI initiatives align with the organization's broader purpose.

Strategies to Maintain Balance

- **Set Clear AI Objectives**: Leaders should define both short- and long-term objectives for AI initiatives. While efficiency gains and process automation are valuable, AI should also contribute to sustainable growth, improved customer experiences, or other strategic goals.

- **Evaluate ROI Beyond Financials**: Leaders can look beyond financial returns when evaluating AI's impact. Metrics such as employee engagement, customer satisfaction, and innovation rates provide a fuller picture of how AI is supporting the organization's vision.

- **Iterate and Reassess**: AI-driven transformation should be an ongoing process. Leaders should regularly evaluate AI projects and adjust strategies as needed, ensuring alignment with the organization's evolving goals.

Leading an organization through AI-driven transformation comes with unique challenges, from managing resistance and skill gaps to addressing ethical considerations. By actively engaging employees, providing growth opportunities, and establishing a strong ethical foundation, leaders can overcome these obstacles and build a culture that embraces AI with enthusiasm and responsibility.

AI-Augmented Leadership

AI-augmented leadership is about leveraging these tools to improve decision-making, foster stronger team dynamics, and even support personalized leadership development. By incorporating AI into their daily practices, leaders can work more effectively and make more informed, strategic decisions.

Data-Driven Decision-Making

AI equips leaders with data-driven insights, enabling them to make well-informed decisions based on real-time analytics and predictive models. Rather than relying on intuition or past experience alone, leaders can now use AI to analyze market trends, customer behavior, and operational metrics with precision. For instance, a retail CEO might use AI to track inventory patterns and optimize supply chain management, minimizing costs and improving efficiency. This data-driven approach ensures that leaders have a clear, objective view of their organization's performance, helping them make proactive, strategic choices.

Enhanced Employee Insights

AI tools allow leaders to gain deeper insights into their teams, identifying strengths, skills gaps, and areas for growth. With AI-powered sentiment analysis, for example, leaders can gauge employee morale by analyzing feedback from surveys, social platforms, and emails. This gives leaders a nuanced view of team dynamics, helping them address potential issues early and make adjustments to maintain a positive work culture. In addition, AI can help leaders identify high-potential employees, enabling them to tailor development plans and provide targeted support for career growth.

Personalized Leadership Development

AI-driven platforms are also transforming leadership development. Personalized programs powered by AI can assess a leader's current strengths and areas for improvement and then suggest tailored learning paths or coaching resources. For example, an AI platform might analyze a leader's communication style and recommend specific modules to enhance interpersonal skills. By providing these tailored learning experiences, AI helps leaders build relevant competencies faster and more effectively, supporting continuous growth and adaptability.

CDiGlobal Consulting's services are positioned to enhance leadership through personalized, AI-driven development programs tailored to individual strengths and growth areas. With AI's capabilities to analyze and interpret complex data, CDiGlobal can create bespoke leadership pathways that address the specific needs of each leader, aligning their personal development with the organization's strategic goals.

1. **Tailored Leadership Assessments**: By leveraging AI to assess leaders' skills—such as communication style, decision-making, and emotional intelligence—CDiGlobal can offer targeted feedback and developmental resources. The AI-driven insights allow leaders to focus on their unique improvement areas, resulting in a more effective and relevant learning experience.

2. **Custom Learning Paths and Coaching**: CDiGlobal's responsible AI strategy includes deploying adaptive learning modules that adjust as leaders progress, providing immediate, data-driven recommendations for further growth. For instance, if the platform identifies a leader's need for enhanced interpersonal skills, it might recommend specific training modules or connect them with specialized coaching resources.

3. **Alignment with Corporate Strategy**: Integrating AI into leadership development helps ensure that these

efforts are not only personalized but also aligned with the organization's broader mission. CDiGlobal's consulting services are designed to support companies in weaving responsible AI initiatives and leadership development into their corporate strategy. This ensures that the leadership pipeline is robust, strategically focused, and capable of driving ethical AI implementation across the organization.

4. Continuous Growth and Adaptability: The dynamic nature of AI-driven platforms enables CDiGlobal to support leaders in real-time, adapting learning paths as organizational needs and individual competencies evolve. This real-time adaptability promotes continuous growth, helping leaders stay agile and responsive to changes in their industry or company landscape.

By integrating responsible AI into leadership development, CDiGlobal Consulting provides organizations with a powerful framework that fosters both technical proficiency and ethical responsibility in their leaders. This ensures leaders are well-equipped to guide their teams through the challenges and opportunities of a technology-driven future.

Future of Leadership

As AI continues to evolve, so too will the role and requirements of leadership. Here are some predictions on how leadership will transform as AI reshapes organizational landscapes.

From Operational to Strategic Focus

As AI takes on more operational and administrative tasks, leaders will increasingly focus on big-picture strategy and vision. Routine responsibilities—such as data analysis, report generation, and even some aspects of performance management—will be augmented or handled by AI systems. This shift allows leaders to spend more time on strategic initiatives, cultural development, and building relationships within and outside the organization. Leaders of the future will be expected to prioritize foresight and long-term planning over daily management.

Emphasis on Ethical and Human-Centered Leadership

With AI's ability to automate and optimize, leaders will need to serve as ethical stewards of technology. This means leaders will be more active in establishing and upholding ethical standards, particularly around data privacy, algorithmic bias, and transparency. Future leaders will be valued for their strategic insights and commitment to ethical AI use, ensuring that technology serves the broader interests of employees, customers, and society.

Increased Need for Cross-Disciplinary Knowledge

In a future where AI impacts every facet of the organization, leaders will need a broader understanding of various domains, from technology and data science to human resources and compliance. This cross-disciplinary knowledge will enable leaders to make balanced decisions that consider the technological, human, and operational aspects of any AI-related strategy. Leaders will be expected to collaborate with data scientists, engineers, and ethicists, blending insights from different fields to drive integrated, responsible AI initiatives.

Focus on Continuous Learning and Adaptability

As AI and other technologies evolve at an accelerated pace, leaders must commit to continuous learning and adaptability. Future leaders will need to stay updated on AI advancements, industry shifts, and new management approaches. This learning mindset will help them remain agile, ready to pivot as new opportunities and challenges emerge. Organizations will likely expect leaders to engage in ongoing development, with AI-powered platforms offering tailored resources to support this growth.

Strengthening Soft Skills and Emotional Intelligence

With AI handling much of the technical work, the importance of **soft skills** will only increase. Leaders will need to excel in areas like empathy, communication, and emotional intelligence to connect with employees, understand diverse perspectives, and foster a supportive culture. These skills will be critical in helping teams navigate AI-driven changes, ensuring that employees feel valued, supported, and engaged in their work. The human touch will be central to future leadership, balancing AI's efficiency with compassion and understanding.

AI-augmented leadership is not just about using new tools; it's about reimagining what leaders can accomplish. By embracing AI for data-driven decisions, personalized growth, and deeper employee insights, today's leaders can position themselves and their organizations for success. As AI advances, leadership roles will continue to evolve, requiring a blend of ethical vision, adaptability, and soft skills that make leaders effective decision-makers and inspiring, human-centered guides through the AI-driven future.

Measuring Leadership Effectiveness in AI-Driven Transformation

In the context of AI-driven transformation, measuring leadership effectiveness requires a combination of both quantitative and qualitative metrics. To capture this multifaceted role, organizations should implement metrics that evaluate leaders' ability to drive results, promote a learning culture, and maintain a people-first approach.

Quantitative Metrics

Quantitative metrics provide clear, data-driven insights into leadership effectiveness by tracking progress and results in measurable terms. I have mentioned below some key quantitative metrics to consider:

- **Transformation Progress and Milestones**: Tracking the completion of AI transformation goals is essential. These metrics can include the percentage of AI initiatives completed on time, successful integration of AI tools, or specific project milestones reached. This helps measure a leader's ability to drive AI projects forward efficiently.

- **Adoption and Engagement Rates**: Gauging the adoption rates of AI tools among employees can provide insights into how effectively a leader has encouraged and managed the integration of AI within the organization. Engagement rates in training sessions, workshops, or feedback forums also show how well leaders have motivated employees to embrace AI.

- **Employee Retention and Turnover Rates**: High turnover or low retention rates can indicate potential issues in leadership, especially during transformative phases that may create employee anxiety. Leaders who effectively support their teams through change tend to maintain stable retention rates, signaling a positive work environment despite the disruption that AI transformation may bring.

- **Productivity and Efficiency Gains**: Effective leadership in AI-driven transformation should lead to measurable improvements in productivity and operational efficiency. Tracking key performance indicators (KPIs) related to cost savings, output rates, or time savings in processes impacted by AI provides a clear picture of how leadership is contributing to the organization's growth.

Qualitative Metrics

Quantitative data tells part of the story, but **qualitative metrics** capture the subtler aspects of leadership, such as employee sentiment, ethical alignment, and the overall culture fostered by the leader. Here are several qualitative metrics to include:

- **Employee Feedback and Sentiment Analysis**: Gathering feedback through surveys, one-on-one meetings, or group discussions can provide insights into how employees feel about AI-driven changes and the leader's approach to guiding them. AI-powered sentiment analysis tools can help interpret large volumes of feedback, identifying themes that reveal employee morale, trust, and engagement levels.

- **Innovation and Learning Culture**: Leaders who are effective in AI-driven transformation foster a culture of experimentation and continuous learning. Conducting surveys or focus groups to assess whether employees feel encouraged to experiment, propose ideas, and develop new skills can help determine if a leader is nurturing an innovative, adaptable environment.

- **Ethical Alignment and Transparency**: Evaluating a leader's commitment to ethical AI use is essential. Leaders should be assessed on their transparency about AI's impact on roles, privacy concerns, and data usage. Surveys or feedback sessions with employees can reveal whether the leader is perceived as upholding ethical standards, fostering trust, and addressing concerns openly.

- **Cross-Functional Collaboration and Inclusion**: Effective leaders break down silos and encourage collaboration across departments, especially during transformations that impact multiple areas of the business. Interviewing department heads, team leads, or project managers about the leader's support for cross-functional collaboration can provide insights into how well they are fostering a unified approach to AI adoption.

Combining both quantitative and qualitative metrics provides a holistic view of leadership effectiveness. For instance, a leader might achieve high engagement rates in AI training (quantitative) but receive feedback that some employees feel overwhelmed by the pace of change (qualitative). Together, these insights allow leaders to adjust their approach, balancing rapid AI adoption with a more supportive and personalized strategy.

Regularly evaluating leadership effectiveness is critical during AI-driven transformation. Organizations should implement ongoing evaluation processes to capture real-time insights rather than conducting annual reviews alone. Monthly or quarterly pulse surveys, feedback forums, and performance reviews help leaders stay responsive to emerging challenges and ensure their approach aligns with employee needs and organizational goals.

Developing Homo Magister leadership capabilities requires a commitment to self-reflection, skill-building, and real-world application. Here's a step-by-step action plan to help leaders cultivate these qualities:

1. Self-Assessment: In high-performance teams, starting at the individual level, I always say, "Conduct a SWOT analysis on yourself! Start by evaluating your current leadership style, strengths, and areas for improvement. Reflect on past experiences and gather feedback from colleagues or team members to gain insights into your approach. Key areas to assess include your communication style, adaptability, decision-making approach, and your ability to mentor and inspire others. This baseline understanding will help you set specific goals for your development journey.

2. Set Targeted Development Goals: Based on your self-assessment, set clear, actionable goals. For example, if you find that you need to improve your adaptability in tech-driven environments, your goal might be to gain more hands-on experience with AI tools. Another goal could be to enhance your mentoring skills by actively engaging with team members, guiding them through projects, and offering constructive feedback.

3. Build Technological Literacy: As AI transforms businesses, Homo Magister leaders need a working understanding of emerging technologies. Enroll in foundational courses on AI and data analytics through platforms like Coursera or LinkedIn Learning. This literacy will allow you to engage meaningfully with tech teams, ask informed questions, and better understand AI's applications and limitations within your organization.

4. Develop Mentorship and Communication Skills: Mentorship is at the core of the Homo Magister approach. Seek out opportunities to mentor junior employees, focusing on their growth and skills development. Engage in active listening, provide tailored guidance, and encourage their ideas. Additionally, work on your communication style by practicing transparency, empathy, and clarity. Participating in leadership workshops or communication training can strengthen these skills.

5. Practice Ethical Decision-Making: AI brings unique ethical challenges, from data privacy to algorithmic bias. Commit to developing a strong ethical framework by studying AI ethics and privacy best practices. Engage in discussions around these topics with peers and team members to broaden your perspective. Use frameworks such as the Fairness, Accountability, and Transparency (FAT) model to approach ethical dilemmas thoughtfully.

6. Engage in Cross-Functional Projects: AI impacts multiple facets of business, requiring leaders to think beyond their specific areas of expertise. Seek out cross-functional projects that allow you to collaborate with different departments. Working closely with teams from operations, HR, and data science, for example, gives you valuable experience in integrating AI solutions across the organization and helps you become more versatile in your leadership.

7. Apply and Iterate: Regularly apply your learning in real-world scenarios. Reflect on your actions, assess the outcomes, and be open to adjusting your approach. Ask for feedback from colleagues and team members after key projects or decisions, and use these insights to refine your Homo Magister capabilities continuously.

Reflections:

To assess your alignment with the Homo Magister approach and identify areas for development, consider these thought-provoking questions:

- How would I describe my current leadership style? Does it include elements of mentorship and empowerment?

- How well do I understand AI and emerging technologies, and how comfortable am I in discussing them with my team?

- Am I actively creating learning opportunities for my team members? How can I enhance my role as a mentor?

- Do I prioritize ethical considerations in my decision-making process? How can I ensure that AI initiatives align with my organization's values?

- In what ways have I encouraged cross-functional collaboration? What steps can I take to increase my involvement in multi-disciplinary projects?

- How adaptable am I when faced with new challenges, and how do I respond to feedback on my leadership style?

The journey to becoming a Homo Magister leader is one of continuous growth, adaptability, and purpose. As organizations face the challenges of AI-driven transformation, leaders who prioritize technological understanding, ethical decision-making, mentorship, and collaboration will be the most prepared to steer their teams through change. By embracing these Homo Magister capabilities, leaders can inspire trust, drive meaningful innovation, and create a balanced approach where technology and human values align. Ultimately, Homo Magister leaders not only adapt to the evolving demands of the AI era—they shape it and set a standard for thoughtful, responsible leadership in a world of constant change.

Chapter 10: Ensuring Responsible AI Use

A group of doctors gathered to discuss a recent recommendation from their new AI-driven healthcare system. The AI analyzed the symptoms, medical history, and similar cases to suggest an aggressive and out-of-the-ordinary treatment plan. The recommendation was data-driven and detailed, but it raised concerns among the doctors.

The patient was an older man with a complex background and would face serious risks if they followed this course of action. Some doctors doubted the AI's approach and worried it might overlook critical human judgment.

As they debated the next steps, bigger questions emerged. If they followed the AI's recommendation and it led to complications, who would be held responsible? Should they trust the AI, given its advanced data processing abilities? Or should human experience and caution take priority, especially in a high-risk situation? A few doctors argued in favor of AI, pointing out its accuracy in past cases. However, others felt the risks were too significant without a closer look and believed that human judgment should always balance AI decisions.

This situation brought forward an important ethical challenge in using AI in healthcare. While AI can offer powerful insights, it lacks the empathy and moral understanding that humans bring to difficult cases. The case made the team think about how they could combine AI's strengths with human expertise, aiming for a balanced approach that protects both safety and responsibility.

The Current AI Ethics

The field of AI ethics has rapidly evolved alongside advances in artificial intelligence, marking a growing emphasis on ensuring that AI technologies align with human values, rights, and societal needs. Basic ethical principles, international teamwork, evolving rules, and the need to stay actively involved all play a big role in how we approach AI. Below, we explore key facets of this dynamic field, highlighting how ongoing efforts aim to balance innovation with ethical considerations.

Key Principles of AI Ethics

The principles guiding AI ethics serve as foundational values that inform policy, regulation, and implementation practices. While variations exist, several core principles have emerged as widely accepted pillars for ethical AI development and deployment:

1. Transparency and Explainability

AI systems should be transparent and explainable to ensure that users and regulators can understand how decisions are made. Explainability also builds trust and accountability, as it allows stakeholders to question and understand AI's impact.

2. Fairness and Non-Discrimination

Fairness involves developing AI that does not perpetuate or amplify biases, ensuring that all users are treated equitably. Addressing biases in datasets and algorithms is critical to prevent discrimination, especially concerning race, gender, and socio-economic background.

3. Accountability

The concept of accountability requires clear frameworks to determine who is responsible for the actions and consequences of AI systems. Mechanisms for redress and accountability frameworks, such as assigning roles for oversight, help address issues arising from AI decisions.

4. Privacy and Data Protection

Privacy principles emphasize the need to protect personal data, advocating for responsible data collection, storage, and use. AI technologies often require large datasets, increasing the potential for privacy infringements, thus making this principle fundamental.

5. Human-Centered Design

AI should be designed and deployed with human values at the center, emphasizing that these technologies serve societal good and do not infringe on individual freedoms.

Human-centered design also prioritizes safety, intending to minimize harmful effects on people.

6. Safety and Security

Safety protocols aim to ensure that AI systems operate reliably and securely, particularly in high-stakes applications like healthcare and transportation. This principle includes safeguards to prevent the malicious use of AI and to protect against cybersecurity risks.

Global Initiatives Shaping AI Ethics

Recognizing the universal implications of AI, several global initiatives have emerged to guide ethical standards and best practices:

1. The European Union (EU)

The EU is a leading figure in AI regulation, with the proposed **Artificial Intelligence Act (AIA)** setting a precedent for regulating AI in high-risk applications. This legislation categorizes AI systems based on risk, imposing strict requirements for high-risk categories. The EU also enforces the **General Data Protection Regulation (GDPR)**, setting strong standards for data privacy, which influence how AI systems handle personal data globally.

2. The OECD Principles on Artificial Intelligence

The Organization for Economic Co-operation and Development (OECD) has developed a set of AI principles endorsed by over 40 countries, which focus on transparency, fairness, and accountability. These principles aim to promote a human-centered approach to AI, encouraging member countries to adopt responsible AI policies and practices.

3. UNESCO's Recommendation on the Ethics of Artificial Intelligence

UNESCO adopted its first global standard on AI ethics in 2021, which addresses issues like transparency, accountability, and human rights. This recommendation calls for member states to implement measures that ensure AI development aligns with ethical and human-centered values, focusing especially on marginalized communities.

4. IEEE Global Initiative on Ethics of Autonomous and Intelligent Systems

The IEEE has published several ethically aligned design guidelines for AI, helping developers prioritize values like transparency and inclusiveness. This initiative is also notable for its emphasis on embedding ethical thinking in engineering education and practice, bridging technical standards with social values.

5. World Economic Forum (WEF) Centre for the Fourth Industrial Revolution

WEF's AI and Machine Learning platforms foster international collaboration to develop governance frameworks and ethical AI use cases. Through multistakeholder partnerships, the WEF addresses the intersection of AI ethics and policy, encouraging responsible innovation.

Emerging Regulations and Policy Developments

Countries and regions around the world are enacting legislation to govern the ethical use of AI, reflecting the urgency and complexity of these issues. Some of the most notable developments include:

1. The European Union's Artificial Intelligence Act

The proposed AIA is a revolutionary regulatory approach to AI, classifying applications into categories like high-risk, limited-risk, and minimal-risk.

High-risk systems (such as those used in law enforcement or critical infrastructure) will require stringent oversight, transparency, and risk management measures, making this Act a potential global model.

2. United States: Blueprint for an AI Bill of Rights

The U.S. White House released a Blueprint for an AI Bill of Rights, which lays out protections concerning privacy, algorithmic discrimination, and the need for clear explanations of AI decisions.

While not legally binding, it offers guidance for federal agencies and private organizations on ethical AI practices.

3. China's AI Regulations

China's regulatory framework for AI includes guidelines on data protection and ethical development, with a focus on AI security.

The **Personal Information Protection Law (PIPL)** in China regulates data processing, and AI systems must comply, especially concerning user consent and data handling.

4. AI Regulation in Canada

Canada has proposed the **Artificial Intelligence and Data Act (AIDA),** which aims to establish clear standards for AI and data handling.

AIDA focuses on balancing innovation with ethical safeguards, particularly in high-impact sectors like healthcare and finance.

5 Sector-Specific Policies

Various industries, such as healthcare, finance, and autonomous vehicles, are seeing sector-specific policies to manage the unique ethical challenges posed by AI.

For instance, in healthcare, policies emphasize accuracy, accountability, and patient data protection, given the sensitivity and potential risks involved.

The Evolving Nature of AI Ethics

AI ethics is inherently dynamic, influenced by rapid technological advances, shifting social norms, and growing public awareness. This evolving nature means that ethical standards and regulations must remain adaptable, with active, ongoing engagement among stakeholders. Key aspects of this evolution include:

- **Continuous Monitoring and Evaluation**: AI systems require regular assessment to address new ethical challenges that arise as technologies advance.

- **Public Engagement and Inclusion**: The voices of diverse communities are critical to ensuring AI development reflects a broad spectrum of human experiences and values.

- **Multidisciplinary Collaboration**: AI ethics necessitates collaboration across fields like law, philosophy, computer science, and sociology, promoting holistic solutions to ethical dilemmas.

- **Proactive Research on Emerging Risks**: As new AI applications emerge, research into potential social, economic, and environmental impacts is essential to preemptively address ethical concerns.

Given the transformative nature of AI, ongoing engagement in ethical discussions is essential to balance innovation with ethical responsibility. Stakeholders—including policymakers, developers, ethicists, and the public—must collaborate to keep pace with advancements. This engagement can take several forms:

- **Policy Iteration and Revision**: Governments and regulatory bodies must periodically update AI regulations to accommodate new challenges and applications.

- **Public Education and Awareness**: Enhancing public understanding of AI ethics can lead to more informed discussions, enabling individuals to advocate for ethical AI.

- **Industry Responsibility and Self-Regulation**: Tech companies are encouraged to self-regulate by adopting ethical guidelines and conducting impact assessments for AI products.

- **Academic and Research Contributions**: Continuous research into ethical frameworks and interdisciplinary studies will enrich the AI ethics field, addressing both current and emerging issues.

While these efforts aim to build a responsible AI ecosystem, the field must remain adaptable to address the rapid advancements in AI technologies. A commitment to ongoing engagement across disciplines and geographies is essential to ensure that AI aligns with ethical standards, protects human rights, and serves the common good. This continuous, collective effort is the cornerstone of building a future where AI technologies are not only innovative but also ethically grounded.

Ethical Pitfalls in AI Implementation

As AI becomes more common in various sectors, it's essential to understand the ethical challenges that come with adopting this technology. Key ethical issues, like bias, privacy violations, lack of transparency, and job displacement, can have serious consequences for people and society. I have mentioned these issues in detail, along with real-world examples that illustrate the impact.

1. Bias in AI

AI systems can unintentionally adopt biases present in the data they are trained on. This happens when historical or societal biases(often around race, gender, or socioeconomic status) are reflected in the data, leading the AI to make unfair or biased decisions.

- **Example**: In the U.S., a health algorithm used by hospitals to prioritize patient care was found to be biased against Black patients. Because the algorithm used past healthcare costs as a measure of healthcare needs, it overlooked the fact that Black patients often have less access to care due to systemic inequality. As a result, Black patients received lower priority, even when they had similar health conditions.[37]

- **Consequence**: Bias in AI can lead to unequal access to services, unfair treatment, and a loss of trust in AI

---

[37] https://pubmed.ncbi.nlm.nih.gov/31649194/

systems, especially in critical areas like healthcare, hiring, and law enforcement.

2. Privacy Violations

AI often relies on large amounts of personal data to learn and make predictions. However, collecting and using this data can raise privacy concerns, especially when it involves sensitive information or lacks user consent.

- **Example**: Facial recognition technology, used in public spaces for surveillance, has sparked controversy worldwide. In London, a facial recognition system used by law enforcement captured and stored images of countless people without their consent. This raised serious privacy concerns, as many people did not know they were being monitored or that their images were being stored.[38]

- **Consequence**: Privacy violations can lead to a loss of personal freedom and security. People may feel constantly watched, which can affect their behavior. Additionally, data leaks or misuse can expose individuals to identity theft or other risks.

---

[38]https://www.bbc.com/news/uk-51237665

3. Lack of Transparency

AI systems are often complex, making it difficult to understand how they reach certain decisions. This lack of transparency, sometimes referred to as the "black box" problem, can be problematic, especially when AI is used to make important decisions that affect people's lives.

- **Example**: In the judicial system, some courts in the U.S. use AI-based tools to assess the likelihood of reoffending when determining bail or sentencing. However, these tools often lack transparency. People affected by the decisions may not understand how the system reached its conclusions, and judges may not fully understand the tool's limitations or biases.[39]

- **Consequence**: When AI lacks transparency, it becomes harder to hold the system accountable for mistakes. People affected by the decisions may feel powerless, and the lack of clarity can undermine trust in the entire process.

4. Job Displacement

AI has the potential to automate many tasks, which can be beneficial for productivity but also leads to concerns about job displacement. As AI takes over certain roles, workers in those positions face the risk of losing their jobs, which can have significant economic and social impacts.

---

[39] https://www.propublica.org/article/machine-bias-risk-assessments-in-criminal-sentencing

- **Example**: In the manufacturing industry, companies are increasingly using robots and AI for tasks that were once performed by human workers. For instance, in automotive assembly lines, AI-driven robots have replaced many manual roles, leading to job losses in areas that rely heavily on manufacturing jobs.[40]

- **Consequence**: Job displacement due to AI can lead to economic hardship, especially in communities where affected jobs are a major source of income. This shift can also widen social inequality, as workers without advanced skills may struggle to find new opportunities.

The ethical challenges in AI adoption are serious and require thoughtful solutions. Addressing issues like bias, privacy, transparency, and job displacement is crucial to ensure that AI serves society fairly and responsibly. With ongoing awareness and effort, organizations and policymakers can work toward minimizing these ethical pitfalls and making AI a force for positive change.

Explainable AI

Explainable AI (XAI) is a branch of artificial intelligence focused on making AI systems more understandable for people. Unlike traditional "black box" AI, which makes decisions in ways that are hard to interpret, explainable AI

---

[40]https://www.mckinsey.com/featured-insights/future-of-work/the-future-of-work-in-america-people-and-places-today-and-tomorrow

aims to show clearly how it arrives at a result. This is especially important in cases where AI affects real-life outcomes, like deciding if someone gets approved for a loan or determining the priority level for a patient's medical treatment. Explainable AI helps people understand and trust the decisions made by machines, ensuring that AI is transparent and accountable.

Explainable AI Functionality

Explainable AI works by using methods that reveal the reasoning behind an AI model's predictions or decisions. One common approach is **feature importance**. This means showing which parts of the data most influenced the AI's decision. For instance, if an AI model decides whether someone qualifies for a mortgage, feature importance would indicate factors like income, credit score, or debt levels that played key roles in the decision. Another technique is **counterfactual explanations**, which describe how a slight change in the input data might alter the result. For example, it might show that if someone's credit score were just a few points higher, they would have been approved for a loan. Both methods provide clearer insights into how the AI system is thinking, which makes it easier for users to follow its logic.

Applications of Explainable AI

Explainable AI is used in areas where high-stakes decisions are involved, and transparency is critical. In **healthcare**, for example, doctors rely on XAI to help interpret AI-based diagnoses. If an AI tool suggests a possible disease, XAI can explain which symptoms or data points influenced that suggestion, helping doctors to confirm or question the AI's recommendation. In **finance**, banks use explainable AI to clarify why a loan or credit application was approved or denied, which is essential both for customer trust and regulatory compliance. Explainable AI is also applied in **criminal justice**, where risk assessment tools are used to evaluate the likelihood of reoffending. XAI can help explain these risk scores to ensure that they are fair and unbiased.

Limitations of Explainable AI

Despite its benefits, explainable AI has limitations. One of the main challenges is that, in making a model easier to understand, we sometimes lose accuracy. Highly accurate models, like deep learning networks, are often complex and less transparent. Simplifying them to make them explainable can reduce their effectiveness. Another issue is that not every AI system can be fully explained. Deep learning models, especially, are built from many layers of complex computations that are hard to interpret, even with advanced XAI techniques.

Additionally, the explanations provided by XAI might still be too technical for everyday users, meaning that while the AI's logic may be clearer to an expert, it's still difficult for a layperson to understand. Finally, explainable AI cannot fully remove bias. If the data used to train an AI system contains bias, then the explanations will reflect that bias. Transparency does not necessarily fix this underlying issue; it simply makes it visible.

Explainable AI is a valuable tool for making AI decisions more understandable and trustworthy. By shedding light on how AI systems work, XAI can improve accountability, especially in critical areas like healthcare, finance, and criminal justice. However, it also has its limits, especially with complex models and biased data. Explainable AI, therefore, should be part of a broader ethical approach, ensuring not only transparency but also fairness and responsibility in AI decision-making.

Organizational Impact of Ethical AI

Prioritizing ethical AI is increasingly important for organizations across industries, affecting several key areas, from product development to customer relationships and regulatory compliance. Ethical AI, which includes principles like fairness, accountability, and transparency, is not just a technical matter but a strategic priority that influences an organization's culture, structure, and reputation.

Impact on Product Development

Organizations that prioritize ethical AI often incorporate fairness and transparency principles from the start of the development process. For example, when creating new AI-powered products, ethical guidelines might require diverse datasets to ensure that the system works fairly across different demographics. This could mean additional steps in the development phase, like conducting fairness audits or bias testing. While these processes may lengthen the time it takes to bring products to market, they help ensure that the final product does not inadvertently harm or exclude certain groups. Moreover, ethical AI standards lead companies to build AI systems that can explain their decisions to users, which can add another layer of complexity but also enhance trust in the product.

Customer Trust and Brand Reputation

Ethical AI practices are increasingly linked to customer trust and loyalty. In a time when consumers are more aware of privacy and bias issues, organizations that adopt ethical AI practices are likely to gain a competitive advantage. For example, a company that openly communicates how its AI respects user privacy and avoids bias can differentiate itself from competitors who may be less transparent. This commitment to ethics helps foster customer loyalty, as consumers are more likely to trust and engage with brands that demonstrate responsibility. Ethical AI also reduces the risk of public relations crises stemming from unethical AI behavior, like data misuse or biased decisions, which can severely damage an organization's reputation.

Regulatory Compliance and Legal Risks

As governments implement stricter regulations around AI, prioritizing ethical practices helps organizations stay compliant and avoid legal repercussions. Regulations like the EU's Artificial Intelligence Act require companies to follow ethical guidelines, especially when deploying high-risk AI systems. By proactively adopting ethical AI standards, organizations can ensure they meet these regulations, reducing the likelihood of fines or lawsuits. This approach also aligns with preparing for future regulations, which are expected to increase as AI becomes more integrated into daily life.

Internal Culture and Employee Morale

Adopting ethical AI standards can also improve an organization's internal culture. Employees increasingly prefer working for companies that uphold ethical standards, and fostering an ethical AI culture can boost morale and retention. When employees see their company prioritizing ethics, it reinforces a sense of pride and shared values, which strengthens team cohesion. Ethical AI practices can lead to the formation of specialized roles and departments, such as ethics officers or fairness teams, creating new opportunities for employees to engage in socially impactful work.

As AI continues to evolve, organizations prioritizing ethics in their AI strategy will experience long-term benefits in trust, compliance, and innovation.

Homo Magister Perspective on AI Ethics

When it comes to AI, leaders who embody the Homo Magister ideal have a crucial role. They are the ones who can lead AI adoption in ways that prioritize both innovation and ethics. By doing so, they ensure that AI supports positive change and respects values that benefit everyone.

Balancing Innovation with Responsibility

Homo Magister leaders understand that technology has great potential but also significant risks. They look beyond the immediate benefits of AI, such as efficiency and profit, and consider the longer-term effects on people and society. For instance, while AI can streamline operations, leaders with a Homo Magister mindset will also ask how it impacts employees, customers, and the community.

These leaders ensure that AI solutions are safe, fair, and transparent. They push for using unbiased data and keep a close eye on potential problems, like how AI might treat different groups unfairly. For example, if a new AI model is developed for hiring, a Homo Magister leader will check that the model treats all candidates fairly and doesn't disadvantage anyone based on race, gender, or background. This balance of progress and responsibility requires careful planning, but it's essential for ensuring that AI serves everyone fairly.

Encouraging an Ethical Culture in the Organization

Leaders who follow the Homo Magister ideal don't just make ethical decisions themselves; they also create a culture that values ethical thinking across the organization. They do this by setting clear ethical standards for AI and ensuring every team member understands and values these principles. This means promoting transparency in AI development, encouraging feedback, and supporting team members who speak up about ethical concerns.

These leaders actively involve teams in discussions about the ethical implications of AI. They don't just give orders; they engage employees in conversations about why ethical AI matters and how it affects the company's reputation. When employees feel a part of these discussions, they are more likely to take ownership of the ethical standards and apply them in their work.

A Homo Magister leader in the tech industry might prioritize creating explainable AI models, even if they take more time or resources to develop. Instead of rushing a product to market, they would ensure that the AI is transparent and fair to build customer trust. In industries like healthcare, a Homo Magister leader would ensure that AI systems used for diagnosis are clear in their reasoning and designed to complement doctors' expertise, not replace them so that patients receive the best care.

Leaders who adopt this perspective focus on creating a positive impact through AI, ensuring it's both innovative and ethical. They guide their organizations toward responsible AI practices, promote a culture of openness and fairness, and remind everyone that AI should work for the good of all. This kind of leadership can be a powerful force in making AI a tool that builds a better future.

Developing an Ethical Framework for AI

At CDiGlobal Consulting, we prioritize the responsible use of AI and have developed a comprehensive ethical framework to guide its implementation. This framework is essential to ensure AI aligns with core values like fairness, transparency, and accountability, addressing both organizational and societal needs. By fostering stakeholder engagement, defining ethical principles, and implementing actionable strategies, we help our clients adopt AI responsibly, mitigating risks and fostering trust. Here's a step-by-step guide that we use for creating and maintaining an ethical AI framework, detailing each phase from stakeholder involvement to principle formulation and strategy deployment.

1. Engaging Stakeholders

The first step is to gather input from all groups who may be impacted by AI use. This includes internal stakeholders, like employees, and external ones, like customers, communities, and even regulators. Engaging these groups early helps ensure that the ethical framework reflects diverse perspectives and addresses real concerns.

- **Identify Key Stakeholders**: List people or groups who have a stake in how AI is used in the organization. This can include data scientists, legal teams, HR, marketing, customers, and community representatives.

- **Conduct Consultations**: Hold discussions or workshops to gather feedback. Ask questions like, "What concerns do you have about AI?" or "What values should AI reflect in our organization?" These consultations provide valuable insights into what matters most to those affected by AI.

- **Build Consensus**: Use this feedback to identify common themes or concerns. This consensus-building process helps align everyone's expectations and ensures the framework is grounded in shared values.

2. Formulating Ethical Principles

With input from stakeholders, the next step is to define the ethical principles that will guide AI use. These principles are the framework foundation and should be clear, practical, and aligned with organizational values and public expectations.

- **Identify Core Values**: Based on stakeholder feedback, determine core values such as fairness, privacy, transparency, accountability, and safety. These values form the ethical basis for AI practices in the organization.

- **Define Clear Principles**: Translate these values into actionable principles. For example:

    o   **Fairness**: Ensure AI systems treat all groups equitably.

    o   **Transparency**: Make AI processes understandable and open to inspection.

    o   **Privacy**: Protect user data and obtain consent for its use.

    o   **Accountability**: Assign clear responsibility for AI-related decisions and outcomes.

- **Prioritize Principles**: Sometimes, ethical principles can conflict (e.g., transparency vs. privacy). Prioritize them according to the organization's mission and values. This prioritization helps guide decision-making when trade-offs are necessary.

3. Developing Implementation Strategies

With principles in place, the next step is to establish strategies for putting these principles into practice. This includes setting policies, creating processes, and building tools to support ethical AI use.

- **Create Clear Policies**: Draft policies that specify how each ethical principle should be applied in practice. For instance, a policy for transparency might require explainable AI models for certain applications or mandate that customers be informed about AI's role in decisions affecting them.

- **Establish Review Processes**: Implement regular reviews to assess AI systems against ethical standards. This could include:

  o **Data Audits**: Check for bias in the data used for AI training.

  o **Algorithm Audits**: Assess AI models for fairness and accuracy.

  o **Impact Assessments**: Evaluate how AI affects different groups, including potential unintended effects.

- **Provide Training and Resources**: Equip teams with the knowledge and tools to apply ethical principles in their work. This might involve training on topics like bias detection, privacy practices, or explainable AI techniques. Providing guidelines and checklists can also help teams adhere to the framework.

- **Assign Ethical Oversight Roles**: Designate people or teams responsible for ethical oversight. For larger organizations, this could be an ethics board or an AI ethics officer. These roles help ensure continuous alignment with ethical standards.

4. Monitoring and Continuous Improvement

AI is an evolving technology, so the framework must adapt to new challenges and insights. Continuous monitoring and improvement are essential to keep the framework effective and relevant.

- **Set Up Feedback Mechanisms**: Create channels for feedback from employees, customers, and other stakeholders on the ethical aspects of AI. This feedback helps identify areas for improvement.

- **Conduct Regular Audits and Updates**: Regularly audit AI systems and processes to ensure they comply with the ethical framework. Update the framework as new ethical concerns arise or as technology and societal expectations evolve.

- **Stay Updated with Industry Standards**: Monitor developments in AI ethics from sources like industry standards, government regulations, and academic research. Incorporate new best practices or legal requirements into the framework as necessary.

Developing an ethical framework for AI requires engaging with diverse stakeholders, setting clear principles, implementing practical strategies, and committing to ongoing improvement. This approach helps ensure that AI technologies align with organizational values and public expectations, promoting trust and responsibility in AI use. As technology evolves, so should the framework, enabling organizations to navigate the ethical complexities of AI in a thoughtful, informed way.

Responsible AI Adoption Strategies

As AI becomes more integrated into various aspects of business, organizations need responsible adoption strategies to ensure that AI is used ethically and in ways that benefit both the company and society. Here are key strategies organizations can adopt for responsible AI use, including training programs, cross-functional ethics committees, and external audits.

1. Training Programs for AI Ethics and Best Practices

Training programs ensure that employees understand the ethical issues surrounding AI and are equipped to make responsible choices when developing or using AI systems.

- **Ethics Training for All Employees**: All employees, from executives to customer service, should understand the basics of AI ethics, including issues like bias, transparency, and data privacy. This promotes a culture where everyone is aware of AI's potential impact and risks.

- **Technical Skill Development for AI Specialists**: Specialized training in ethical AI development is essential for data scientists, engineers, and other technical roles. This includes courses on avoiding bias in data sets, using explainable AI techniques, and implementing privacy safeguards. Training can also cover relevant regulatory requirements, such as data protection laws, to ensure compliance.

- **Regular Updates and Refresher Courses**: AI technology and regulations are constantly evolving. Regularly updating training materials and providing refresher courses can help employees stay informed about new developments and best practices. This ongoing education reinforces a commitment to ethical standards.

2. Establishing Cross-Functional Ethics Committees

A cross-functional ethics committee brings together people from different departments to oversee AI practices and address ethical concerns. These committees ensure that AI decisions consider various perspectives and impact different areas of the organization.

- **Involving Diverse Teams**: An ethics committee should include representatives from IT, legal, human resources, marketing, and customer support, as well as AI specialists. Each department brings unique insights—legal may flag compliance issues, while marketing might highlight customer trust concerns. Including a diverse team helps prevent blind spots in ethical decision-making.

- **Defining the Committee's Role and Responsibilities**: The committee should have a clear mission, such as overseeing AI projects to ensure they align with ethical guidelines, reviewing potential risks, and approving AI applications before deployment. By setting these responsibilities upfront, the committee can check AI practices.

- **Regular Ethics Reviews and Consultations**: The committee should conduct periodic reviews of all AI-related projects and be available for consultations when new projects or challenges arise. This continuous oversight helps maintain ethical standards and addresses concerns early before AI systems are widely deployed.

- **Encouraging Open Dialogue**: Cross-functional committees foster open communication, which allows employees to voice concerns about ethical issues without fear of reprisal. This transparency encourages a proactive approach to ethical AI, where potential issues can be addressed before they become problems.

3. Conducting External Audits for Objective Insights

External audits provide an impartial review of an organization's AI practices, helping to identify potential ethical and compliance issues that may be overlooked internally. These audits also demonstrate a commitment to transparency and accountability, which is essential for building public trust.

- **Hiring Independent Auditors**: External audits are most effective when performed by independent organizations with expertise in AI ethics and regulatory compliance, like CDiGlobal Consulting. These auditors can evaluate the organization's AI models, data practices, and impact assessments to ensure they align with industry standards and ethical guidelines.

- **Assessing Data and Algorithms for Bias**: A key part of an audit is reviewing data sources and algorithms to detect biases that may unfairly affect certain groups. Independent auditors can offer an objective analysis, identifying biases that may be difficult for internal teams to spot due to their familiarity with the system.

- **Evaluating Compliance with Regulations**: External auditors can also verify compliance with laws and regulations, such as data protection standards (e.g., GDPR). This is particularly important for organizations working in regulated industries, like finance or healthcare, where ethical lapses or non-compliance can lead to severe consequences.

- **Public Reporting for Transparency**: Some organizations choose to share the findings of external audits with the public. This openness fosters trust and accountability, showing stakeholders that the company is dedicated to responsible AI use and willing to correct any identified issues.

In addition to training, ethics committees, and external audits, there are other strategies that organizations can adopt to strengthen their responsible AI practices:

- **Developing Ethical AI Guidelines**: Create clear guidelines that outline ethical AI principles, such as fairness, privacy, and transparency. These guidelines can serve as a reference for teams and help standardize practices across the organization.

- **Building an AI Ethics Helpdesk**: Establish an internal support channel where employees can seek advice on ethical questions related to AI projects. This could be a dedicated email or a helpdesk staffed by members of the ethics committee.

- **Implementing Continuous Monitoring**: Even after AI systems are deployed, regular monitoring is essential to catch any issues that arise. Automated checks, like bias detection tools, can be integrated into systems to continuously evaluate AI performance against ethical standards.

Adopting responsible AI requires intentional strategies that address ethical concerns and promote accountability. These strategies build a strong foundation for ethical AI, ensuring that it aligns with company values and public expectations.

Change Management for Ethical AI

Adopting ethical AI practices often requires a shift in mindset and new ways of working, not just for tech teams but for everyone involved. Change management in this area means helping employees and other stakeholders understand the importance of ethical AI, addressing any concerns they may have, and building a culture that values responsible innovation. Here are some key strategies for guiding this change effectively.

1. Open Communication and Education

One of the first steps is to communicate clearly about what ethical AI is and why it matters. This means sharing information on what ethical AI looks like, what kinds of issues it addresses (like privacy and fairness), and how it benefits everyone, from employees to customers. Regular workshops, webinars, or informational sessions can help people learn about these concepts and how they affect their work.

It's also important to listen to employee concerns. Some might worry that ethical AI practices could make their work harder or slow down projects. Creating spaces for open discussions allows these concerns to be heard and addressed. When people feel their opinions are valued, they're more likely to support the changes.

2. Leadership Support and Role Modeling

Change is easier when leaders actively support and model the behavior they want to see. Leaders should not only talk about ethical AI but also demonstrate their commitment through actions. For example, they could take part in training sessions, ask questions about the ethical impact of new AI projects, or share success stories of ethical AI within the company. When employees see leaders prioritize ethics, they understand it's not just a policy but a core value of the organization.

3. Aligning Ethical AI with Company Goals

To make ethical AI adoption easier, it helps to show how it aligns with the organization's larger goals. For instance, if a company values customer trust, then ethical AI practices like transparency and fairness support that goal by ensuring customers feel respected and safe. When employees see that ethical AI directly contributes to their work and the company's success, they're more motivated to adopt these practices.

4. Incentives and Recognition

Recognizing employees who embrace ethical AI practices can make a big difference. Incentives, like awards or acknowledgment in team meetings, show employees that their efforts are valued. For example, a team that successfully completes an AI project while following ethical guidelines could be celebrated. These small rewards reinforce a culture that values responsible and ethical AI use.

Guiding employees and stakeholders through the adoption of ethical AI practices requires open communication, supportive leadership, and practical steps that connect these practices to the organization's goals. With a strong change management approach, ethical AI can become part of everyday work, empowering teams to make decisions that not only drive progress but also uphold integrity and respect for all.

AI Ethics Governance Structures

To keep AI use ethical over the long term, organizations need strong governance structures. These structures provide rules, oversight, and accountability, ensuring that ethical principles aren't just talked about but actually applied in everyday practices. Here's a look at some governance models that can help ensure ongoing ethical AI use.

1. Ethics Boards or Committees

An ethics board or committee is a group of people dedicated to overseeing AI practices within the organization. This team often includes individuals from different departments, such as technology, legal, HR, and customer service, as well as external experts if needed. Their role is to review AI projects, identify ethical risks, and ensure that AI aligns with the organization's values. They also provide a space where employees can raise ethical concerns. By having a specific group in charge of AI ethics, organizations show that ethical AI use is a priority and not just a passing concern.

2. Regular Ethical Audits

At CDiGlobal Consulting, we conduct regular ethical audits for client organizations to ensure their AI systems uphold the highest ethical standards. These audits involve a thorough review of data sources, algorithms, and model impacts, assessing alignment with key principles like fairness, privacy, and transparency. Our intervention enhances objectivity as external auditors, adding an unbiased perspective that bolsters credibility and public trust. By identifying and addressing potential issues early, we help our clients make timely adjustments to maintain accountability and stay true to their ethical commitments in AI deployment.

3. Integrating AI Ethics with Existing Compliance

AI ethics governance should work with existing compliance and risk management systems. This integration helps avoid duplication of effort and keeps AI ethics aligned with other important company policies, such as data privacy or anti-discrimination practices. For example, the legal team might already conduct regular reviews for compliance with data protection laws; adding an AI ethics review as part of this process can help ensure AI systems respect user privacy.

4. Ongoing Training and Updates

AI ethics is a constantly evolving field, so regular training and updates are necessary for everyone involved. As new regulations, standards, or ethical challenges arise, the governance structure should adapt and provide updated guidance to the teams working with AI. This could mean annual ethics training sessions, as well as briefings on any new laws or industry best practices. Keeping teams informed helps maintain a strong ethical foundation and ensures that everyone understands their responsibilities.

5. Creating an Ethics Helpline

Some organizations set up a helpline or online platform where employees can report ethical concerns about AI projects. This gives employees a safe way to voice their worries if they believe an AI system is being used in a harmful or unfair way. Having a helpline shows that the organization takes ethical concerns seriously and is committed to addressing them promptly.

Establishing solid governance structures for AI ethics, such as ethics boards, regular audits, and integration with compliance processes, ensures that ethical considerations remain front and center as AI systems evolve. These structures provide accountability and ongoing oversight, helping organizations navigate ethical challenges with clarity and responsibility. Organizations can create a lasting commitment to responsible AI use by integrating ethics within existing frameworks and encouraging transparent practices that promote trust and integrity in all AI-related activities.

Take Microsoft, for instance. Microsoft is widely recognized as a leader in ethical AI practices thanks to its comprehensive approach to responsible AI. The company has invested in ethical AI frameworks, built internal governance systems, and prioritized transparency and fairness in its AI technologies. This case study examines how Microsoft developed its ethical AI strategy, the challenges it faced, and the positive impact of these efforts on its business and stakeholder trust.

Microsoft's commitment to ethical AI began with the creation of its AI, Ethics, and Effects in Engineering and Research (AETHER) Committee in 2017. This committee includes representatives from engineering, research, and policy departments who collaborate on ethical issues related to AI. The AETHER Committee works alongside the Office of Responsible AI, a department that enforces AI ethics policies and coordinates efforts to align AI products with ethical standards. Together, these groups ensure that AI ethics is part of every stage in Microsoft's product lifecycle, from research and development to deployment.

Microsoft has also set up six core principles for AI, including fairness, reliability and safety, privacy and security, inclusiveness, transparency, and accountability, which serve as guidelines for all AI-related projects. The company requires teams to evaluate these principles regularly when building or deploying AI systems. For instance, Microsoft's Azure Machine Learning platform has built-in tools for bias detection and explainability, helping users understand and trust AI models.

Implementing ethical AI on a large scale came with significant challenges. One of the main obstacles Microsoft faced was integrating ethical standards without slowing down the pace of innovation. Ensuring that every AI system aligned with ethical principles meant adding extra steps in development, such as testing for bias or implementing explainable AI models. This required balancing speed with careful ethical review, which Microsoft achieved by automating some of these checks and embedding ethical considerations into the engineering process from the start.

Another challenge was staying adaptable to emerging issues. As AI technology evolves, new ethical concerns frequently arise. Microsoft addresses this by continuously updating its AI ethics policies and conducting ongoing research. For instance, when privacy concerns related to facial recognition technology became prominent, Microsoft was one of the first companies to call for regulatory guidance on the use of facial recognition, showcasing its commitment to transparency and responsible innovation.

Microsoft's strong stance on ethical AI has positively impacted its business and enhanced stakeholder trust. Customers and partners have increasingly chosen Microsoft's AI solutions over competitors, citing trust in the company's ethical commitments. By being transparent about its AI practices and engaging with stakeholders on ethical concerns, Microsoft has strengthened its reputation as a responsible AI provider, which has been a key factor in retaining customer loyalty and attracting new clients.

Microsoft's comprehensive approach to ethical AI demonstrates the value of building a robust framework, overcoming challenges through innovation, and consistently prioritizing stakeholder trust. This commitment to responsible AI use has differentiated Microsoft in the tech industry and set a standard for ethical AI practices that other companies strive to emulate.[41]

Overcoming Resistance to Ethical Constraints

Introducing ethical practices for AI can sometimes face resistance within organizations. Some teams might feel that ethical guidelines slow down innovation or make their work more complicated. However, by showing the clear benefits of ethical AI and aligning these practices with the company's core values, organizations can encourage broader support. Mentioned below are some key strategies to address resistance to ethical AI constraints.

1. Show the Business Value of Ethical AI

Customers today are more concerned than ever about how their data is used and whether technology respects their privacy and rights. By following ethical AI practices,

---

[41]https://www.researchgate.net/publication/375744287_Artificial_Intelligen ce_and_Ethics_A_Comprehensive_Review_of_Bias_Mitigation_Transparency _and_Accountability_in_AI_Systems

companies can build trust with customers, which leads to stronger loyalty and brand reputation. Ethical AI also helps avoid public scandals or legal issues, which can cost a company both money and reputation. When employees see that ethics can lead to greater customer trust and reduce risks, they are more likely to support it.

2. Share Success Stories

Sharing examples of companies that have succeeded by adopting ethical AI can make a big impact. For instance, Microsoft's commitment to ethical AI has helped it stand out as a trusted leader in tech. Stories like these can inspire employees by showing that ethics and success can go hand-in-hand. Real-world cases also help make ethical issues more relatable and tangible, showing teams the long-term benefits of responsible practices.

3. Connect Ethical AI to Company Values

Another important strategy is to link ethical AI with the organization's core values. For example, if a company values "customer trust" or "innovation with integrity," then ethical AI is a natural extension of these values. When ethical practices are presented as part of what the company already stands for, they're easier for teams to accept and support. This approach also helps foster a sense of pride among employees, as they see their work contributing to the organization's positive impact on society.

4. Provide Training and Resources

Sometimes, resistance comes from a lack of understanding of what ethical AI really means. Providing training and resources can help clear up confusion and make ethical guidelines more approachable. Training can cover why ethics matter in AI, how to identify ethical risks, and ways to ensure fairness, transparency, and accountability in AI projects. When employees feel equipped with knowledge and tools, they're more likely to support ethical guidelines.

Overcoming resistance to ethical AI requires clear communication, practical examples, and alignment with organizational values. Providing training and resources further empowers employees, making it easier for teams to integrate responsible AI practices into their work. With these strategies, organizations can ensure that ethical AI becomes a valued and respected part of their operations.

Future of AI Ethics

As AI continues to evolve, so too will the field of AI ethics. The future of AI ethics will likely bring new challenges and opportunities for shaping how AI impacts society. Here are some predictions about where AI ethics may be headed and the role of global cooperation in guiding ethical standards.

1. Addressing New Ethical Challenges

As AI becomes more advanced, it will present new ethical questions that we may not yet fully understand. For example,

AI systems that can make complex decisions, like self-driving cars or AI-powered medical tools, will need strict ethical guidelines to ensure safety and fairness. Another emerging area is AI's role in influencing public opinion and information. With tools like deepfakes and content generation, AI could be used to spread misinformation, creating a need for guidelines to manage these risks.

Additionally, as AI becomes more integrated into personal devices, ethical concerns around privacy and data use will grow. People will want assurances that AI systems respect their privacy and don't misuse sensitive information. Addressing these challenges will require updated ethical standards and regulations that are flexible enough to adapt as technology changes.

2. Increased Global Cooperation

As AI affects people worldwide, global cooperation will be essential in setting common ethical standards. Organizations like the United Nations, the European Union, and the World Economic Forum are already working on international AI ethics guidelines, and this trend is likely to grow. Global standards would help ensure that AI systems are safe, fair, and respectful of human rights, no matter where they're used.

This cooperation is important because AI doesn't have borders. For example, an AI system created in one country can quickly be used in another, making it necessary for countries to agree on certain ethical basics, like privacy and accountability. International agreements can help prevent conflicts and make it easier for companies to develop AI that meets the standards of multiple regions rather than navigating different regulations for each country.

3. Ethical AI Becoming a Competitive Advantage

In the future, companies that prioritize ethical AI could gain a strong competitive edge. As customers become more aware of data privacy and the social impact of AI, they are more likely to choose brands that demonstrate responsibility and transparency. Ethical AI can, therefore, become a key selling point, giving companies that invest in ethical practices an advantage over competitors who ignore these concerns.

4. New Roles and Responsibilities for AI Ethics

As AI ethics becomes a priority, we may see new job roles focused specifically on responsible AI. Positions like "AI Ethics Officer" or "Ethics Program Manager" could become common in companies to ensure that AI practices meet ethical guidelines. These roles would oversee AI projects, conduct regular reviews, and educate teams on ethical standards. Having dedicated roles for AI ethics helps ensure that ethical principles remain a priority as technology advances.

The future of AI ethics will bring new challenges and exciting opportunities for global cooperation. As AI grows more powerful and integrated into daily life, ethical guidelines must evolve to address emerging issues like data privacy, misinformation, and the safe use of AI in critical areas. Companies can set a course that benefits business and society, building trust and creating a positive impact by prioritizing ethics as AI advances.

Measuring Ethical AI Performance

Evaluating the ethical performance of AI systems is essential to ensure that they align with an organization's values and ethical guidelines. Here are some commonly used metrics for measuring ethical AI performance:

- **Bias Detection**: Track the fairness of AI models by examining their outputs across different demographic groups. A common metric is **disparity ratio**, which compares outcomes for protected groups (e.g., gender, race) to identify potential bias. If results significantly differ between groups, the model may need adjustments.

- **Transparency and Explainability**: Measure how well users can understand AI decisions. This can be evaluated through **explainability scores** that assess the clarity of model explanations or through feedback surveys where users rate how understandable the AI's decision-making process is.

- **Privacy Compliance**: Track adherence to data privacy regulations (like GDPR). KPIs in this area may include **consent rate** (percentage of users who give consent for data use) and **data retention**

metrics (how long data is stored). Monitoring these metrics helps ensure that AI systems handle user data responsibly.

- **Accountability and Redress Mechanisms**: Evaluate how easily users can report issues with AI and receive support. **Response time to ethical complaints** and the **resolution rate** of AI-related issues are useful metrics that show how well an organization handles concerns.

- **Impact on Stakeholder Trust**: Surveys or feedback scores can help measure whether stakeholders (like customers or partners) trust the AI systems. A **trust index** based on survey responses can provide insights into how ethical AI practices are perceived externally.

These KPIs help organizations measure the ethical impact of their AI systems and support continuous improvement.

Adopting ethical AI practices requires a clear, step-by-step approach to ensure that each aspect of AI implementation aligns with ethical standards. Here's a practical action plan we use for organizations looking to implement ethical AI:

1. **Initial Assessment**: Begin by evaluating your current AI practices and identifying ethical risks, such as data biases or privacy concerns. A quick audit of existing AI models can help highlight any immediate issues.

2. **Set Ethical AI Goals and KPIs**: Define your organization's ethical goals and the KPIs you'll use to measure success. Decide which metrics are most relevant, like fairness, privacy, and transparency, and set clear benchmarks for each.

3. **Form an AI Ethics Committee**: Create a cross-functional ethics committee to oversee AI initiatives. This team should include representatives from tech, legal, compliance, and HR to provide diverse perspectives on ethical risks and solutions.

4. **Develop and Document Ethical Guidelines**: Create clear guidelines outlining the ethical principles your AI systems should follow. This could include rules for data collection, model explainability, and privacy protections. Make these guidelines accessible to all teams involved in AI development.

5. **Implement Ethical Reviews and Testing**: Add ethical checks at different stages of AI development, such as bias testing during model training and explainability testing before deployment. This ensures that ethical considerations are part of the process, not an afterthought.

6. **Continuous Improvement**: Set up a feedback loop to gather input from users and stakeholders. Regularly review AI systems and update ethical guidelines as new issues or technologies emerge.

This action plan provides a structured approach to building ethical AI from the ground up, helping organizations minimize risks and foster responsible AI practices.

Reflections:

To help readers apply ethical AI concepts in their own organizations, here are some reflection questions that encourage deeper thinking and planning:

1. What are the main ethical risks in our current AI practices? Consider areas where your organization's AI might affect fairness, privacy, or transparency.

2. How do our company values align with our AI initiatives? Reflect on how ethical AI fits within the organization's core mission and values.

3. Who are the key stakeholders impacted by our AI systems? Think about the individuals or groups who might be affected by your AI systems, including customers, employees, and the public.

4. What specific metrics can we use to measure ethical performance in our AI systems? Identify which KPIs make the most sense for your organization and how you'll track them.

5. What structures or teams do we need to establish to oversee AI ethics? Consider who within your organization should be responsible for ethical AI

governance and how to build a support system for ethical reviews.

6. How will we address ethical issues as they arise? Think about what processes need to be in place to handle ethical concerns promptly and effectively.

These questions encourage thoughtful planning, helping leaders and teams identify areas for improvement and build a roadmap for ethical AI.

Adopting ethical AI practices requires a thoughtful approach, from setting clear performance metrics to building structured action plans and fostering ongoing reflection.

As AI becomes an integral part of business and society, the importance of ethical AI practices cannot be overstated. Ethical AI ensures that technology respects human rights, promotes fairness, and builds trust with stakeholders. Establishing a culture of ethical AI is essential for encouraging long-term success, safeguarding the rights of individuals, and contributing to a future where technology serves the common good.

Chapter 11: Assessing AI's Business Impact

A company's leadership team was under pressure at a quarterly board meeting. They had poured substantial resources into advanced AI systems, intending to revolutionize their customer service, streamline operations, and give the company a competitive edge. However, as the CFO presented the recent financials, the anticipated ROI from AI wasn't as clear-cut as they had hoped. Although there were improvements in certain areas, quantifying the exact impact of AI on the company's bottom line was proving difficult. The board members looked skeptical, questioning whether the investment was delivering real value.

The CEO and tech leads were in a complicated situation. Traditional metrics like revenue growth and cost savings weren't fully capturing the benefits that AI was bringing, which included enhanced customer experiences, quicker service resolution, and more insightful analytics. These advantages were hard to quantify in immediate financial terms, yet they were crucial to the company's long-term strategy.

As they discussed the issue further, the team recognized that measuring AI success required a different approach. Unlike more conventional technologies, AI's value often lies in its ability to provide insights, automate processes, and support complex decision-making, all of which are challenging to reduce to dollar figures on a quarterly report. It became clear that they needed to develop new key performance indicators (KPIs) that could reflect AI's broader impact, such as customer satisfaction scores, efficiency improvements, or employee productivity boosts.

The discussion with the board underscored an important reality: traditional measurement tools weren't enough for AI-driven initiatives. They needed a comprehensive framework that could demonstrate AI's value beyond immediate financial returns, capturing both tangible and intangible benefits. As the team left the meeting, they understood that if they were to continue investing in AI, they'd need to establish these new metrics—ones that would accurately reflect the complex, transformative impact AI was intended to have on the business.

Evolution of Performance Measurement

Performance measurement in organizations has come a long way. In the early days, companies mainly looked at financial metrics(things like profit, revenue, and costs) to assess how well they were doing. While these numbers are important, they only tell part of the story. Financial metrics can show whether a company is making money, but they don't capture other factors that contribute to long-term success, like customer satisfaction, employee engagement, or innovation.

In the 1990s, the balanced scorecard approach became popular. This method expanded performance measurement beyond financial results to include four key areas: financial, customer, internal processes, and learning and growth. The balanced scorecard allowed companies to track how well they served customers, how efficiently they operated, and how they were developing new skills and capabilities. This helped organizations see where they were succeeding and where they needed improvement across different areas, not just financially.[42]

Now, in the AI era, companies face new challenges with performance measurement. AI can impact everything from customer interactions to decision-making and operations, but it's hard to measure these impacts with traditional metrics. For example, AI might improve customer service response times or provide insights that lead to smarter strategies, but these benefits aren't always reflected in immediate profits. AI's contributions are often complex and gradual, making it hard to capture their full value through existing measures.

There's a growing need for new types of metrics that can track AI's impact as AI plays a bigger role in business. This might include metrics that measure customer engagement, data quality, efficiency gains, or how well AI supports decision-making. Just as the balanced scorecard expanded performance measurement beyond finances, the AI era calls for a new approach that captures the broader effects of AI on business success.

---

[42]https://www.hbs.edu/ris/Publication%20Files/10-074_0bf3c151-f82b-4592-b885-cdde7f5d97a6.pdf

KPIs for AI

As companies invest more in AI, it's becoming clear that traditional KPIs (Key Performance Indicators) don't always capture the full impact of these initiatives. AI can transform processes, improve decision-making, and enhance customer experiences, but its benefits often go beyond simple metrics like revenue growth or cost reduction. To measure AI's true value, organizations need to rethink KPIs to better capture the visible and hidden effects of AI.

Conventional KPIs focus mostly on financial and operational metrics, such as profits, sales, and productivity. While these metrics are important, they often miss the value AI brings. For example, AI can help a company make smarter decisions by analyzing massive amounts of data, but the quality and speed of decision-making are difficult to measure directly. Traditional KPIs also don't capture improvements in areas like customer satisfaction, personalization, or employee productivity, which can be positively impacted by AI but don't immediately show up in financial reports.

Another challenge with traditional KPIs is that AI's benefits are often long-term or indirect. For instance, a predictive maintenance AI system in manufacturing can reduce unexpected equipment failures, saving costs over time, but these benefits accumulate gradually and might not be visible in short-term metrics. Similarly, an AI-driven customer service chatbot might enhance customer experience and lead to greater loyalty and retention in the long run, but these outcomes aren't instantly reflected in revenue numbers.

New KPIs to Capture AI's Impact

To fully understand the value AI brings, organizations need to create or adapt KPIs that reflect AI's unique contributions. Mentioned below are some examples of new or redefined KPIs that can help measure AI-driven transformation:

1. **Decision-Making Speed and Accuracy**: AI helps process data faster and can make decisions based on complex patterns. KPIs like "time to decision" or "decision accuracy" can show how AI is improving the quality and speed of business choices.

2. **Customer Engagement and Satisfaction**: AI often plays a direct role in customer interactions, such as personalized recommendations or automated support. Metrics like "customer satisfaction scores," "engagement rates," and "response time" for AI-driven customer service solutions can provide insights into how AI is enhancing customer experience.

3. **Operational Efficiency**: While cost savings are commonly tracked, more specific KPIs can show how AI improves efficiency. For instance, "processing time per task" or "accuracy of output" can measure how AI automates and enhances routine processes, resulting in smoother operations.

4. **Innovation and Adaptability**: AI can be a key driver of innovation, helping companies develop new products, services, or ways of working. KPIs like "time to market for AI-driven products" or "number of AI-powered solutions deployed" can show how AI contributes to a company's ability to innovate and adapt.

5. **Data Quality and Usage**: Data is the foundation of AI, so tracking data quality is essential. Metrics like "data completeness," "data accuracy," and "frequency of data updates" can help ensure the data used by AI systems is reliable and up-to-date, which is crucial for effective AI performance.

6. **Employee Productivity and Satisfaction**: AI tools can support employees by taking on repetitive tasks, allowing them to focus on more valuable work. KPIs like "time saved per task" or "employee satisfaction with AI tools" can reveal how AI is boosting productivity and job satisfaction.

When AI is implemented, its impact often reaches many parts of the business, but these effects can be hard to quantify in financial terms. For example, an AI system might help detect fraud faster, improving security and customer trust. Metrics like "number of fraud cases detected" or "reduction in fraudulent activity" can provide a clearer picture of AI's impact on security.

By broadening KPIs to include these types of metrics, companies can capture the hidden value AI brings, which makes it easier for stakeholders to communicate this value. This approach also supports a more comprehensive understanding of AI's role in driving innovation and maintaining competitive advantage.

Redefining KPIs for AI is essential for organizations that want to accurately measure and maximize the benefits of their AI investments. Traditional metrics, while still important, don't capture the full picture of how AI transforms processes, decision-making, and customer experiences. By developing new KPIs focused on decision speed, customer engagement, data quality, and operational efficiency, organizations can create a more meaningful framework for evaluating AI's impact.

AI Impact Framework

This framework provides a complete way to evaluate the impact of AI across different parts of an organization. It looks at how AI affects financial performance, day-to-day operations, customer satisfaction, and innovation. By using this framework, companies can get a clear picture of how AI is changing their business.

Financial Metrics

The framework includes traditional financial metrics to see how AI is boosting revenue or cutting costs. Financial impacts are usually easy to measure, so these metrics help highlight the direct value AI brings.

Operational Metrics

AI can make operations smoother and faster, so it's important to track metrics like processing speed, accuracy, and efficiency. These metrics show where AI is helping improve workflows and reduce errors.

Customer Metrics

Since AI often plays a big role in customer experience, this framework looks at customer satisfaction scores, engagement rates, and response times. These metrics help reveal how AI affects customer loyalty and brand reputation.

Innovation Metrics

Lastly, the framework considers how AI drives new ideas and growth, measuring things like the number of new AI-driven products or the time to market for AI-powered solutions. This part of the framework highlights AI's role in making the company more competitive and forward-thinking.

Using this framework, companies can see the full picture of AI's impact across all key areas, giving them insights into how AI is really working to strengthen their organization.

Balancing Short-Term and Long-Term Metrics

When companies invest in AI, they often face pressure to show quick results. While some AI benefits may appear quickly, many changes, like improvements in customer loyalty or operational efficiency, take time. Balancing short-term wins with a focus on long-term transformation is essential for fully understanding AI's impact. Here's a breakdown of strategies to help manage this balance, along with the challenges organizations face in measuring AI initiatives with longer payoffs.

Set Clear Short- and Long-Term Goals

The first strategy is to establish both short-term and long-term goals for AI projects. Short-term goals should focus on easily measurable benefits, like improved processing speed or reduced error rates in specific tasks. These results help demonstrate quick progress. For the long term, goals should include more strategic transformations, like increased customer satisfaction or innovation in product offerings.

Use Different KPIs for Short- and Long-Term Success

Another strategy is to use different key performance indicators (KPIs) for short-term and long-term impacts. Short-term KPIs might include metrics like cost savings, error reduction, or processing time improvements. These KPIs show the early successes of an AI initiative. For the long-term, focus on metrics like customer loyalty, market share growth, or the number of new products enabled by AI. Long-term KPIs provide insights into how AI is changing the business over time. Having distinct KPIs for each phase helps teams stay focused and ensures that both types of outcomes are valued.

Regular Reviews and Adjustments

To balance both timelines, it's helpful to conduct regular reviews of AI initiatives. Quarterly check-ins can track short-term gains and ensure projects are on course. Annual reviews provide a chance to assess longer-term progress. These regular reviews create flexibility, and if a short-term metric doesn't show the expected result, teams can adjust the approach. For long-term metrics, reviews can reveal gradual trends, which would help the team understand the full scope of AI's impact.

Communicate Short-Term Wins to Keep Momentum

One of the challenges with long-term AI projects is maintaining support from stakeholders who want to see quick results. A good strategy here is to share short-term wins regularly, even if they are small. Highlighting improvements in speed, cost savings, or productivity gives stakeholders confidence that the AI initiative is moving forward. These updates keep morale high and help secure continued investment and support from leadership.

Invest in Tools for Long-Term Tracking

AI projects often involve complex, long-term data analysis. Investing in tools that track trends over time, like data visualization software, can be essential. These tools help make long-term impacts visible. For example, a tool might reveal how customer satisfaction gradually increases after implementing an AI-driven personalization feature.

Having the right tools makes it easier to capture the broader impact of AI.

Measuring AI initiatives with long-term payoffs can be challenging. AI's benefits are often gradual, and it can be hard to tie improvements directly to specific projects. Additionally, some impacts, like improved customer trust, are harder to quantify. Another challenge is maintaining patience and support for projects that may take years to show their full value. Balancing short-term and long-term metrics requires careful planning, clear communication, and the right measurement tools.

Balancing short- and long-term metrics allows companies to capture both the immediate wins and the lasting benefits of AI. By setting clear goals, using the right KPIs, and sharing progress regularly, companies can keep projects on track and show how AI contributes to both current operations and future growth.

Measuring Intangible Benefits of AI

AI adoption often brings benefits that are hard to quantify directly. These intangible benefits, including better decision-making, enhanced customer experience, and greater agility in responding to change, add significant value, yet they can be challenging to measure. Organizations need effective techniques to capture these impacts in order to understand the full contribution of AI. I have mentioned below methods for quantifying these hard-to-measure benefits.

1. Measuring Improved Decision-Making Quality

One of the most valuable but intangible effects of AI is enhanced decision-making. AI helps by providing insights based on large amounts of data, which allows leaders to make decisions with better information. Quantifying this impact requires indirect approaches.

- **Surveys and Feedback**: Regular feedback from decision-makers and employees can reveal how AI tools contribute to decision-making. Surveys can ask leaders if they feel more confident in their decisions, if AI insights are helpful, and if decision times have shortened. This qualitative data can then be quantified by tracking positive responses over time.

- **Decision Speed and Accuracy Metrics**: AI often speeds up the decision-making process. Metrics like "time to decision" or "reduction in decision errors" can provide numerical insight into how AI affects the quality and efficiency of choices. Comparing past decision-making times and error rates before and after AI adoption can reveal improvements.

- **Outcome-Based Measurement**: By tracking specific outcomes associated with AI-assisted decisions, such as increased project success rates or improved forecasts, companies can indirectly measure decision quality. For instance, if AI-supported forecasting leads to fewer product shortages, the value of that better decision-making becomes measurable.

2. Enhancing Customer Experience

AI is widely used to improve customer experiences, from personalization in marketing to quicker responses in customer support. However, customer experience is also a somewhat intangible benefit, making it harder to directly measure.

- **Customer Satisfaction Scores (CSAT)**: Customer satisfaction surveys, particularly those with ratings on a scale (such as 1 to 10), can show how AI-driven improvements influence customer happiness. By comparing CSAT scores before and after implementing AI in customer interactions, companies can gauge AI's impact on satisfaction.

- **Net Promoter Score (NPS)**: NPS surveys ask customers how likely they are to recommend the company to others. If AI-driven tools like personalized recommendations or faster service are making a difference, companies should see improvements in their NPS. Tracking this score over time provides insight into how AI boosts customer loyalty.

- **Engagement Metrics**: AI can improve customer experience by making interactions more engaging. Metrics like session length, frequency of engagement, and customer return rates can all serve as indicators. For instance, if an AI-powered recommendation system leads customers to spend more time on the website, it shows that AI is enhancing the user experience.

3. Increasing Organizational Agility

AI can make organizations more agile, allowing them to respond faster to changes and adapt to new challenges. However, organizational agility isn't easy to measure directly, so companies need to use related metrics.

- **Response Time to Market Changes**: Tracking how quickly the organization reacts to shifts in the market—such as changes in customer demand or competitor actions—can reflect increased agility. AI-powered data analytics can make these responses faster, and response time metrics can provide a concrete way to measure that agility.

- **Time to Market for New Products**: AI can speed up product development by automating research, data analysis, and testing. Tracking "time to market" for new products before and after adopting AI tools can reveal whether AI is making the company more responsive to new opportunities.

- **Project Turnaround Time**: Shortening the time it takes to complete projects is another indicator of organizational agility. Metrics that track project duration from start to finish can show how AI contributes to faster execution of tasks and projects, especially when AI-driven automation or data insights are involved.

- **Employee Adaptability Surveys**: Surveying employees about how easily they can adapt to changes in processes or tools, thanks to AI support, can reveal internal agility improvements. If employees feel AI has enabled them to handle change more easily, that's a measurable outcome showing how AI improves flexibility.

Since intangible benefits are hard to measure directly, companies often need to combine multiple metrics to get a complete picture. For example, if an organization wants to understand AI's impact on decision-making, it might look at survey feedback, decision speed, and actual outcomes together. By triangulating these metrics, companies can gain more reliable insights into how AI-driven improvements in intangible areas are benefiting the organization as a whole.

However, I would like to mention here that quantifying intangible benefits is not without challenges. One issue is that intangible impacts, like enhanced customer loyalty or increased adaptability, may develop gradually. It's also hard to tie these benefits directly to AI alone, as other factors like employee training or market conditions play a role. To address these challenges, companies should track these metrics consistently over time, look for patterns, and adjust metrics as needed to capture evolving AI impacts.

While intangible benefits like improved decision-making, customer experience, and organizational agility are challenging to measure, they represent significant parts of AI's value. Companies can start to quantify these impacts by using surveys, performance metrics, and tracking response times. Combining these metrics gives a fuller picture of AI's role in the organization, highlighting the value of AI investments. This approach helps companies justify their AI initiatives and demonstrates the broader, lasting impact of AI on organizational success.

Tesla, for instance, has been a pioneer in AI-driven technologies, particularly in the development of autonomous driving systems and highly automated manufacturing processes. Traditional metrics, such as vehicle sales or production costs, don't fully capture the value and impact of Tesla's AI initiatives. Tesla has, therefore, developed new metrics focused on safety, autonomy, and production efficiency to assess its progress and ensure continuous improvement. This case study explores Tesla's approach, the challenges it encountered, and the resulting impact on its strategy and operations.

Tesla needed metrics that would better reflect the progress and effectiveness of its AI-driven innovations. The company developed specific metrics to evaluate safety improvements, levels of autonomous driving, and production efficiency, allowing Tesla to track the success of its AI technologies.

1. **Safety Metrics for Autonomous Driving:** Tesla introduced metrics like miles driven per accident and collision avoidance success rate to evaluate the performance and reliability of its autonomous driving system. By focusing on safety-related metrics, Tesla could assess the

real-world effectiveness of its AI-powered Autopilot and Full Self-Driving (FSD) features.

2. Autonomy Level Metrics: To track progress in autonomous driving, Tesla uses metrics to indicate the degree of autonomy in its vehicles. For example, Tesla monitors the percentage of miles driven in autonomous mode and the frequency of human interventions. These metrics help Tesla understand how often and effectively its AI systems operate without human assistance, indicating advancements in autonomous technology.

3. Manufacturing Efficiency Metrics: In its AI-powered manufacturing processes, Tesla tracks metrics like time per vehicle assembly, defect rate, and energy usage per vehicle produced. These metrics reflect how AI and automation improve manufacturing efficiency, reduce errors, and streamline production, which are crucial for Tesla's competitive advantage.

One of the key challenges Tesla faced was ensuring that its new metrics aligned with regulatory standards and public expectations, especially for autonomous driving safety. As Tesla's AI technology pushes the boundaries of what's possible with self-driving, regulators and the public expect transparency and accountability. Tesla addressed this by openly sharing some of its safety metrics in quarterly vehicle safety reports, which highlight the safety performance of its autonomous features compared to human driving.

Another challenge was managing the technical complexity of measuring autonomy accurately. Autonomous systems require large-scale data collection and advanced analytics to evaluate performance, which means Tesla needs robust data processing capabilities. Tesla overcame this by leveraging its fleet of vehicles to collect real-world data and by building powerful data analytics tools to process and interpret these metrics efficiently.

By redefining its success metrics, Tesla gained deeper insights into the effectiveness of its AI technologies. Safety and autonomy metrics provided Tesla with valuable feedback for refining its AI algorithms, helping the company prioritize safety improvements and enhance autonomous capabilities. The manufacturing metrics allowed Tesla to optimize its production lines, reduce waste, and lower costs, aligning with its strategy to make electric vehicles affordable and accessible.

Tesla's transparency in sharing its safety metrics also strengthened trust among customers and stakeholders, reinforcing Tesla's position as a leader in autonomous driving technology. This strategic approach to metrics not only helped Tesla improve its AI performance but also provided a solid foundation for regulatory discussions and future advancements in autonomous driving.

Tesla's redefinition of metrics for AI-driven innovation in autonomous driving and manufacturing showcases the importance of creating specialized KPIs to measure the unique benefits of AI. By focusing on safety, autonomy levels, and manufacturing efficiency, Tesla can more accurately capture the value of its AI initiatives, drive continuous improvement, and maintain a competitive edge in the industry. This case study demonstrates how customized metrics can support both operational success and strategic growth, helping companies like Tesla lead in technology-driven transformation.[43]

AI-Specific Performance Indicators

Traditional metrics often fall short in evaluating its unique contributions as AI becomes more integrated into organizations. AI-specific Key Performance Indicators (KPIs) provide a more accurate picture of AI's effectiveness, addressing factors like model accuracy, bias, decision quality, and the efficiency of AI-human collaboration. Mentioned below are some key AI-specific performance indicators and how they can be measured and interpreted.

Model Accuracy

Model accuracy is one of the most straightforward indicators of AI performance, reflecting how often the AI makes correct predictions or classifications. For instance, in a medical AI application, accuracy can be measured by comparing the AI's diagnostic predictions against actual diagnoses. An accuracy rate of 95% indicates the model correctly identifies the diagnosis 95% of the time. High accuracy is crucial in high-stakes applications like healthcare and finance, where mistakes can have serious consequences. However, accuracy alone doesn't tell the

---

[43] https://techcrunch.com/

whole story; it must often be balanced with other metrics to ensure comprehensive performance.[44]

Bias Detection

AI models can unintentionally reflect biases present in their training data, which may lead to unfair outcomes. Bias detection KPIs help track and mitigate this risk. For example, a hiring AI might show bias if it favors certain demographic groups over others in its recommendations. Bias can be measured by analyzing decision outcomes across different demographic groups and ensuring they meet fairness standards, such as similar acceptance rates across race or gender. Tools that audit and visualize bias patterns help interpret these results, allowing teams to adjust the model or training data to reduce bias.

Decision Quality

Beyond accuracy, decision quality measures how effectively AI supports decision-making. It can be assessed by comparing decisions made with and without AI assistance to see if AI improves outcomes. For instance, in loan approvals, decision quality can be measured by looking at the default rates of AI-approved loans versus those made without AI input. A lower default rate for AI-assisted decisions suggests that AI is providing valuable insights. Decision quality can also be interpreted through user

---

[44]https://towarddatascience.com/accuracy-precision-recall-or-f1-331fb37c5cb9

feedback, where human decision-makers rate the AI's impact on their choices.[45]

AI often works in tandem with humans, so measuring collaboration effectiveness is key. This metric evaluates how well AI supports and enhances human roles, often using user satisfaction surveys and task completion times. For example, in a customer service setup, AI-human collaboration effectiveness can be measured by tracking average response times, where faster times suggest AI is helping agents address queries more quickly. Feedback from users on how helpful they find AI assistance also provides insight into this KPI. Interpreting these results helps organizations fine-tune AI's role to optimize productivity and satisfaction.

Homo Magister Perspective on Measurement

The Homo Magister plays a critical role in shaping how AI performance is measured, ensuring that metrics are balanced with a broader, ethical perspective. Leaders embodying this ideal understand that while quantitative metrics are essential, they should be complemented by qualitative insights to get a fuller picture of AI's impact on people and society.

Balancing Quantitative and Qualitative Assessments

Leaders with a Homo Magister perspective recognize that AI metrics must go beyond numbers. While metrics like

---

[45]https://www.mckinsey.com/capabilities/quantumblack/our-insights/the-state-of-ai

accuracy and bias detection offer concrete insights, qualitative assessments—such as employee and customer feedback—are equally important. For instance, an AI that scores high on accuracy but receives negative feedback for being overly complex or intrusive may not be serving its intended purpose. Homo Magister leaders encourage gathering these softer data points to assess the human impact of AI. By combining quantitative results with qualitative feedback, they ensure that AI systems are evaluated not just for efficiency but for alignment with ethical values and human needs.

Fostering an Inclusive Approach to Measurement

A Homo Magister leader values input from diverse stakeholders, ensuring that AI performance measurements consider the perspectives of those directly affected by the technology. For example, in an AI-powered hiring system, this leader would seek feedback from HR professionals, candidates, and even external diversity consultants. This inclusive approach ensures the AI's performance metrics reflect fairness and respect for all involved. Such leaders actively involve cross-functional teams in developing metrics, making sure the criteria reflect the organization's core values and social responsibilities.

Guiding Ethical Metrics Development

Homo Magister leaders emphasize that performance indicators should encourage responsible AI use. They might advocate for including KPIs that measure unintended effects, like whether the AI influences employee morale or how it impacts customer trust. For example, in a healthcare setting, alongside measuring diagnostic accuracy, a Homo Magister leader might track patient feedback on the AI's role in their care, ensuring that the technology is seen as supportive rather than invasive. By pushing for these ethical metrics, they create an AI measurement framework that prioritizes positive societal impacts and avoids unintended harm.

Emphasizing Continuous Improvement and Accountability

These leaders see AI measurement as a continuous process, recognizing that AI's impact can evolve over time. They promote regular reviews of AI performance metrics and advocate for updates as new ethical considerations emerge. For instance, as AI applications expand in sensitive areas like finance or healthcare, new metrics may be needed to capture evolving ethical standards. Homo Magister leaders encourage transparency in reporting.

AI-specific KPIs provide organizations with a way to track critical aspects of AI performance, from accuracy and bias detection to decision quality and collaboration effectiveness. Meanwhile, leaders with a Homo Magister mindset guide the development of AI measurement frameworks that combine quantitative rigor with qualitative insights. By balancing efficiency with ethical considerations, they help organizations adopt AI responsibly, ensuring that it enhances both performance and human values.

Data Collection and Analysis for AI Metrics

Collecting and analyzing data to measure AI performance is essential for understanding its effectiveness and impact. However, gathering the right data and interpreting it correctly can be challenging, given AI's complexity and the range of performance metrics involved. Here's a look at strategies for collecting and analyzing data for AI metrics, including using AI itself to aid this process.

Data Collection Strategies

Effective AI performance measurement begins with gathering relevant and high-quality data. This involves identifying the specific metrics to track, such as model accuracy, bias, decision quality, and user engagement. Data sources vary depending on the application—for instance, user interaction logs can reveal how customers engage with AI, while feedback forms can provide insights into decision quality. In more complex AI setups, data from sensors, network logs, and real-time system outputs may also be relevant. To ensure accuracy, organizations should regularly review data sources and validate data quality to avoid incorrect metrics.

Automated Data Analysis Using AI

As AI applications grow more complex, using AI tools to analyze performance data can be incredibly valuable. AI-driven analytics tools can process large datasets quickly, detecting patterns and anomalies in performance metrics that might not be immediately obvious. For example, natural language processing (NLP) algorithms can analyze customer feedback to gauge satisfaction with AI-driven services, while machine learning models can identify trends in decision-making accuracy over time. Additionally, AI can automatically flag potential issues, such as increases in bias or drops in accuracy, enabling faster responses and adjustments.

Real-Time Monitoring and Dashboards

For ongoing AI projects, real-time monitoring provides insights into performance as it happens. Dashboards powered by AI analytics offer live updates on key metrics, making it easy to track metrics like response time, error rates, and data throughput. By continuously collecting and analyzing performance data in real-time, organizations can adjust AI systems to maintain optimal performance and address emerging issues immediately.

Periodic Evaluation and Adjustments

Beyond real-time monitoring, periodic evaluations—such as monthly or quarterly assessments—offer a deeper look at trends in AI performance. Analyzing these trends allows organizations to refine models, update training data, or adjust algorithms to better meet performance goals. This cyclical review process helps organizations maintain high performance and address any shifts in AI system behavior.

Effective data collection and analysis are essential for accurately measuring AI performance and understanding its impact. This approach allows for adjustments, optimizes AI effectiveness, and provides actionable insights that drive continual improvement. Well-executed data collection and analysis not only support the success of AI initiatives but also ensure that AI's role aligns with organizational goals and user expectations.

Ethical Considerations in AI Measurement

Measuring AI performance raises ethical concerns that organizations must address to ensure responsible practices. These ethical considerations include data privacy, the risk of metric manipulation, and the impact of measurement practices on employee well-being. Here's a closer look at some of the main ethical issues and strategies to address them.

Privacy Concerns in Data Collection

Collecting data to evaluate AI performance can pose risks to privacy, especially when sensitive user or employee data is involved. For example, tracking customer interactions with AI-powered services may require gathering personal information, while monitoring employee productivity with AI tools can infringe on personal privacy. To address this, organizations should prioritize data minimization, collecting only what is necessary to assess performance. Anonymizing or aggregating data whenever possible is another important strategy to protect privacy. Additionally, clear consent mechanisms and transparent communication about data collection can help build trust with users and employees.

Potential for Metric Manipulation

Like any performance measurement, AI metrics can be manipulated if individuals or teams focus solely on achieving specific targets rather than on genuine performance improvement. For instance, if accuracy is the primary metric for an AI system, teams might optimize for accuracy at the expense of fairness or transparency. Similarly, if customer satisfaction scores are the focus, it could lead to neglecting other critical factors like data security. To prevent this, it's crucial to use a balanced set of metrics that represent a well-rounded view of AI performance, including accuracy, bias, fairness, and transparency. Regular reviews and audits of AI performance metrics can help ensure integrity in measurement.

Impact on Employee Well-Being

In some cases, measuring AI performance can indirectly impact employees, especially if metrics are used to evaluate productivity or decision-making accuracy. For example, in customer service environments, AI can monitor response times or interaction quality, potentially putting pressure on employees to meet specific targets. This can lead to stress, reduced morale, and even burnout if not managed carefully. To address this, organizations should involve employees in discussions about AI metrics and ensure that performance measurement is fair, realistic, and supportive of employee well-being. Including metrics that reflect teamwork, adaptability, and employee feedback can help create a more balanced and humane approach to AI performance evaluation.

Ensuring Fairness and Avoiding Bias

As AI continues to influence decision-making, it's essential to ensure that measurement practices do not reinforce biases or unfair treatment. For instance, if an AI model consistently shows higher accuracy in certain demographics but lower accuracy in others, focusing on aggregate accuracy alone can mask underlying biases. Organizations should prioritize metrics that assess fairness and equality of outcomes across different groups. Conducting regular bias audits and providing transparency on AI performance across demographics can help mitigate these risks, ensuring that measurement practices promote fairness.

Addressing ethical considerations in AI measurement is key to responsible AI implementation. Organizations can build trust and accountability in their AI practices by prioritizing privacy, minimizing the risk of metric manipulation, and focusing on employee well-being. Balancing a variety of metrics ensures that AI performance reflects a holistic and fair approach rather than focusing solely on isolated metrics. Taking these ethical issues seriously supports a culture of transparency and respect, ensuring that AI's impact aligns with organizational values and societal expectations.

Communicating AI Success

Effectively communicating the success of AI initiatives is crucial for gaining ongoing support from various stakeholders, such as executives, employees, customers, and investors. Each group has different interests and levels of technical knowledge, so it's essential to tailor the messaging accordingly.

For Executives

When presenting to executives, focus on how AI contributes to the organization's overall goals, such as increasing revenue, reducing costs, or improving customer satisfaction. Use key performance indicators (KPIs) that align with the company's strategic objectives and highlight tangible outcomes. Summarizing the return on investment (ROI) of AI initiatives is often effective, as executives prioritize value and impact. Visuals, such as graphs or charts, can help illustrate growth trends and performance improvements.

For Employees

Employees need to understand how AI affects their roles and benefits their day-to-day work. Emphasize how AI streamlines tasks, reduces repetitive work, or enables more informed decision-making. Including specific examples of how AI has positively impacted team productivity or quality of work makes the message relatable. Encouraging feedback and open discussions also help employees feel engaged with AI initiatives, promoting a sense of ownership and reducing resistance to AI integration.

For Customers

Customers are interested in how AI improves their experience, whether through personalized recommendations, faster service, or enhanced security. Communicating AI success to customers should focus on the benefits they directly experience. For instance, a message highlighting how AI improves response times in customer service or personalizes product suggestions makes the technology's impact more tangible and builds trust in the company's commitment to quality.

For Investors

Investors are primarily interested in how AI initiatives drive growth, create competitive advantages, and increase shareholder value. When communicating to investors, highlight AI's impact on market positioning, revenue generation, and cost savings. Use data that demonstrates how AI initiatives contribute to future scalability and long-term profitability. Showing how the company is prepared to lead in AI adoption within the industry can reassure investors about sustained growth and innovation.

Clear and targeted communication strategies help convey AI's value to each stakeholder group, ensuring continued support and alignment with the organization's AI goals.

Communicating the success of AI initiatives effectively requires a customized approach for each stakeholder group. Clear and targeted communication fosters support and understanding, helping build trust in AI initiatives and aligning them with organizational goals. This approach ensures that everyone sees the value AI brings to the table and encourages a culture of ongoing AI innovation and adoption.

Future of AI Performance Measurement

As AI technology advances, the way we measure AI performance is likely to evolve significantly. Here are some key predictions for how AI performance measurement may look in the future.

Real-Time, AI-Driven Performance Optimization

In the future, we can expect AI performance measurement systems to operate in real-time. These systems will not only monitor AI's metrics continuously but also make immediate adjustments based on real-time data. For instance, an AI-driven system might automatically adapt algorithms or resource allocation to maintain optimal performance without human intervention. This approach will enable AI systems to self-correct and improve in real-time, leading to higher efficiency and consistency.

Holistic and Multidimensional Metrics

Future AI performance measurement will likely involve a broader range of metrics that go beyond accuracy and efficiency. There may be more emphasis on ethical dimensions, such as fairness, transparency, and user trust. Metrics related to environmental impacts, like energy consumption and sustainability, might also become standard. This multidimensional approach will help organizations gain a fuller understanding of AI's impact and align AI initiatives with broader societal goals.

Integration with Business Intelligence (BI) Tools

AI performance metrics are expected to become more integrated with business intelligence platforms, providing seamless access to data across departments. This integration will allow organizations to link AI metrics directly to overall business outcomes, such as revenue, customer satisfaction, and operational efficiency. Leaders and teams will be able to access real-time performance data within existing BI systems, enabling faster and more informed decision-making.

Personalized AI Performance Dashboards

As AI becomes increasingly essential across various departments, there may be personalized AI dashboards for specific roles within organizations. For example, a customer service manager might have a dashboard showing AI performance in response times and customer satisfaction, while a data scientist might view metrics on model accuracy and training data quality. Tailored dashboards would provide relevant insights to each user, ensuring that performance metrics align with their goals and responsibilities.

The future of AI performance measurement points toward real-time, adaptive systems and a shift toward holistic, multidimensional metrics. As AI-driven performance optimization becomes more advanced, organizations will gain new tools to ensure their AI systems are continuously improving. This evolution in measurement will support a more responsible and strategic use of AI, integrating ethical considerations and aligning AI metrics with broader business objectives.

Overcoming Measurement Challenges

Measuring AI success comes with unique challenges, from ensuring data quality to accurately attributing outcomes to AI and even facing resistance to new ways of measurement. Here are strategies to tackle these obstacles effectively.

Improving Data Quality

One of the biggest issues in measuring AI performance is poor data quality. Incomplete, biased, or inconsistent data can skew results and reduce the accuracy of metrics. To address this, organizations should establish data quality standards before launching AI initiatives. This might include regular data audits to ensure accuracy, implementing automated data-cleaning processes, and training employees on data handling best practices. Clear guidelines help maintain data quality across the board, which is essential for reliable AI performance measurement.

Handling Attribution Problems

AI often contributes to a result alongside other factors, making it difficult to pinpoint exactly how much AI itself is responsible for specific outcomes. To tackle this, organizations can adopt a blended measurement approach. By using a combination of direct metrics (such as how many decisions AI directly influences) and indirect indicators (like overall process improvement), it's possible to get a clearer view of AI's specific impact. Testing with control groups can also help. For example, comparing outcomes between teams using AI and those without can provide insights into the real effect of AI.

Overcoming Resistance to New Measurement Approaches

Some teams might resist new measurement methods, especially if they're accustomed to traditional metrics. To ease this transition, it's essential to communicate the value of AI-specific metrics and demonstrate how they provide more accurate insights. Start by introducing one or two new metrics alongside existing ones to allow gradual adjustment. Training sessions and open discussions can help employees understand and appreciate the purpose of these new measurements, fostering acceptance and support for the change.

Organizations can overcome key obstacles and establish a more accurate and comprehensive approach to AI measurement by implementing these strategies.

You would require a structured approach that begins with defining metrics and moves through data collection, analysis, and continuous improvement to create an effective AI measurement framework. A step-by-step guide is mentioned below to develop AI-era performance measurement in your organization.

1. Define Clear AI Metrics: Start by identifying the goals of your AI initiative and defining metrics that align with those goals. For instance, if AI is implemented to improve customer service, focus on metrics like response time, customer satisfaction, and error reduction. Ensure the metrics you choose are specific, relevant, and achievable within your organization's context.

2. Establish Data Collection Methods: Once metrics are defined, determine how you will collect the necessary data. This might involve integrating data sources, setting up dashboards, or implementing automated data capture processes. Ensure you have quality checks in place to verify the data's accuracy. It's also helpful to create a clear schedule for data collection, such as weekly or monthly, to maintain consistency.

3. Analyze and Interpret Results: With data in hand, the next step is to analyze it to understand how well your AI is performing. Use data visualization tools to make patterns more visible and highlight any trends. Comparing current metrics with past results or benchmarks can provide insights into AI's effectiveness over time. For more detailed analysis, consider using AI-powered analytics tools to detect patterns that might not be immediately visible.

4. Refine Metrics and Adjust Goals: As your AI initiative progresses, revisit and refine your metrics to ensure they remain relevant. This might involve adjusting metrics based on new business goals or adding new metrics to capture emerging benefits. Regular reviews will keep your measurement framework aligned with organizational objectives and the evolving nature of AI projects.

5. Report Findings and Gather Feedback: Share results with stakeholders to communicate AI's impact clearly and gather feedback. Customizing reports for different audiences like executives, team leads, and employees can make the information more accessible and meaningful. Feedback can provide valuable insights for further refinement and improvements to the measurement framework.

6. Establish a Continuous Improvement Cycle: AI performance measurement isn't a one-time task. Set up a continuous improvement cycle to track progress, update metrics, and adapt to new challenges. Regular evaluation helps ensure your AI measurement approach remains effective and supports your organization's growth and innovation.

Following these steps provides a strong foundation for implementing a robust AI measurement framework that supports meaningful insights and sustainable AI success.

Reflections:

To help apply these AI measurement concepts to your organization, here are some reflection questions to consider:

1. What are the main goals of our AI initiatives, and how can we create metrics that directly align with those goals? Consider specific outcomes you want to achieve and think about metrics that reflect both immediate and long-term impacts.

2.   What data sources are available to us, and do we have the right tools to capture and analyze this data effectively? Assess whether existing data collection methods are sufficient or if new tools or processes might be needed for reliable measurement.

3.   How can we address potential resistance to new AI-specific metrics within our teams? Reflect on ways to communicate the benefits of AI metrics and involve employees in the transition to foster buy-in.

4.   How can we ensure our AI metrics remain relevant as our organization's goals or AI projects evolve? Think about a process for regularly reviewing and updating metrics to keep pace with organizational changes.

5.   What steps can we take to ensure ethical data collection and avoid potential privacy issues when measuring AI performance? Consider safeguards to protect privacy and handle data responsibly, such as anonymization and transparency with stakeholders.

These questions encourage a thoughtful approach to help you align AI measurement strategies with your organization's needs and challenges.

Measuring performance requires new approaches that go beyond traditional metrics. As organizations integrate AI, they must adopt measurement strategies that capture the unique contributions of these technologies while addressing challenges like data quality, privacy, and organizational buy-in.

Chapter 12: Adapting to Ongoing Change

A century-old company with a strong reputation and loyal customer base was known for its reliability and tradition. But, suddenly, it was hit by a massive disruption due to a sudden technological breakthrough.

For decades, it had been a leader in its industry, known for consistent quality and trusted by generations. But then, a new AI-driven innovation technology entered the market, disrupting everything. This technology offered faster, more efficient, and far cheaper solutions, which the company's traditional methods couldn't match. Almost overnight, what had once seemed like a stable and successful business was at risk of becoming irrelevant.

The leadership team faced a harsh reality. They had to either adapt or risk falling behind permanently. They knew they needed to incorporate AI and other advanced technologies to stay competitive. However, it wasn't just about adopting new tools; it required a complete overhaul of how the business operated. Many employees had been with the company for decades and were loyal to established methods. Shifting to new systems and rethinking operations felt like an enormous technical and cultural challenge.

This turning point highlighted the critical need for adaptability and forward-thinking. The company's once rock-solid foundation wasn't enough in a world where technology was advancing rapidly. To survive, the organization realized it had to embrace AI, promote a culture open to change, and stay agile to meet future disruptions. The company's path forward now depended not just on its past strengths but on its willingness to innovate and reinvent itself for a new era.

Future-proofing allowed the company to remain competitive and resilient in an unpredictable market. Recognizing that relying on past successes wasn't enough, especially as technology evolved rapidly, the company adopted a forward-thinking approach centered on adaptability and innovation. This shift involved incorporating AI, which brought smarter decision-making, streamlined processes, and a stronger customer experience. By integrating AI into various operations, the company could analyze data in real-time, make accurate forecasts, and adjust strategies based on emerging trends.

In addition to AI, the company promoted a culture open to continuous learning and flexibility, which encouraged employees to embrace change rather than resist it. The company restructured workflows, prioritized cross-functional collaboration, and invested in regular training programs to stay agile. This agile mindset allowed it to respond more quickly to new challenges and technological advances, ensuring it remained at the forefront of industry developments.

Future-Proofing in the AI Era

In the context of AI and rapid technological change, future-proofing refers to the strategies and practices organizations adopt to stay resilient and relevant.

Future-proofing is about more than just preparing for the future; it's about building a structure and mindset that can adapt to unexpected changes without major disruptions. This approach emphasizes a balance between preparedness(having the right skills, technologies, and systems in place) and flexibility(the ability to pivot and respond to new developments as they happen).

For companies, future-proofing often means investing in scalable technologies like cloud computing, modular systems, and advanced data analytics. These allow organizations to grow and evolve without overhauling their entire infrastructure every time a new technology emerges. For example, by implementing AI platforms that can be updated and expanded, a company can integrate new advancements in AI without disrupting existing operations.

Another key part of future-proofing in the AI era is continuous learning and development. As AI capabilities expand, organizations need teams that are equipped to understand, implement, and manage these technologies. Training employees in digital skills, data literacy, and AI management prepares the workforce to handle both current and future technologies, enabling a smoother transition as new tools become essential.

Future-proofing also involves a mindset of constant innovation and open-mindedness. Companies that cultivate a culture of experimentation and flexibility are more likely to recognize and capitalize on new opportunities. Instead of rigid, long-term strategies, these organizations adopt agile planning, allowing them to adjust goals and processes as new developments arise.

Ultimately, future-proofing in the age of AI is about building a resilient organization that doesn't just react to change but is structured to thrive within it. It requires a blend of proactive readiness and adaptive agility, ensuring that the organization can meet the demands of today while staying prepared for tomorrow's challenges and opportunities.

This need for resilience and adaptability is not new; in fact, organizational adaptability has evolved significantly over time. Initially, companies relied on rigid, long-term planning to guide their actions. This traditional strategic planning involved setting multi-year goals and crafting careful strategies to achieve them. It worked well in relatively stable environments where changes were predictable and gradual, allowing organizations to make decisions with a high degree of certainty. However, as markets grew more dynamic, so did the need for flexible and responsive approaches.

However, as markets became more dynamic and technology began advancing rapidly, traditional planning methods started to fall short. Organizations needed ways to respond more quickly to unexpected changes, whether from new competitors, economic shifts, or technological breakthroughs. This need for faster responses gave rise to agile methodologies in the 1990s, initially within software development but soon expanding to other areas of business. Agile approaches emphasize iterative development, cross-functional collaboration, and continuous feedback, allowing companies to adjust plans frequently and make incremental improvements.

Scenario Planning

In recent years, scenario planning has emerged as a critical tool for navigating uncertainty, particularly as digital transformation introduces new complexities. Unlike traditional planning, this approach involves crafting multiple potential future scenarios and developing strategies tailored to each. However, this has proven to be a daunting task for many organizations. As a result, they often turn to us to lead the effort, leveraging tools such as AI-powered scenario simulations and predictive analytics to enhance accuracy, inform decision-making, and build resilience in the face of unpredictability.

Today, organizational adaptability involves a combination of these methods, uniting the long-term vision of strategic planning with the flexibility of agile and the foresight of scenario planning. Together, these approaches enable companies to face the challenges of the digital age, making them better equipped to handle rapid change and stay competitive in an era defined by constant innovation.

Scenario Planning Techniques for Technological Disruptions

Scenario planning is a powerful technique that helps organizations prepare for future uncertainties, particularly in the face of rapid technological disruptions. Unlike traditional planning, which assumes a single, predictable future, scenario planning involves creating multiple plausible scenarios. This approach helps companies identify potential disruptors, imagine a variety of outcomes, and develop strategies to adapt regardless of which scenario unfolds.

Here's a closer look at how to use scenario planning to stay resilient and prepared in a technology-driven world.

Identifying Potential Disruptors

The first step in scenario planning is to identify potential disruptors, i.e., events or changes that could significantly impact the organization. In the context of technology, disruptors may include advancements in AI, shifts in data privacy laws, new competitors entering the market, or breakthroughs in digital platforms. To spot these disruptors, organizations can track trends, monitor industry reports, and gather insights from experts within and outside the company. Brainstorming sessions with cross-functional teams can also help bring diverse perspectives to the table, ensuring that no potential disruptor is overlooked.

Constructing Plausible Scenarios

Once potential disruptors are identified, the next step is to construct plausible scenarios based on these disruptors. Scenarios should cover a range of possibilities, from the most optimistic outcomes to the most challenging ones. A good practice is to create at least three to four distinct scenarios that span a variety of conditions.

For example, if the focus is on AI as a disruptor, one scenario might envision a world where AI dramatically improves productivity, while another imagines a scenario where regulatory restrictions limit AI's use. In yet another scenario, AI adoption might be slow due to high costs or ethical concerns. Each scenario should include basic elements, such as key players, market conditions, customer behavior, and technological advancements, to provide a clear picture of how different futures might look.

Developing Adaptive Strategies

With these scenarios in hand, organizations can begin developing adaptive strategies that would work well across multiple scenarios. The goal is not to create separate plans for each scenario but to identify flexible strategies that can be adjusted as conditions change. These strategies may include building a scalable tech infrastructure, investing in employee training for new skills, or establishing partnerships to access emerging technology.

For instance, if AI is a potential disruptor, a flexible strategy might involve investing in AI upskilling for employees so they're prepared to work alongside new technologies. Another adaptive approach might be to build a modular IT system that can integrate new AI tools easily if AI adoption accelerates. If regulatory concerns grow, a strategy might include establishing a compliance team focused on staying up-to-date with AI regulations.

Testing and Refining Strategies

Scenario planning is most effective when it's treated as an ongoing process rather than a one-time exercise. As new information emerges or conditions change, organizations should revisit and refine their scenarios and strategies. Periodic reviews allow companies to test their assumptions and adapt their strategies accordingly. Testing scenarios with "what-if" questions or small pilot projects can also reveal the strengths and weaknesses of each approach, helping organizations adjust before committing to large-scale changes.

Scenario planning equips organizations with the flexibility needed to adapt to technological disruptions. By identifying potential disruptors, constructing a range of plausible scenarios, and developing adaptive strategies, companies can prepare for a variety of outcomes. This proactive approach enables organizations to stay resilient, respond to change effectively, and thrive in a rapidly evolving technological landscape.

Building Adaptive Capacity

Organizations must be able to adapt quickly to new challenges and opportunities. Building adaptive capacity means embedding adaptability into the core of the organization and making it a fundamental part of how the company operates, makes decisions, and responds to change.

Develops a Culture of Experimentation

A key element of adaptive capacity is encouraging a culture where experimentation is valued. In an organization with a strong culture of experimentation, teams are empowered to test new ideas and learn from successes and failures. This mindset allows the organization to explore creative solutions and stay agile in the face of unexpected changes.

To promote this culture, leaders can implement "safe-to-fail" experiments—small, controlled projects where teams are encouraged to test innovative ideas without fear of significant setbacks. Celebrating learning outcomes from both successful and unsuccessful projects is essential for embedding adaptability. When employees see that they're supported in trying new approaches, they are more likely to explore innovative solutions that keep the organization flexible and forward-thinking.

Developing Dynamic Capabilities

Dynamic capabilities are the skills and processes that enable an organization to sense change, seize opportunities, and reconfigure resources in response. These capabilities include everything from quick decision-making to the ability to shift resources between projects as priorities change. Developing dynamic capabilities ensures that the organization can pivot smoothly when new demands or challenges arise.

Training employees in adaptable skills, such as problem-solving, digital literacy, and cross-functional teamwork, strengthens these capabilities. Encouraging collaboration between departments and offering resources for continuous learning further supports this goal. Dynamic capabilities also extend to leadership, where leaders need to be open to new information and able to adjust strategies based on data and feedback. By building a team that's skilled in recognizing change and responding effectively, organizations can stay resilient in a rapidly evolving environment.

Creating Flexible Organizational Structures

Organizational structures play a critical role in either supporting or hindering adaptability. Traditional and hierarchical structures can make it difficult to respond quickly, as decisions often get bogged down in layers of approval. In contrast, flexible structures like cross-functional teams or project-based groups allow for faster responses and a more collaborative approach to change.

In a flexible structure, teams can be formed or restructured around specific projects or goals as needed, which makes it easier to adapt to shifting demands. For instance, if a new technological opportunity arises, a cross-functional team can be assembled with members from IT, marketing, and product development to evaluate and act on the opportunity quickly. Additionally, decentralizing decision-making allows teams closer to the issue to make informed, timely choices, reducing bottlenecks and increasing responsiveness.

Building adaptive capacity requires an organization to embrace a mindset of continuous learning, flexible structures, and dynamic capabilities. These strategies enable organizations to not only respond to change but also to anticipate it, positioning them to thrive in a world where agility and resilience are essential.

Amazon exemplifies adaptive capacity through a culture of experimentation, dynamic capabilities, and a flexible organizational structure. Known for its "fail fast, learn faster" approach, Amazon encourages teams to try new ideas and take calculated risks. This allows the company to identify successful innovations rapidly. This experimentation led to key offerings like Amazon Prime and AWS. Small, cross-functional teams, known as "two-pizza teams," operate with autonomy, enabling quick decision-making and helping the company act swiftly on new ideas without lengthy approvals.

Amazon's dynamic capabilities also fuel its adaptability. A customer-centric, data-driven approach enables Amazon to sense changes in customer needs and make timely adjustments. For instance, when demand for fast delivery surged, Amazon responded by building its own logistics network and introducing same-day delivery options. During the COVID-19 pandemic, the company quickly scaled logistics to prioritize essential goods. This commitment to flexible structures and responsiveness has made Amazon resilient, allowing it to thrive in a rapidly changing environment.

Continuous Learning Strategies

Organizations need continuous learning to stay competitive and innovative. Institutionalizing this mindset involves creating systems and opportunities that allow employees to keep growing, adapt to new technologies, and develop fresh skills. Key strategies to foster continuous learning include establishing internal learning platforms, partnering with educational institutions, and implementing job rotation programs.

1. Internal Learning Platforms: Internal Learning Platforms have become integral to many organizations, offering employees access to tailored resources such as online courses, skill-building workshops, and training on industry-specific tools, trends, and critical skills like data analysis or AI. These platforms are designed to align with the organization's needs, making it convenient for employees to engage with training materials on their own schedules and embedding continuous learning into their routines. To ensure these resources remain relevant, effective, and aligned with market demands, we are frequently invited as consultants to provide an external perspective. Our periodic reviews help organizations maintain their competitive edge, adapt to customer needs, and ensure their teams remain proficient and aligned with evolving systems.

2. Partnerships with Educational Institutions: Partnering with universities and other educational bodies allows organizations to bring in external expertise and cutting-edge research. These partnerships often include joint training programs, research collaborations, or certificate courses tailored to industry needs. For example, a company could collaborate with a university's AI department to offer specialized workshops or co-create custom certification programs. These partnerships bring in fresh perspectives and ensure that employees stay informed about the latest industry developments and innovations.

3. Job Rotation Programs: Job rotation is another powerful tool for continuous learning, enabling employees to gain experience in different areas of the organization. By rotating through various roles or departments, employees build a broader skill set, gain insights into different functions, and develop a more holistic view of the organization's operations. This flexibility strengthens individual skill sets and fosters a culture of adaptability as employees become more versatile and ready to take on new challenges.

Together, these strategies build a foundation for continuous learning and reinvention, ensuring that the organization remains agile and ready for change. By embedding learning opportunities into the organizational fabric, companies can cultivate an engaged, skilled, and equipped workforce to thrive in a rapidly changing world.

IBM, established in 1911, has demonstrated remarkable resilience over the years by successfully overcoming technological disruption. Its strategic adaptability and forward-thinking leadership have been essential in maintaining its status as a leader in the technology sector.

One of IBM's major turning points came in the 1990s, during the rise of the internet, when then-CEO Lou Gerstner led the company's transition to e-business. Recognizing the transformative potential of the internet, Gerstner shifted IBM's focus from traditional hardware to internet-based solutions and services. This strategic pivot involved creating the IBM Internet Division and positioning e-business at the core of IBM's operations. By 1996, IBM had become a market leader in helping businesses adopt network-centric e-business models, a shift that set the stage for its continued evolution and success.

In the 2010s, IBM foresaw the importance of cloud computing and artificial intelligence and made bold investments in these areas. The acquisition of Red Hat in 2019, a significant $34 billion investment, expanded IBM's cloud capabilities and underscored its commitment to cloud computing as a core business component. At the same time, IBM developed its AI platform, Watson, to offer advanced analytics and cognitive computing solutions. These moves strengthened IBM's position in the emerging cloud and AI markets, securing its competitive advantage as new technologies reshaped the industry.

IBM's approach to sustained success has always included a commitment to continuous transformation and innovation. The company consistently identifies new disruptive technologies, such as cloud, analytics, mobile, and social technologies, and adapts its business model accordingly. This perspective has led IBM to undergo multiple internal transformations over the years, allowing it to remain relevant and competitive in a rapidly evolving technological landscape.[46]

Homo Magister's Role in Future-Proofing

Leaders who embody the **Homo Magister** ideal have an important role in future-proofing their organizations. These leaders bring an ability to balance long-term vision with the need for short-term adaptability. Their approach ensures that while the organization remains flexible in the face of immediate challenges, it also builds a foundation for enduring success.

---

[46]https://www.wsj.com/articles/ibm-makes-6-4-billion-bet-on-hashicorp-to-boost-cloud-management-offerings-495a5095?utm_source=chatgpt.com

One of the key strengths of Homo Magister leaders is their commitment to a long-term vision that aligns with core values and sustainable practices. These leaders understand that future-proofing isn't just about reacting to current trends but about building a resilient organization that can thrive through ongoing transformations. With this in mind, they invest in areas that support sustained growth, such as workforce development, ethical technology adoption, and responsible innovation. For example, a Homo Magister leader may prioritize employee upskilling in digital technologies, ensuring that the organization's talent base is prepared for future shifts rather than relying solely on quick fixes or short-term hires.

At the same time, Homo Magister leaders excel in short-term adaptability. They recognize that while long-term strategies are essential, organizations must remain agile to navigate immediate changes and seize new opportunities. To foster this adaptability, they encourage a culture of experimentation and continuous learning within the organization, empowering teams to innovate without fear of failure. These leaders also promote flexible organizational structures, such as cross-functional teams, which allow the company to respond swiftly to market shifts and technological advancements. By balancing the long-term with the short-term, Homo Magister leaders make future-proofing a proactive, strategic process rather than a reactionary one.

In essence, the Homo Magister leader combines a forward-looking vision with a practical, adaptable approach. This balance allows organizations not only to prepare for future challenges but also to evolve through them with integrity and purpose. Through their wisdom and ethical grounding, these leaders create resilient, responsible, and equipped organizations to thrive in a constantly changing world.

AI's Role in Organizational Resilience

AI technologies play an important role in building organizational resilience by enhancing adaptability, foresight, and responsiveness. Organizations can anticipate changes, identify potential risks, and prepare strategies to face uncertain futures through tools like predictive analytics and AI-powered scenario simulations. These capabilities make AI a tool for operational efficiency and a critical asset for long-term resilience.

Predictive Analytics for Anticipating Change

Predictive analytics is one of the core ways AI boosts resilience. By analyzing vast amounts of data, predictive AI models can identify emerging trends and forecast shifts in customer behavior, market demand, and industry conditions. For example, in retail, predictive analytics can alert companies to changes in consumer preferences before they become widespread, enabling businesses to adjust inventory, refine marketing strategies, and better serve their customers.

This anticipatory capability gives organizations a strategic edge and allows them to make proactive adjustments rather than simply reacting to changes after they occur.

AI-Powered Scenario Simulations for Strategic Foresight

AI-powered scenario simulations take foresight a step further by creating models of different future possibilities. This helps organizations to prepare for a range of outcomes. These simulations enable leaders to explore the potential impacts of various scenarios, such as economic downturns, supply chain disruptions, or shifts in technology. In industries like finance or manufacturing, AI-powered simulations help organizations identify vulnerabilities in their operations and develop contingency plans, creating a framework for quick responses.

Enhancing Real-Time Decision-Making

In addition to predictive capabilities, AI can also improve decision-making speed and precision within organizations, making them more responsive to real-time changes. Machine learning algorithms can analyze real-time data, detect anomalies, and provide instant insights that help decision-makers adjust strategies on the fly. This ability to analyze and respond to current conditions with speed and accuracy supports resilience by ensuring that companies can adapt as conditions evolve.

AI is a powerful tool for strengthening organizational resilience. By integrating AI into resilience strategies, companies are better equipped to withstand disruptions and thrive in an increasingly unpredictable world.

Ethical Considerations in Future-Proofing

While future-proofing aims to prepare organizations for long-term success, these strategies bring up important ethical concerns, particularly around job security and the responsible use of predictive technologies. Leaders must consider how future-proofing can affect employees, customers, and society to ensure these efforts are both effective and ethically sound.

Impact on Job Security

One of the most significant ethical challenges in future-proofing is the potential impact on job security. As organizations adopt new technologies and automate processes, some roles may become redundant, leading to job displacement. For instance, integrating AI and automation can increase efficiency, but it can also mean fewer roles for human employees in tasks that are easily automated. Companies focused on future-proofing must balance technological advancement with the well-being of their workforce. Ethical future-proofing requires that organizations plan for these changes by providing reskilling and upskilling opportunities, helping employees adapt to new roles rather than simply replacing them. Offering career transition support or training in digital skills is an ethical approach that allows employees to thrive in the evolving workplace rather than being left behind.

Responsible Use of Predictive Technologies

Another ethical consideration in future-proofing is the responsible use of predictive technologies, such as AI-powered analytics. Predictive tools enable companies to forecast trends, identify risks, and make proactive decisions, which can be extremely beneficial. However, these technologies also raise ethical questions about privacy, fairness, and accountability. For example, predictive algorithms can sometimes reinforce existing biases if they're trained on biased data, leading to unfair outcomes in hiring, lending, or other critical decisions. Additionally, predictive technologies often rely on vast amounts of personal data, which can raise privacy concerns if data collection isn't transparent or properly managed.

To use predictive technologies ethically, organizations should implement clear data privacy policies and prioritize transparency in how they collect and use data. Ethical guidelines, regular audits, and bias checks can help ensure that these tools serve fair and unbiased purposes. Additionally, organizations should involve diverse teams in the development and testing of predictive models to ensure that various perspectives and potential risks are considered.

Ethical considerations are crucial in future-proofing strategies, as they shape how responsibly organizations navigate change. By addressing the potential impact on job security and practicing responsible use of predictive technologies, companies can ensure that future-proofing efforts support not just organizational resilience but also the well-being of employees, customers, and society at large. Balancing technological advancement with ethical responsibility creates a more sustainable and socially conscious approach to future-proofing.

Measuring Future-Readiness

Measuring an organization's future readiness involves establishing metrics that assess how well-prepared it is to handle change, adopt new technologies, and continually learn. Here's a guide to establishing key metrics in each area.

Indicators of Adaptive Capacity

Adaptive capacity reflects an organization's ability to respond quickly and effectively to new circumstances, whether they come in the form of market shifts, economic changes, or technological disruptions. To gauge adaptive capacity, organizations can track metrics like decision-making speed, resource flexibility, and innovation frequency:

- **Decision-Making Speed**: Measuring how quickly teams can respond to emerging challenges can reveal organizational agility. This can be tracked by assessing the average time taken to make critical decisions during periods of change.

- **Resource Flexibility**: This metric shows how easily resources—such as talent, budget, or tools—can be redirected to meet new demands. High flexibility indicates that the organization can quickly shift focus or scale resources as needed.

- **Innovation Frequency**: Tracking how often the company develops new products, services, or processes indicates its commitment to innovation. A steady flow of new ideas and implementations shows that the organization is continuously adapting to market needs.

Indicators of Technological Foresight

Technological foresight measures how well an organization can anticipate, plan for, and adopt new technologies. This dimension focuses on forward-looking strategies and investment in emerging technologies. Metrics in this area include R&D investment, technology adoption rate, and competitive tech positioning:

- **R&D Investment**: Organizations with high future readiness often invest consistently in research and development. Tracking the percentage of revenue allocated to R&D can provide insight into the organization's commitment to innovation and technological progress.

- **Technology Adoption Rate**: This measures the speed at which new technologies are adopted across the organization. By assessing how long it takes to implement new tech, from planning to execution, companies can gauge how open and prepared they are to integrate emerging tools and systems.

- **Competitive Tech Positioning**: Benchmarking the organization's technology stack against industry peers provides insight into its competitive stance. By evaluating where it stands in terms of technology adoption, companies can determine if they're leading or lagging in their sector.

Indicators of Learning Agility

Learning agility is the ability of an organization and its workforce to learn quickly, adapt new skills, and apply them effectively. Measuring this aspect involves looking at metrics related to employee development, knowledge sharing, and responsiveness to feedback:

- **Employee Development and Training Hours**: The number of hours employees spend in training, skill-building workshops, or online courses is a direct measure of how seriously the organization takes learning. Regular development opportunities indicate a commitment to preparing the workforce for future challenges.

- **Knowledge Sharing and Collaboration**: Measuring the frequency and quality of knowledge-sharing initiatives—such as workshops, internal forums, or cross-departmental projects—reflects how well the organization supports a learning culture. High engagement in knowledge-sharing activities indicates that employees are committed to learning from each other and staying updated on new insights.

- **Feedback Responsiveness**: Tracking how quickly and effectively the organization acts on feedback from employees and customers shows its openness to continuous improvement. This can be measured by the average time taken to implement suggestions or address issues raised, signaling how agile the organization is in adjusting to internal and external needs.

Measuring future readiness provides valuable insights into an organization's resilience, adaptability, and preparedness for change. These indicators help organizations identify areas for growth, invest wisely in innovation, and build a culture that supports continuous learning and adaptability, positioning them for sustained success in an evolving landscape.

Overcoming Obstacles to Future-Proofing

Future-proofing initiatives are essential for organizations aiming to thrive in a fast-evolving world, but implementing these strategies comes with its own set of challenges. Common obstacles like short-term thinking, resource constraints, and resistance to change can hinder efforts to build long-term resilience. Here are strategies to address each of these challenges effectively.

Addressing Short-Term Thinking

One of the biggest hurdles in future-proofing is the focus on immediate results over long-term resilience. Leaders may prioritize short-term gains, especially in competitive or financially driven environments, leaving future-oriented initiatives underfunded or ignored. To counteract this, organizations can embed long-term goals into performance metrics and incentive structures. For instance, integrating future-proofing milestones—such as technology adoption targets or innovation benchmarks—into executive and team performance evaluations can align short-term actions with long-term priorities. Additionally, communicating the benefits of future-proofing in terms of both immediate and future rewards can help stakeholders appreciate the value of a balanced approach.

Managing Resource Constraints

Resource limitations, whether financial, technological, or human, often restrict the scope of future-proofing efforts. To overcome this, organizations can adopt phased implementation and strategic partnerships. A phased approach allows for gradual investment, where smaller, manageable steps can be taken toward larger goals without straining current resources. For example, a company might first invest in a scalable technology that can be expanded over time rather than overhauling systems all at once. Strategic partnerships, such as collaborating with tech vendors, educational institutions, or industry experts, can also provide access to resources and expertise without significant upfront costs. These alliances help organizations leverage external capabilities while keeping future-proofing initiatives affordable.

Overcoming Resistance to Change

Resistance to change is a common barrier in future-proofing, as employees and even leadership may feel uncomfortable with new practices, technologies, or structural adjustments. Building a culture of openness to innovation and encouraging employee involvement are key strategies to address this. Leaders should emphasize the importance of adaptability and actively involve employees in future-proofing projects, giving them a voice in shaping changes that impact their roles. Offering training and upskilling programs also help ease concerns, showing employees how future-proofing initiatives can enhance their skills and career opportunities. When employees understand and feel included in the process, they're more likely to embrace change rather than resist it.

While obstacles like short-term thinking, limited resources, and resistance to change can challenge future-proofing efforts, organizations can overcome these barriers with thoughtful strategies. By aligning incentives with long-term goals, using phased approaches and partnerships, and fostering an open culture of change, companies can make future-proofing a realistic and achievable objective. These strategies help build a resilient organization that's equipped to adapt and thrive in the face of ongoing change.

Future of Future-Proofing

In the future, AI-powered predictive analytics will play an even larger role in future-proofing efforts, enabling organizations to forecast potential disruptions and prepare accordingly. With advanced machine learning models, companies will be able to predict market changes, supply chain vulnerabilities, and shifts in customer behavior more accurately. This will allow for real-time adjustments and proactive planning.

Another anticipated shift is the increasing focus on automated, continuous learning systems. Rather than traditional training, companies may adopt AI-driven platforms that personalize learning and skill-building for employees, automatically adapting to new tools and knowledge areas as they arise. Additionally, resilience strategies are expected to incorporate collaborative ecosystems as businesses form partnerships to share resources, knowledge, and technology. In a future where digital transformations happen at a rapid pace, companies may also adopt "resilience-as-a-service" models, outsourcing parts of their future-proofing strategies to specialized firms that can provide expertise in managing technological change.

Building a resilient, future-ready organization requires a clear, structured approach. Here's a step-by-step guide to help organizations begin their future-proofing journey:

1. **Conduct an Initial Assessment**: Start by evaluating the organization's resilience and identifying strengths and weaknesses in technology, workforce adaptability, and operational flexibility. Conduct surveys, review performance metrics, and hold discussions with key stakeholders to comprehensively view the organization's current state.

2. **Identify Key Future Trends and Disruptors**: Research industry trends, technological advancements, and potential disruptors that could impact the organization. This might include developments in AI, regulatory changes, or shifts in consumer expectations. Engaging with industry reports and consulting with experts can help pinpoint relevant trends to address.

3. **Define Future-Proofing Goals**: Based on the assessment and identified trends, establish clear future-proofing goals. These might include enhancing digital skills within the workforce, adopting specific new technologies, or increasing operational flexibility. Goals should be specific, measurable, and aligned with the organization's broader strategic vision.

4. **Develop a Multi-Phased Strategy**: Create a phased action plan to achieve future-proofing goals gradually. For instance, start with foundational improvements like upskilling teams and upgrading essential technologies, and

then move toward more advanced steps like implementing predictive analytics or building collaborative networks.

5.   Allocate Resources and Establish Partnerships: Assign the necessary resources, budget, and personnel to support future-proofing initiatives. Explore partnerships with tech vendors, educational institutions, or consultants to access specialized expertise and technology cost-effectively.

6.   Implement and Track Progress: Begin implementing each phase of the strategy, ensuring that key stakeholders are involved and engaged. Set up regular check-ins to track progress and make adjustments as needed. Use metrics tied to the organization's goals to evaluate the success of each initiative.

7.   Review and Adapt: Future-proofing is an ongoing process. Regularly review the strategy, assess emerging trends, and adjust goals as the organization and its environment evolve. Keeping a flexible approach allows the organization to adapt and refine its resilience strategies over time.

Reflections:

To apply future-proofing concepts within their specific context, here are some thought-provoking questions for readers to consider:

1.   What are the biggest potential disruptors in my industry, and how could they impact my organization? Reflect on technological, regulatory,

or market changes that could significantly alter the organization's future.

2. How adaptable is our current workforce, and what steps can we take to strengthen their resilience to change? Consider the skills, flexibility, and mindset of the workforce. Think about how upskilling or cross-training could enhance adaptability.

3. What technologies or innovations are we currently missing that could enhance our long-term resilience? Identify areas where adopting new technologies, such as AI or cloud solutions, could improve operations or provide a competitive advantage.

4. How can we integrate continuous learning into our organizational culture to ensure future readiness? Explore ways to make learning and development a regular part of work, encouraging employees to keep evolving with industry demands.

5. What partnerships or collaborations could help us achieve our future-proofing goals more effectively? Think about industry allies, tech providers, or educational institutions that could add value to future-proofing efforts through collaboration.

6. What metrics should we use to measure our future readiness, and how will we track progress over time? Consider the specific indicators that would demonstrate adaptability, learning agility, and technological readiness in your organization.

Reflecting on these questions and incorporating the outlined strategies will help organizations prepare for challenges and capitalize on new opportunities, ensuring a sustainable and adaptable path forward.

Future-proofing has become essential for organizations seeking to remain competitive and resilient in a world of rapid technological change and constant uncertainty. Companies can better navigate disruptions and seize emerging opportunities by building adaptability into their operations, investing in continuous learning, and leveraging predictive tools. Future-proofing isn't just about preparing for the unknown; it's about creating a foundation that allows organizations to thrive, regardless of what the future holds.

Conclusion: Seizing the AI Opportunity

Looking back at the opening scenario, where a CEO grappled with the decision to implement an AI system that would bring both productivity gains and potential workforce reductions, the concepts and strategies explored throughout this book offer a way forward with a more balanced and positive outcome. By applying future-proofing principles, focusing on ethical considerations, and developing a culture of continuous learning, the CEO could approach AI integration to maximize benefits while supporting employees through the transition.

Instead of viewing AI implementation as an all-or-nothing decision, the CEO could start by gradually introducing the technology to allow the organization and its people to adapt. For instance, reskilling and upskilling programs could be implemented well before full automation, preparing employees to take on new roles that the AI system can't fulfill. Job rotation and internal training platforms could help address the skills gap, ensuring employees gain the expertise needed to align the company's evolving demands. Additionally, the CEO could build trust and reduce resistance by promoting transparent communication about these changes, creating an environment where employees feel valued and supported throughout the transformation.

Additionally, the CEO could leverage the company's enhanced productivity and profitability to invest in innovative roles focused on areas like AI oversight, ethics, and customer engagement. This approach not only preserves the workforce but also aligns with a long-term, ethically grounded strategy that prioritizes the well-being of both the organization and its people. In this way, the company doesn't just survive the AI transition; it builds a culture of adaptability and resilience, positioning itself as an agile, future-ready organization in an AI-driven world.

Skillful Pivots Recap

Learning skillful pivots is essential for organizations aiming to remain relevant, resilient, and competitive. This summary revisits the key strategies and themes covered throughout the book to offer a comprehensive guide for leaders and organizations.

Recognizing Digital Shifts

- **Identifying Technological Trends**: Organizations must stay vigilant to digital shifts, acknowledging how rapid tech advancements can impact markets.

- **Embracing Change Proactively**: Moving beyond physical products or manual processes helps businesses stay competitive by integrating technology strategically.

Embracing New Leadership Models

- **Homo Magister Ideal**: Leaders are encouraged to act as mentors and strategists, balancing human judgment with AI's capabilities.

- **Fostering a Learning and Ethical Culture**: Leaders guide teams to embrace change responsibly, prioritizing ethical decision-making and adaptability.

Building Technological Foundations

- **Laying Infrastructure for AI**: Establishing foundational technology, from digital tools to predictive analytics, prepares organizations for AI integration.

- **Developing Digital Skills**: Training teams to use digital tools empowers employees, enhances decision-making, and improves customer service capabilities.

Fostering Organizational Flexibility

- **Creating Agile Structures**: Using agile methodologies and cross-functional teams enables organizations to adapt swiftly to changes.

- **Promoting a Culture of Continuous Learning**: Organizations that value adaptability and learning can pivot quickly as market conditions shift.

Making Data-Informed Choices

- **Data-Centric Culture**: Establishing data-driven insights as a cornerstone supports informed decisions across departments.

- **Leveraging Predictive Analytics**: Organizations benefit from predictive tools, enabling proactive adjustments to align with business goals.

Ensuring Responsible AI Use

- **Balancing Ethics with Innovation**: Leaders must implement AI responsibly, ensuring that technology aligns with human judgment and ethical considerations.

- **Maintaining Fair and Transparent Practices**: Responsible AI use involves ongoing evaluation of bias, transparency, and data privacy.

Cultivating Human Capital and Continuous Learning

- **Upskilling and Digital Literacy**: Continuous learning initiatives, such as upskilling programs, ensure a workforce that can adapt to technological advancements.

- **Educational Partnerships**: Collaborations with institutions help organizations access cutting-edge knowledge, equipping teams with essential AI-era skills.

Skillful pivots in the AI era require a holistic approach, including ethical foresight and a continuous learning culture. By embedding these strategies, organizations can remain resilient and promote a workforce and operational structure capable of evolving alongside technological advancements.

Transformation Journey Map

The Transformation Journey Map is a strategic tool that visually outlines the steps an organization takes to become a future-ready, AI-enabled business. It highlights key milestones, identifies potential challenges, and defines critical success factors to guide the digital transformation process. By leveraging this map, leaders can effectively communicate the transformation strategy, align teams around shared objectives, and proactively address obstacles to ensure a seamless transition. At CDiGlobal, we also craft these maps, enabling client organizations to navigate their transformation journey with clarity, precision, and confidence.

Initial Assessment and Vision Setting

The journey begins with an initial assessment and vision setting, where organizations conduct a thorough analysis of their current state, capabilities, and readiness for change. Establishing a clear, future-focused vision that aligns with organizational values and goals is a crucial success factor at this stage, providing a unifying direction. However, without a cohesive vision, departments may become misaligned, which can slow the transformation process.

Building a Digital and Technological Foundation

Next, organizations focus on building a digital and technological foundation by investing in essential infrastructure, such as digital tools and foundational AI capabilities like data analytics and automation. Ensuring that these systems are scalable and flexible allows for future technology integration. Yet, an overinvestment in complex tools without a clear implementation strategy can waste valuable resources and derail progress.

Developing a Skilled Workforce

As the transformation journey continues, developing a skilled workforce becomes essential. By launching training programs and reskilling initiatives, organizations prepare employees for new roles in an AI-enhanced environment. A culture that supports learning and upskilling helps employees adjust to new technological demands. However, resistance to change or fear of job displacement can affect employee engagement in training efforts, posing a significant challenge.

Fostering a Culture of Experimentation and Innovation

With a skilled workforce in place, organizations then focus on developing a culture of experimentation and innovation. This involves implementing agile practices and cultivating a mindset that values creativity, experimentation, and learning from failure. Creating safe-to-fail environments where teams feel comfortable testing new ideas is critical to this phase. However, if the organization's culture harbors a fear of failure, innovation can be stifled, limiting the adaptability and growth necessary for transformation.

Integrating Data-Driven Decision-Making

In the next phase, integrating data-driven decision-making becomes a focal point. Embedding data-centric practices across departments supports predictive analytics and informed choices. Encouraging data literacy throughout the organization ensures that teams can effectively leverage insights. Challenges arise when data silos or a lack of analytical skills prevent teams from making the most of data-driven strategies.

Implementing AI with Ethical Considerations

The transformation journey also requires implementing AI with ethical considerations in mind. Organizations must balance automation with human oversight and responsibility, ensuring AI use aligns with ethical standards. Maintaining transparency, addressing biases, and protecting privacy are critical to responsible AI adoption. Neglecting these ethical considerations can damage trust in the organization and reduce AI's effectiveness.

Ensuring Organizational Flexibility and Agility

To further enhance adaptability, organizations work on ensuring flexibility and agility by establishing adaptable structures, such as cross-functional teams that can respond quickly to change. By empowering teams to make decentralized decisions, organizations foster the ability to pivot effectively. If rigid hierarchies remain in place or teams lack autonomy, response times to market shifts may be hindered, which would eventually reduce organizational resilience.

Evaluating Impact and Pursuing Continuous Improvement

Regular assessments of transformation efforts allow organizations to measure outcomes against defined objectives, ensuring the strategy's effectiveness. Adopting a continuous improvement approach enables organizations to refine their strategies based on feedback and evolving needs. However, neglecting to revisit and adjust the transformation strategy can lead to stagnation, missing new opportunities, and limiting growth.

The Transformation Journey Map connects each milestone to critical success factors, such as fostering a learning culture and ensuring ethical AI use, and highlights potential pitfalls, like resource wastage or resistance to change. Leaders can chart a clear course for AI adoption, ensuring that each phase contributes to building a stronger, more resilient organization equipped for the future.

Homo Magister Evolution

As AI and technology advance, the role of Homo Magister, the wise, guiding leader, will become even more essential in steering organizations through ethical and responsible AI adoption. While AI can automate tasks, process massive amounts of data, and provide insights, it still lacks the human qualities of empathy, ethical judgment, and strategic foresight. As a result, leaders embodying the Homo Magister ideal will need to blend technological understanding with a strong ethical compass to guide their organizations.

In the coming years, the Homo Magister role is likely to expand to include not just strategic oversight but also a mentorship focus, helping teams navigate the shifts that AI brings to the workplace. As organizations adopt AI, these leaders will need to advocate for responsible AI use, ensuring that technologies align with the company's values and respect human rights. They will act as intermediaries, balancing technological possibilities with the human and social implications, addressing concerns such as bias, privacy, and transparency. Additionally, Homo Magister leaders will prioritize the ongoing development of their workforce, fostering a culture of continuous learning to prepare employees for new roles that emerge alongside AI. Ultimately, the Homo Magister leader will play a pivotal role in ensuring that AI is implemented ethically, transparently, and effectively, with a strong emphasis on safeguarding the human aspects of the organization.

As AI and emerging technologies continue to reshape the business world, several potential future scenarios illustrate the need for adaptive leadership and skillful pivots. In one scenario, AI becomes deeply integrated into all business operations, automating complex processes across sectors such as healthcare, finance, and manufacturing. In this world, organizations that have invested in AI-driven transformation will enjoy heightened efficiency, predictive insights, and improved customer experiences. However, the need for human oversight will remain critical, as Homo Magister leaders will be essential in addressing the ethical and social challenges that accompany such deep integration of technology.

In another possible future, ethical and regulatory challenges slow AI adoption as governments and industry bodies implement strict guidelines on AI's scope and use. This scenario would require leaders to adapt quickly to changing regulations, balancing innovation with compliance and ethical considerations. Leaders who excel at skillful pivots will be well-positioned to adjust to these new constraints, finding ways to innovate responsibly within regulatory frameworks.

In a third scenario, AI leads to unexpected social and economic shifts, such as significant job transformation across industries. Here, Homo Magister leaders will need to focus on reskilling, upskilling, and redefining roles within the organization, ensuring that employees can transition into new positions created by the AI-driven economy. In each of these potential futures, AI will require leaders to make thoughtful, adaptive decisions guided by a clear vision for ethical and effective AI use. These scenarios underscore the ongoing need for skillful pivots, highlighting that while technology will continue to evolve, the role of human leadership remains indispensable.

Quick Recap of Key Case Studies

Throughout this book, various case studies have illustrated the real-world application of future-proofing strategies and adaptive leadership in the AI era. These examples reinforce how organizations across different industries have successfully navigated complex challenges, showcasing the practical value of the concepts and strategies discussed.

1. Microsoft's Transition to Cloud and AI: Microsoft's pivot from a traditional software company to a leader in cloud computing and AI-driven services demonstrated the power of adaptive capacity. By investing in cloud infrastructure and launching Azure, Microsoft transformed its business model, enhancing both resilience and scalability. This case underscores the importance of aligning long-term vision with technological foresight, as well as fostering a culture that embraces continuous learning and innovation.

2. Netflix's Use of Predictive Analytics: Netflix serves as a prime example of leveraging AI-driven insights to stay competitive in a dynamic market. By using predictive analytics and recommendation algorithms, Netflix tailored content suggestions to individual users, significantly improving customer satisfaction and retention. This case highlights the value of data-informed decision-making and demonstrates how AI can enhance customer experience while reinforcing the company's market position.

3. Unilever's Commitment to Ethical AI Use: Unilever's approach to responsible AI adoption, particularly in recruitment, showcased the importance of ethical considerations in future-proofing strategies. By implementing bias detection tools in its hiring processes, Unilever ensured fair and transparent recruitment practices, balancing efficiency with fairness. This case study illustrates the role of Homo Magister leadership in guiding ethical AI practices, ensuring that technology is aligned with company values and societal expectations.

4. Amazon's Experimentation Culture: Amazon's "two-pizza teams" and safe-to-fail experimentation culture allowed it to pivot and adapt quickly to changing market demands. Through initiatives like Amazon Prime and AWS, the company demonstrated how fostering a culture of agility and innovation can drive continuous growth. This case reinforces the importance of organizational flexibility and empowering teams to make decentralized decisions, enabling Amazon to respond swiftly to new opportunities.

5. IBM's Evolution Through Technological Disruption: IBM's journey through multiple waves of technological change, from mainframes to AI and quantum computing, underscores the value of a long-term vision coupled with short-term adaptability. By investing in emerging technologies and continuously reinventing its business model, IBM stayed resilient in a highly competitive industry. This case study highlights the critical role of future-proofing through ongoing transformation and the strategic integration of new capabilities.

Each of these case studies provides a practical example of how organizations can successfully apply the strategies discussed, from developing adaptive capacity and ethical AI practices to embracing a culture of experimentation. Together, these real-world examples underscore the relevance and effectiveness of future-proofing strategies, demonstrating their potential to guide organizations toward sustainable growth and resilience in the face of continuous change.

Ethical Leadership Imperative

As organizations increasingly adopt AI and other advanced technologies, the role of ethical leadership becomes more essential than ever. Ethical considerations are not just a component of AI strategy; they are a foundation that ensures AI is used in ways that benefit both organizations and society as a whole. Leaders who embody the values of integrity, fairness, and transparency serve as the moral compass of their organizations, guiding the responsible implementation of AI and overseeing its impacts on employees, customers, and society at large.

Throughout the book, the concept of ethical AI adoption has been highlighted across multiple facets, from ensuring data privacy and mitigating algorithmic bias to creating an inclusive and fair workplace. Ethical leaders recognize that while AI can drive efficiency and profitability, it also brings risks, such as job displacement, privacy concerns, and potential biases in decision-making. To mitigate these risks, leaders must prioritize transparency in AI processes, invest in technologies that can detect and prevent biases, and implement guidelines that protect the rights and well-being of all stakeholders. By integrating these ethical considerations into AI strategies and organizational transformations, leaders ensure that technology serves a positive role, advancing both business goals and social responsibility.

Furthermore, ethical leadership is crucial for building trust. In an era where AI and digital transformation affect nearly every aspect of our lives, stakeholders—from employees to consumers to regulators—are increasingly concerned with how AI is being used. Leaders who demonstrate commitment to ethical AI use and communicate openly about these technologies' potential benefits and limitations foster trust and credibility. This ethical approach doesn't only safeguard the organization's reputation; it also establishes a sustainable path for future innovations that align with human values and societal needs.

Global Impact Perspective

The widespread adoption of skillful pivots and ethical AI practices holds transformative potential for society, the economy, and global challenges. As more organizations embrace adaptability, prioritize ethical considerations, and harness AI responsibly, we can anticipate positive ripple effects that extend beyond individual companies.

From an economic perspective, organizations that adopt skillful pivots will be better equipped to drive innovation and create jobs in emerging sectors. By fostering an adaptable workforce and prioritizing continuous learning, these companies contribute to a more resilient labor market, preparing workers with skills that match the demands of a technology-driven world. This shift can help reduce the skills gap, making economies more competitive and better prepared for future disruptions. Moreover, as businesses create ethically sound AI solutions, they open up new markets for technology that is trusted and valued for its positive impact, driving sustainable growth.

On a societal level, responsible AI adoption can enhance quality of life and address pressing global challenges. For instance, ethically guided AI applications in healthcare can improve diagnostic accuracy, provide better patient outcomes, and make healthcare more accessible. In sectors like agriculture, AI-driven innovations can optimize food production, helping to address food security challenges. Leaders committed to ethical AI practices ensure these technologies are deployed equitably and inclusively, bridging divides rather than exacerbating them. By focusing on transparency, fairness, and accountability, organizations contribute to a world where AI fosters social good and reduces disparities.

Ultimately, a global shift toward ethical leadership and adaptive strategies will create a collaborative environment for tackling complex global issues, from climate change to social inequality. As companies and leaders around the world prioritize ethical considerations in their transformative journeys, they help build a sustainable, equitable, and resilient global ecosystem. This collective commitment to ethical and skillful pivots creates not only stronger businesses but also a more responsible and humane world where technology and humanity move forward together.

Personal Reflection Prompts

The journey toward AI-driven transformation starts with introspection, as effective leaders must first understand their own approach and their organization's readiness. The following reflection prompts help readers evaluate their personal leadership style, ethical priorities, and their organization's capacity for change. Consider the following questions:

- **Leadership and Ethics**: How do I approach ethical considerations in decision-making? Am I prepared to prioritize ethical concerns over short-term gains when implementing AI?

- **Adaptability and Openness to Change**: Am I fostering a culture of adaptability and openness to learning within my team? What specific actions am I taking to prepare myself and my organization for rapid technological shifts?

- **Employee Empowerment**: How can I support my employees' growth and ensure they feel secure, rather than threatened, by AI-driven changes? What initiatives can I implement to promote reskilling or upskilling?

- **Alignment with Long-Term Vision**: How does my vision for AI align with my organization's broader goals? Am I balancing immediate benefits with the pursuit of sustainable, long-term value?

- **Trust and Transparency**: What steps can I take to ensure that my organization uses AI transparently and responsibly, building trust with employees and stakeholders?

Reflecting on these questions allows leaders to better align their leadership practices with ethical AI adoption and prepares them to guide their organizations through transformational change.

Action Planning Framework

To lead AI-driven transformation effectively, leaders need a structured action plan that integrates the key concepts and strategies discussed throughout the book. This action planning framework provides a practical guide for readers to chart a clear course for implementing AI responsibly and effectively within their organizations.

1. **Assess Organizational Readiness**: Begin with a comprehensive assessment of your organization's current technology infrastructure, workforce capabilities, and cultural openness to change. Identify strengths and areas that need improvement to prepare for AI integration.

2. **Set a Clear Vision and Ethical Standards**: Define the goals of AI adoption, ensuring they align with the organization's mission and values. Develop ethical guidelines for AI use, prioritizing transparency, data privacy, and bias prevention.

3. **Develop Key Skills and Foster a Learning Culture**: Implement upskilling and reskilling initiatives to prepare employees for the demands of AI-driven roles. Encourage continuous learning by establishing training programs and providing access to learning resources.

4. **Build Flexible Structures and Promote Collaboration**: Create agile, cross-functional teams that can respond quickly to changes and work collaboratively on AI projects. Decentralize decision-making to empower teams, ensuring they have the autonomy to act and adapt.

5. **Integrate Data-Driven Decision-Making**: Embed data-centric practices across departments to support AI-powered insights. Ensure that employees have the tools and training necessary to interpret data effectively and make informed decisions.

6. **Implement and Monitor Ethical AI Practices**: Introduce AI tools with a focus on ethical use, fairness, and transparency. Set up regular audits and feedback channels to monitor AI's impact on the organization and address any ethical concerns that arise.

7. **Regularly Evaluate and Adjust the Strategy**: Future-proofing is an ongoing process, so revisit and refine the action plan periodically. Assess the effectiveness of AI implementation, gather feedback, and make adjustments as necessary to keep pace with technological and organizational changes.

This framework ensures that AI-driven transformation is both strategic and sustainable, aligning short-term actions with a broader vision for long-term growth and resilience.

Resources for Continued Learning

To effectively adapt to the evolving landscape of AI and transformational leadership, leaders benefit from ongoing education and networking. Here's a curated list of resources for readers looking to deepen their knowledge and connect with a community of like-minded professionals.

- **Books**:

  o *Superintelligence: Paths, Dangers, Strategies* by Nick Bostrom – A foundational text on the potential impacts of advanced AI.

  o *Human + Machine: Reimagining Work in the Age of AI* by Paul Daugherty and H. James Wilson – Insights into integrating AI with human roles.

  o *Ethics of Artificial Intelligence and Robotics* edited by Vincent C. Müller – A comprehensive exploration of ethical challenges in AI.

- **Courses / Masterclass**

  o **Skillful Pivots: Leveraging AI and Innovation for Agile Organizational Transformation Masterclass by CDiGlobal Consulting.**

  For inquiries, access to a free toolkit, a downloadable workbook, and to join our email list for social media updates, contact us at **mindful.machines.rai@gmail.com**.

  o **Coursera's AI for Everyone** by Andrew Ng – A beginner-friendly introduction to AI and its applications.

  o **MIT Sloan's Leading Digital Transformation** – A course focused on leadership and strategic planning for digital change.

o **Harvard's Data Science Professional Certificate** – Equips leaders with data analysis skills relevant to AI-driven decision-making.

- **Communities**:

  o **AI for Good** – A global community of innovators working to leverage AI for social impact.

  o **The Association for Computing Machinery (ACM) Special Interest Group on Artificial Intelligence (SIGAI)** – A professional group that offers resources, events, and a network for those interested in AI ethics and technology.

  o **LinkedIn's AI Enthusiasts Group** – A large online community where professionals share insights and trends and discuss AI applications across industries.

These resources support a journey of continuous learning, helping leaders build AI mastery and improve their approach to transformational leadership. By engaging with these books, courses, and communities, leaders can stay informed, refine their strategies, and connect with peers facing similar challenges, fostering a deeper understanding of the AI era's demands and opportunities.

As we stand on the brink of an AI-driven future, you have the opportunity—and the responsibility—to lead your organization through transformative change. Now is the time to embrace your role as a **Skillful Pivoter**, a leader who not only navigates change but steers it with purpose, adaptability, and integrity. You are equipped with the insights, strategies, and ethical frameworks to make decisions that not only drive success but also safeguard the well-being of employees, customers, and society as a whole. This journey may seem daunting, but the impact of your choices will echo far beyond your organization, influencing industries and shaping the future for generations to come.

Your organization's transformation journey begins with small, decisive steps. By prioritizing learning, fostering adaptability, and ensuring ethical AI adoption, you pave the way for sustainable, human-centered progress. Each action you take helps build a workplace that's not only technologically advanced but also rooted in values that people can trust and support. This is your moment to lead with vision, to make a difference, and to contribute to an AI-powered future that advances society. Embrace the challenge, and start shaping a positive AI-driven world today.

As we close this book, it's clear that AI holds tremendous potential to transform our world—but only if guided by responsible, adaptive human leadership. At its core, this book's message is about the enduring role of human values in a world of machine intelligence. When AI is driven by ethical leadership and a commitment to positive impact, it becomes a tool for advancement, improving lives, driving innovation, and addressing global challenges.

The true power of AI lies not in the technology itself but in the leaders who wield it thoughtfully and responsibly. By balancing innovation with ethical considerations, you can unlock AI's full potential while creating a future that respects and uplifts humanity. As you move forward, remember that the impact of AI on our world depends on leaders like you—leaders who choose to pivot with integrity, vision, and compassion. The journey is just beginning, and with the right mindset, the possibilities are limitless.

Synopsis

This book was born from a desire to empower leaders at all levels to embrace the opportunities and challenges brought by artificial intelligence (AI). It is crafted for executives steering large enterprises, team managers overseeing daily operations, and emerging leaders eager to make their mark in an ever-evolving world.

In an era where technology is advancing at an unprecedented pace, leadership must evolve to meet new demands. AI, automation, and data-driven decision-making are no longer the future—they define the present. These transformative tools reshape industries, redefine roles, and challenge traditional business models. Leaders must adapt, innovate, and adopt strategies that surpass the expectations of previous generations. This book is a guide to thriving in this new reality, emphasizing the importance of integrating AI strategy into generic or traditional strategic planning, ensuring that technology complements, rather than replaces, time-tested frameworks.

More than just a technical manual, this book highlights the need for ethical leadership and responsible AI adoption. As AI becomes integral to our lives and workplaces, leaders must navigate critical questions of privacy, fairness, and accountability. It is no longer enough to deploy technology for efficiency; leaders are responsible for ensuring AI-driven decisions respect individual rights and advance the greater good.

Central to the book is the concept of *Homo Magister*—from the Latin words *homo* (human) and *magister* (teacher). This philosophy champions leaders as guides, educators, and catalysts for transformation, merging the timeless human ability to inspire with the unparalleled potential of technology. By harnessing the synergy between human insight and technological breakthroughs, leaders can create environments where innovation thrives, decisions are ethical, and progress is sustainable.

This book aspires to be both a compass and a resource, inspiring leaders to confidently and responsibly navigate a world transformed by AI. It equips you to balance agility with foresight, innovation with ethical responsibility, and human ingenuity with technological mastery. In doing so, it lays the foundation for a new era of leadership that is not only effective but deeply human.

Endorsement for Book:Mindful Machines, Masterful Humans

The Role of Innovations, AI & Tech Mastery in Organisation Transformation by Robert Munjoma

The book comprehensively grapples with a crucial issue virtually all organizations are facing (or very soon will)— how to integrate AI into their workplace or organization in a way that helps more than it harms. Each chapter presents a unique angle on the potential for AI to benefit organizations, and the book empowers leaders to make informed decisions about how they can (and should) integrate AI into their teams. Not only does it provide a wealth of knowledge and evidence, but it also offers insights on the ethical impacts of AI that also provide valuable food for thought. The book contains useful examples and scenarios that strongly resonate with decisions many leaders are facing, and as such, it's a timely resource and valuable read.

- Dr. Professor R. Glenn Cummins

In a world where everyone claims to be an expert on the future of work by spewing anecdotal opinions seemingly pulled out of thin air, Robert Munjoma offers data-driven, actionable guidance for business leaders in the age of AI. In his book, Mindful Machines, Masterful Humans: The Role of Innovations, AI and Tech Mastery in Organizational Transformation, Munjoma synthesizes case studies,

495

innovation insights, and business research to offer leaders a practical playbook on how to future-proof their organizations as well as measure the value and impact of AI implementation on organizational performance. Key takeaways include encouraging leaders to become conversant in AI-adjacent technology and strengthen their teaching, coaching, and change management toolkits to upskill their teams in AI application and mitigate resistance to AI adoption. Munjoma uses non-technical, jargon-free prose to enhance readability and application while including reflection questions to help leaders self-assess where their companies are on their transformation journey and what they should do next. This book illustrates the importance of adaptive, transformational, situational, and servant leadership and a culture of continuous learning as prerequisites for organizations to reap all the benefits of AI-driven transformation.

Eric D. Waters, PhD, MBA

Talent & Organization Consultant, Learning & Leadership-Focused Organizational Development Thought Partner and Solutionator

The book provides the interconnection of human cognitive capabilities and their elasticity in stretching the conceptual potential in humans when aided by the complex tools of Artificial Intelligence and organization transformation.

Rob traces the evolution of leadership and the organic development of leadership competencies. in influencing business and workforce development from 20th-century-based leadership and perspectives into the 21st leadership imperatives.

The centrality of intergenerational workforce dynamics presents huge leadership demands and challenges that call for corporate leadership to enhance conceptual, strategic, and leadership thinking to higher levels. There is no better way to provoke leadership and competence gaps than to expose these in the era of global digitalization, the drive for innovative thinking, and the demands to master corporate transformation in an environment increasingly dominated by Artificial Intelligence, Machine Learning, and human intelligence elasticity to adjust to the tech-based world demands of today's business.

The book masterfully pivots the theme of "homo magister leadership" pillared by multifactor dynamics of technology, human intelligence, business transformation demands, and the need to craft a leadership narrative that inspires continuous learning desired to grapple with the realities of working and living in a digital economy.

Rob's book tackles the often less understood granular elements of Artificial Intelligence and how each piece plays a complementary role in shaping business operational efficiencies and human performance effectiveness guided by the homo magister leadership paradigm.

This book is a huge leadership learning resource for young and middle-aged leadership executives who have to grapple with the need to embrace the Fourth Industrial Revolution dynamics, which call for embracing data analytics for better decision making, use of IA to enhance innovation and influence business growth and performance sustainability through science-based leadership narratives guided by empirically proven tech-based leadership tools and competencies.

Mindful Machines, Masterful Humans: The Role of Innovations, AI, and Tech Mastery in Organisation Transformation is a comprehensively interwoven literary artwork that provokes traditional leadership thinking to visualize and take up the challenges of pushing the frontiers of leadership thinking into technology-driven leadership, which is the new leadership norm of 21st Century corporate transformation imperatives.

By Dr Jeskinus Ziwenge Mukonoweshuro-Lead Consultant, HR, Strategy & Culture, Crowe Chartered Accountants & Advisory, Zimbabwe.

(DBA, MBA, BSc, Grad Dip, Mgt Studies, MIPMZ) author of the Book: Enhancing Leadership Performance Through Soft Skills: A Research-Based Guide, 2019, LAP Lambert.

Genuinely captivating, inspiring, and truly edifying, it weaves the intricate nuances of modern technologies with the possibilities of human capabilities to confront today's societal challenges.

– ***Dr. Professor Dennis Nikisi***

www.ingramcontent.com/pod-product-compliance
Lightning Source LLC
Chambersburg PA
CBHW030449210326
41597CB00013B/592